THE SMALL BUSINESS SURVIVAL GUIDE

How To Manage Your Cash, Profits and Taxes

ROBERT E. FLEURY

SOURCEBOOKS TRADE
NAPERVILLE, ILLINOIS

Bulk copies are available at a discount from the publisher.

Published by:
Sourcebooks Trade
A Division of Sourcebooks, Inc.
P.O. Box 372
Naperville, Illinois, 60566
(708) 961-2161
FAX: 708-961-2168

Editorial: Lynn Brown
Design and Production: The Print Group
Proofreading: Joyce Petersen
Indexing: Lynn Brown

This publication is designed to provide accurate and authoritative information in regard to the subject matter covered. It is sold with the understanding that the publisher is not engaged in rendering legal, accounting, or other professional service. If legal advice or other expert assistance is required, the services of a competent professional person should be sought.

From a Declaration of Principles Jointly Adopted by a Committee of the
American Bar Association and a Committee of Publishers and Associations

Library of Congress Cataloging-in-Publication Data

Fleury, Robert E. (Robert Earl), 1941-
    The small business survival guide : how to manage your cash,
profits and taxes / by Robert E. Fleury.
      p. cm.
    Includes index.
    ISBN 0-942061-11-X : hardcover. --   ISBN 0-942061-12-8 : paperback
    1. Small business--Cash position. 2. Small business--Managment.
 I. Title
HG4028.C45F64   1991
658.15'92--dc20   90-25205
                                          CIP

Printed and bound in the United States of America.

10 9 8 7 6 5 4 3

Acknowledgment

Contributions to this book have been made by many over the years, but there are several whose contribution stands out in helping me bring this book to market. First is Dr. Don W. Arnold who first helped me to organize the No-Entry Users Manual and inspired me to continue development of the book. Next is Jack Holloway who organized the first seminars and whose enthusiasm for no-entry accounting inspired me to continue the work. My daughter Rita spent countless hours in editing a really rough first manuscript. The Hayden Mc Partlands and their Kings Mill Refinishing business provided the finishing touches in pulling the book together as a complete guide book for small businesses. The professional contributions of editor Lynn Brown, publisher Dominque Raccah and consultant Raymond Bennett have turned the work into a book. Their combined contributions are greatly appreciated and hereby acknowledged.

Dedication

This book is dedicated to those who seek to improve their navigational skills before they risk their life savings on a small business venture.

Table of Contents

Introduction

The Small Business Survival Guide: How to Manage Your Cash, Profits and Taxes

What is this book about? I have seriously pondered this question for five years and just cannot bring myself to answer the question in less than a few pages. Real-life stories, plus new concepts and theories, combine with No-Entry Accounting to provide a model of a complete, living, breathing, entrepreneurial adventure. The model is levitating and rotating slowly. It permits the observer to look in from a single perspective from above or below, from the left or the right and come away moved in some new direction.

Experience has shown that each encounter has brought the observer away with something different. Some observers come to realize that an entrepreneurial experience is something they are not well suited for so they save themselves from making a costly mistake. Some adopt the entire package and use it to guide themselves through the development of their entrepreneurial venture. Some apply the new knowledge to their personal affairs. Still others use their new knowledge to better serve their employer and develop a better empathy for the customers they serve.

For example, the bankers have introduced their officers to the world of No-Entry Accounting in seminar form at one-day seminars I have given over the years. Not one of the bankers uses it as an accounting system, but they are among the most enthusiastic endorsers of what comes out of the package. They are impressed by the grand picture that No-Entry Accounting paints. Every bank group that has put its officers through a No-Entry Accounting session has signed up the seminar as a customer education package. The attendees at these bank seminars have come from all walks of life. Some were highly educated, some were illiterate. Some were already wealthy, some were in the grasp of bankruptcy. Some had a very small business or just a hobby. Others were the owners of multimillion dollar operations. But one thing has been consistent. Each seminar has received high marks regardless of the mix. The last two seminars were ranked 9.1 and 9.2 out of a possible 10 by the attendees.

But what is No-Entry Accounting? It is the fastest, simplest method I can think of for learning—and doing—accounting. There are no debits or credits. There are no ledgers or journals. It is an audiovisual, hands-on teaching aid, for students of accounting. It is a nifty lab tool for those who would do their own accounting. It is a road map that guides the entrepreneur through the whole array of accounting and taxes, right down through a perpetually audit-ready filing system. A high-level IRS official (now retired) reviewed the package. He said, "If used as directed, it would meet the standards of the most demanding IRS auditor."

But the No-Entry Accounting system itself is less than half of what this book is all about. Many businesses are already too large for implementation of No-Entry Accounting to be practical. The owner of an independent grocery store, for example, whose annual revenue is over $5 million, taught his son No-Entry Accounting as he was learning to take over the family business. The father, with No-Entry Accounting, was able to teach the son more through the course of the No-Entry Accounting seminar than the son could have learned on the job in months. Both participants both gave it high marks, an example of a great "learning exposure.".

I cannot leave out the young woman who attended a seminar with a small business owner. She was the owner's secretary/bookkeeper who participated for the purpose of helping to streamline the businesses information system. I asked her what she had gained from the seminar since she was not a business owner. Her response, "I learned that I will probably never own my own business. It's not secure enough. I could not live with the thought that tomorrow I might have to start all over again." This example is the "let someone else take the risk" exposure.

An electronics technician who owned a repair shop also attended a seminar. His company's revenue was less than $50,000 a year. This entrepreneur had started his business in the basement and eventually moved into a stripshop where he could get greater visibility. Toward the end of the seminar a light came on in this young man's mind. He stood up abruptly and said to all in attendance, "I wish I knew all this before I moved out of my affordable basement. I see now that most of my profit is going to the landlord. My lease is up at the end of the month and I'm moving back into the basement." This example illustrates a "moving to profitability" experience.

Perhaps this book should be about the two women who were operating a children's clothing store. The very day after attending a my seminar, they closed the doors to their business. They had learned enough at the seminar to realize that they should get out while the getting was good.

Let's call this example a "protect your capital" exposure.

Another lady, a florist, attended one of the seminars held at a bank. She had a blank, depressed stare on her face. She said, "As you are going through these examples, it has just dawned on me why I have not made a decent profit in the years I have been in business. I can visualize my helper this very morning making an attractive bouquet. She sold it for $12.50 right there as I watched. Now as I sit here and price out the flowers in that bouquet, the arrangement had to cost $15.00 without the vase that was included." The seminar group helped her design an arrangement

pricing form right on the spot. This example shows the "realization of what it takes to be in business" experience.

Maybe this book should be about the auto mechanic who was working long hours running a shop for an absentee owner. He had spent years wishing that he had the education to run a business of his own. If only he knew enough about finance and accounting, and taxes. His wife convinced him to attend a seminar because she could see his potential. She could see that he was already doing almost everything. It was only his fear of paperwork and taxes that separated him from the ranks of the entrepreneur. His parting words as he left the seminar were, "Within a year I'll have my own business. Now I can see the whole cycle. It isn't as difficult as I had thought." Let's call this example a "go ahead decision" experience.

A Realtor who had been in business for 10 years attended a bank-held seminar. At the end she was asked to rank the seminar on a scale of 1 to 10. She said, "10 is not high enough. I know now that I have been doing things wrong for ten years. I have never attended a seminar that was so beneficial to me. From now on I'm going to have order. I'm going to know where I am every week. My tax man won't believe my next filing. Instead of a big cardboard box, he will get organization and I will get all the deductions I have coming." This one is a "giant lights on" experience.

Once I met a landscaper whose revenue is over $1 million annually, which puts his business in the top 2% of all the businesses in the United States. Our encounter was ironic, because I had already written a piece about the ideal business. One ideal type would be a nursery and landscape business at the edge of urban sprawl. The business would grow from landscaping the new construction in the area with stock from its own nursery. Once the sprawl had encompassed the nursery, its land value would skyrocket, yielding even greater profit.

This fellow fit the bill perfectly as a test reader for which I had been searching. I asked if he would be interested in reading my rough draft and providing me with any insight he may have to offer. Much to my surprise, he was excited about the task.

A couple weeks had passed when I finally stopped by his nursery to see whether he had read the book and to learn what his comments might be. This successful business owner noted that he identified with the many problem areas that are exposed through real-life situations.

As he stood silently struggling to be kind, I realized that there was nothing particularly new to him, at least not on the spur of the moment. An hour into our conversation I realized a major impact had been made. The techniques about the real costs of business mistakes, which I dub the Real Ratio, had moved this millionaire to take stock of the way he was handling his business. In the two weeks following his return he had tagged and catalogued every piece of motorized equipment he owned. He had set up procedures for handling equipment that needed repairs to facilitate its rapid return to serviceability. A system was developed to keep track of hundreds of nonpowered tools and equipment so that managers could be held responsible for their whereabouts. A catalogued parts inventory system for repair parts and supplies was implemented. Then it happened. Joe made my day with the words, "From now on we are going to do a physical inventory every month." Imagine that: a landscape contractor doing a monthly physical inventory. It turned out that there were over a thousand items, some in large quantities many of considerable value, that were essentially unaccounted for.

This business owner was already successful. But, like so many of the seminar participants and readers of this book, he had been moved to action. Call this example a "frosting on the cake" experience.

Focus of This Book

A primary focus of this book is to enhance your fiscal responsibility. Because small business owners lose billions of dollars each year, they are one of my primary targets. Most of them first decide to open a business and then discover the need to learn how to run it. These risk takers eagerly tie their health, wealth, and well-being to a decision to make it on their own, ready or not! It is generally believed that if they wait until they are fully educated, fully financed, and otherwise fully prepared, the opportunity will bypass them.

This book provides you with the opportunity to catch up fast. Many new concepts—The Real Ratio and the Cycle of Demise, for example—have been developed in Part I of the book to deal with fiscal ignorance in a way that does not require a college education. These new concepts, together with No-Entry Accounting, provide a breakthrough in small business education. This package has been described as, "The meat and potatoes of what it takes to run a business."

The simple basics that No-Entry Accounting provides in Part II are a necessary foundation for learning business concepts beyond accounting mechanics. The artifacts of conventional accounting, debits and credits, ledgers and journals, are abandoned. In their place is left a small business information system that is exceptionally easy to use, is perpetually audit ready, and is faster than doing the work on a computer.

The greatest problem facing the small business owner is simple ignorance. There is nothing particularly difficult about learning to be fiscally responsible. The problem is that there are many small, simple principles which are an absolute necessity to running a fiscally sound entity. An ignorance regarding these simple principles leads directly to failure. While the principles are simple, they are not easy to come by, as they are tidbits derived from many academic disciplines. Parts III and IV of this book tie together these pieces to help you master cash management and achieve profitability.

Why This Book Is Required Reading

Let's begin with two not so well known facts about business.

- 65 percent of the businesses that fail are profitable.
- Most accountants agree that the time required for a business to reach the success level is from five to seven years.

If you proceed with a quest for an understanding of how these statements can be true, the result will be a considerably enhanced opportunity to succeed in any financial venture, be it entrepreneurial or otherwise. Whether personal finance is your consideration or the finances of an employer, whether you are starting or have already created your business, there is something new to gain from these pages.

You can study the important concepts best from the perspective of the entry-level business venture. You can then tune down to the individual or family level, or tune up to the larger corporation level as your business size and sophistication warrant.

Most of the obstacles to financial success develop without apparent warning to the untrained eye. The common problems, however, are quite easy to identify if you spend some time preparing yourself to prevent them. I have noticed three important factors that contribute to the entrepreneurs need to get close to their own accounting.

First, the signals that warn of business failure are within accounting, but they are substantially masked by the manner in which commercially available accounting statements are presented. The accounting product the small business person needs, and is willing to pay for, is not the product the accountants provide. I have worked with approximately 250 practicing accountants. None have provided, as part of their monthly service, the *cash management information* so necessary for achieving success. The problem of masked information is complicated by the time delay that usually occurs between an accounting transaction and that transaction's appearance in a statement. Anything less than monthly statements simply will not do the job! Any system that is less current than two weeks after the canceled checks are available will not suffice either.

Second, the bulk of actual accounting work, perhaps 95 percent, must already be done by the business person before the figures are turned over to an accountant for statement preparation. If this preparation is not done completely and accurately, sufficient error may be introduced that render the statements useless. More importantly, such statements may cause the owner to guide the business directly to failure. Only if basic accounting is understood, can the entrepreneur choose the data which is pertinent and use it to his or her advantage.

Third, the typical practicing accountant is expensive. The work of a CPA firm usually reflects a rate starting at $100 per hour. Specialized work is even more expensive. A CPA who attended a No-Entry Accounting seminar was asked, "Why is the cash management data we develop with No-Entry Accounting not seen as a product in commercially available accounting?" His reply was, "It's too expensive." The mechanics required to back cash data out of conventional accounting is cost prohibitive. It might also require a personal visit each month. This is so because most of the data required for cash analysis is not a part of the balance sheet or income statement.

The relationship between a ship and the captain can be compared to the relationship between an entrepreneur and a business. A good navigator is required to keep the ship from wandering astray and finally crashing on the rocks. If a captain becomes a captain without first being a navigator, the ship is in peril. Unfortunately, most fiscal endeavors (be they personal, small business, large business, or government) are handled by a captain who became captain with no navigational experience. To the captain whose ship has already set sail, the highly condensed No-Entry Accounting method represents the opportunity to learn entrepreneurial navigation at the helm. It may provide damage control for the captain whose ship that is already on the rocks. For the captain who has not yet cast off, No-Entry Accounting represents the opportunity to become profitable on the maiden voyage and remain that way through many ports of call.

Learning to do your own accounting is the act of acquiring entrepreneurial navigation skills. In my opinion, it is the single most effective way to improve the entrepreneur's chance for success. It saves the considerable expense involved in commercial accounting. It teaches the importance of quickly and accurately compiling the financial statements. But most importantly, it teaches entrepreneurs how to obtain and manage their own cash management data. It qualifies the captain in navigation before he or she ends up guiding the ship. Maybe, once the ship gets larger, the captain can afford to hire a navigator who would *help* keep the ship off the rocks.

Begin your navigational training, then, by putting small business into perspective.

Part 1

What Makes a Business Successful

The Small Business Survival Guide deals with existing businesses as well as those about to be started. The advantage of reading this book before you start up a business is that it can help you to avoid many of the early pitfalls that so often tie the hands of entrepreneurs in existing ventures. Existing businesses already experiencing these pitfalls need to learn to identify and recover from them. The concepts in *The Small Business Survival Guide* will quickly help existing businesses to gain control of their venture, attain or enhance their profitability, and increase their opportunity to succeed in the long run.

The underlying principle you must come to grips with is that if you want to run a business successfully, you must run it like successful businesses are run. You must do the things that "businesses" do. If you want to be a carpenter or a hair dresser, that's fine. But if you want to be a carpentry contractor or run a beauty salon, you must become adept at fiscal management. Basic legalities, accounting—and particularly cash management—will have to be added to your proficiencies. To launch a concern with anything less is simply toying with your financial future.

Misconceptions abound in the world of small business and, therefore, so does bad advice. Sometimes it's free; sometimes it's paid for. The purpose of this part is to set straight many of the misconceptions you might have. You will come away with an enhanced ability to be your own judge.

Chapter 1

The Entrpreneurial Challenge

It is important for all owners of small businesses, whether they have already begun or not yet started, to have a perspective on the big picture. Many businesses are started under gross misconceptions that actually preclude any chance for success. Figure 1.1 will help you to define the edges of financial well-being and establish realistic goals for a business enterprise.

The chart depicts the income levels of those working 40-hour work weeks by age and education. A primary indication is that education is certainly helpful in getting to the top. Many small-time entrepreneurs do not have higher education. Compare what you now earn with these national norms to see whether there is room for improvement. My observation is that the best way to the top without that extra education is to own and operate a small business. The primary object of owning a business is to arrive at a higher station in life than one could by working for someone else.

As an entrepreneur you need to be in touch, therefore, with where you are financially relative to the typical wage earner. Owning a business creates many risks that are not a part of being a wage earner. The owner of an existing business, or one who hopes to start a new one, should expect some gain from incurring those risks. It is foolish to accept these extra risks for no change—or worse yet, a decline—in income.

Deciding Whether to Take the Plunge

An indication of whether you should choose a job or a business comes from determining how much opportunity your business affords to accumulate equity as a by-product. Being in business usually provides a significant advantage, both through business write-offs and from tax deductions. For example, employees who earn $35,000 will have just $30,000 (after taxes) pass through their hands. Entrepreneurs who earn $35,000 will likely have had more than $100,000 pass through their

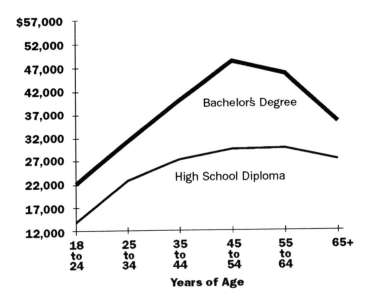

Figure 1.1. Income Comparison for U.S. Wage Earners

hands. A portion of the $65,000 difference would have gone to finance the purchase of business assets, such as land, equipment, and buildings.

Writing off interest expense and depreciating assets will reduce business income and therefore taxes. This process essentially pays in part for equipment, tools, buildings, and so on, while still paying the owner's $35,000 salary. At the same time, many of these assets increase in value through appreciation. An entrepreneur, then, is the benefactor of more than just a $35,000 salary. The sale of a profitable business may generate even more income beyond the owner's salary, company purchased assets, and asset appreciation.

Outside Financing
Venture capital is the term the financial industry uses to describe financing a new business. The industry rates such financing from risky to highly risky. In practice, venture capital generally is not available to businesses that have annual sales under $500,000, which excludes 96 percent of all businesses.

When venture financing is received, it comes as a mixed blessing. Either it is very expensive (high interest rates) or the owner must give up some significant portion of ownership (or both). Many a terrific idea has been lost by an entrepreneur who has momentarily stumbled in a venture capital deal that gives control, even ownership, to the capitalists. For those who have outgrown their personal ability to fund their growing business, the corporation can generate the needed cash by selling stock to investors. But for now let's deal with the 96 percent of all U.S. businesses with annual revenue under $500,000.

Family Net Worth
Figure 1.2 shows the U.S. median net worth by age group of the head of household. Net worth, or *equity*, is the amount left over if you sell everything you own and pay

off everything you owe. Attendees at my seminars often express disbelief that median net worth, or equity, could be so low.

Age of Head of Household	Median Net Worth
Under 35	$6,739
35 to 44	$41,959
45 to 54	$55,509
55 to 64	$68,608
65 or Older	$53,982

Figure 1.2. Family Net Worth

My experience has been that a personal residence is often the collateral for a business loan. The $6,739 in equity for the 35-and-under age group is essentially the value of an automobile. The $41,959 for the 35-to-44 age group includes a car and some equity in a home. Jewelry and personal property such as furniture have not been included.

Using Your Residence to Finance Your Business

A personal residence is considered desirable collateral for all types of loans. It represents a strong personal commitment on the part of the borrower and indicates a measure of confidence the borrower exhibits in the ability to make his or her plan work. Thus, a home can be used to collateralize a small business loan while keeping the interest rate down and keeping control, especially in the beginning. A personal residence has served as the womb for many an entrepreneur who nursed along a hobby or pastime until it bloomed into a business.

There is another reason that owning a home before starting a business is appropriate. The personal residence is undoubtedly the entrepreneur's best tax shelter. An entrepreneur can buy a home and use it to build equity. For many small businesses, part of the home becomes the office or even the physical plant where operations begin. The interest and property tax that are paid through the years are written off on the annual tax return.

These interest and property tax writeoffs save money that would have been spent on income taxes. Usually, the annual savings from these writeoffs typically results in the equivalent of two or three monthly mortgage payments per year.

The down payment and the monthly principal payments are a savings plan or insurance policy that results in a paid-up house. In addition to the principal payments, a home usually appreciates in value over the years. An owner can roll these savings and appreciation into ever larger and more expensive personal residences.

The objective should be to achieve an after-costs appreciation of $125,000. Then, once either spouse reaches age 55, the property can be sold with no tax whatsoever on the $125,000 profit. The costs involved in buying the home and fixing it up might well be paid up by the time an owner reaches age 55. Therefore, a home that sells for $250,000 and began perhaps as a $50,000 handyman special 20 years earlier, could return $250,000 in cash!

The first $125,000 represents the return of the cumulative purchase price and improvements for the various houses, which were paid off with down payments and mortgage payments. The second $125,000 represents untaxed appreciation, profit from the investment in a personal residence. Currently, any appreciation beyond $125,000 is taxed at regular income tax rates. In the meantime, the owner has had use of the net equity in the home to collateralize business loans. It is this collateral and the labor-to-equity transfer (discussed in detail later) that are usually the only means of financing the typical entrepreneurial venture.

Refer again to Figure 1.1. Notice that the peak earning years are in the 45-to-60-year range. The higher one's income level, the higher one's income taxes will be. If taxable income is reduced by property taxes and mortgage interest during these years, an individual will receive greater tax benefits than if the same property taxes and mortgage interest were paid in years of lower earnings. As an individual approaches retirement age, income typically begins to drop off. Therefore, the purchase of as large a home as possible during these high income years essentially permits a home owner to buy a house, at least in part, with money he or she would otherwise be compelled to spend as income tax. The higher the taxable income at the time of ownership, the greater the benefit to the owner.

In summary, there are five reasons why becoming a home owner should be the first step an entrepreneur takes:

1. The first $125,000 earned as the profit from the sale of a personal residence after age 55 is not taxed at all. There is no like business opportunity.

2. The income tax that would ordinarily be due during one's best earning years is reduced by the mortgage interest and property taxes that are paid to buy a home. The amount of these savings in real dollars typically ranges from 15 percent to 25 percent of the annual interest and property tax expense.

3. Any tax that would result from a sale in excess of $125,000 is reduced because the process of paying off the home effectively moved tax on this profit into years in which the individual's tax rate is lower.

4. The benefits of a forced savings plan that a monthly mortgage payment places on the buyer are obvious. Many buyers would be unable to save anything in the absence of a mortgage obligation. This is borne out by the fact that the bulk of an individual's net worth today is the equity in his or her home.

5. The excess of appreciation (increase in value from market forces) and paid up value (mortgage payments that have reduced the original mortgage loan balance) serves as an equity base that can be used to collateralize a business loan.

What Returns to Expect for Your Efforts

Given the substantial risks involved, it is necessary to become versed in what to expect in terms of return from an entrepreneurial venture. Misunderstandings and outright false impressions prevail among would-be small business owners. Many potential business owners have found this next bit of information shocking. The vast majority—98 percent—of American businesses have gross revenue under $1 million. Even more shocking is that 84 percent of these businesses have gross annual revenues under $100,000.

Figure 1.3 lays out the distribution of these businesses based on annual gross revenue. It is important to realize that you do not need a very large business to have a "big" business. The company that has revenues over $100,000 is in the top 16 percent nationally.

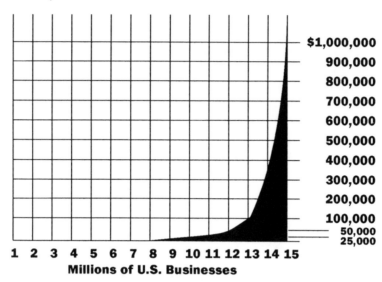

Figure 1.3. Gross Sales for U.S. Nonfarm Businesses

This "big" business mentality has some implications. I have made thousands of cold calls on small businesses over the years. A disturbing and common find was that many entrepreneurs believed their business too small to warrant the regular regimen recommended in this book. This belief is completely erroneous. Regular and accurate financial statements are as important to the small business as they are to a Fortune 500 company. The importance of timely and accurate data is underscored by the lengths to which Fortune 500 companies go to get such data. An example is the increasing use of optical scanners, which instantaneously price and update inventory and compute the cost of sales. Month-end statements can be prepared within days of closing the accounts with this equipment, rather than the weeks it used to take without this equipment. The accuracy of the results is greater than ever before.

Fortune 500 companies readily spend whatever it takes to provide their managers with this instant accuracy. The companies do so because they recognize the importance of timely cash management data. The more quickly a problem can be defined through the financial record, the more quickly—and therefore less expensively—that problem can be solved. Small businesses suffer through the same problems but do not have the financial resources to get the job done electronically. The job, however, is no less important and must be done manually. For some small businesses, the personal computer is a step forward.

In the typical American community with a population of 15,000, from 300 to 500 businesses are in operation. It would be very difficult to drive through such a town and find these businesses, though, because most of them are not in a storefront or office park. Such businesses include the local beautician who operates out of her basement and the welder working from his garage. Most businesses are not mom and pop businesses; rather, they are mom *or* pop businesses.

Figure 1.4 portrays the American business scene, by annual sales, 100 businesses at a time. My objective is to entrench in your mind that your business is not too small to bother managing well. To avoid contributing to the billions of dollars lost annually by small businesses, you need to do like the big guys: Prepare financial statements monthly and ensure that those statements are accurate and timely. Using No-Entry Accounting, most businesses can get this job done (exclusive of taking a physical inventory) in less than one hour per month and have their records automatically in a perpetually audit-ready state.

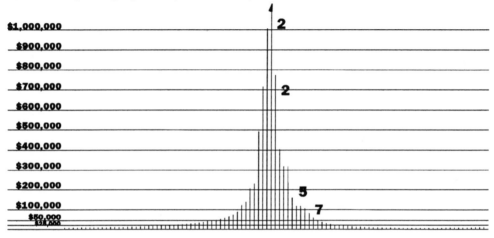

One Hundred Businesses

Figure 1.4. Gross Income Typical of Every 100 U.S. Businesses

Net Profit Study

It may be helpful to the entrepreneur to understand just how ignorant those around him or her are about business. Conduct this simple poll. Ask these people, "How many cents of a dollar in sales represent profit for the typical American business?" The correct answer is charted for a sampling of retail operations in Figure 1.5. If you browse through the *United States Statistical Abstract* (available at every public library) for other business types, you will discover considerable similarity in profit levels.

Three to 5 percent (or $5 profit on $100 in sales) is a very good five-year average for those businesses that are profitable. It is necessary to use a five-year average whenever possible. The practice of pushing a big deal forward into the coming year or forcing it into the books of a current year is common. This practice can make profit look good in any given year. Each year, however, 80 percent of all businesses make no profit at all.

My purpose here is not to scare you away. It is to leave you with some reasonable definition of what to expect once you open your business. This purpose is strengthened by my belief that most owners who make no profit at all fail because of simple ignorance. The presumption is that the owner who is more informed will be more likely to act in a guarded, responsible way. The hope is that the more informed entrepreneur is more able to look after his or her own well-being. The recognition is that those who do are much more likely to find success and prosper in less time.

Note in Figure 1.5 that the percent of net profit is much greater for small stores than it is for larger stores. A higher sales volume rarely represents higher profits as a percent. The net for department stores is a good example. At the $1 million to $2 million range, the average net profit is 2.75 percent. By expanding the business to the $10 million to $20 million range, the average net profit falls more than 50 percent, to 1.3 percent. The *total* profit is, of course, greater with the larger business but so is the commitment, the work, and the risk.

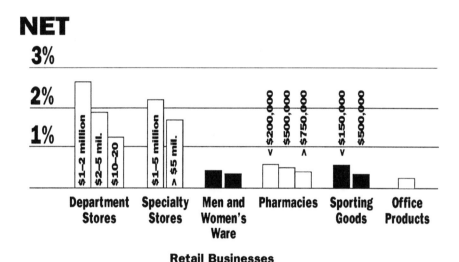

Figure 1.5. Net Profit Comparison for Selected U.S. Retail Businesses

An entrepreneur in a medium-sized midwestern town had spent the best part of his life running a grocery store. His store was located in a growth area of town. It was open 7 days a week, 24 hours a day. It was known as a model of success. The downtown portion of the city had been decaying. City fathers were looking for an investor to move into a large piece of that downtown property with the hope of revitalizing the area. The grocer took up the challenge by building a very large store that included every service a grocery store could offer. It even had a full-sized, upscale cafeteria. The new store opened with great fanfare. Two months later the operation had failed, and a new large corporate owner took over. Revenues were less than half of what was expected.

The problem is that the profits from a successful small operation can easily be overwhelmed by the losses of a much larger operation. A lifetime of working gain can be dissolved in two months with a failed operation. In this case, it even happened within what could be considered the same market as the highly successful operation. It was being operated with many of the same knowledgeable people. However, little thought was given to keeping costs in line with potential revenue. Because the town was being adequately served by several other supermarkets, the only way the new one could succeed was to win the customers away from these other stores. It didn't work! The Real Ratio, discussed later in the text, shows how the declining profit margins of larger operations significantly decrease the chance for success.

Summary

Deciding whether to start a business or to continue in one may well be the most important professional decision of your life. That decision should be based on a realistic assessment of both the risks and benefits involved.

Chapter 2

Preventing Business Failure

It is easier to define what causes businesses to fail than to define what causes them to succeed. This is because the number of failures is far greater than the number of successes. Experts have compiled considerable data about these failures. By inference, then, your chances for success will increase if you learn what to avoid. The fact is, the vast majority of business failures stem from a single cause, *poor cash management*. So if you can find a fast and simple way to properly manage cash, you have a much better chance of beating the odds. Just what are the odds? About one new business startup in five makes it through the fifth year of business.

No-Entry Accounting, which is the subject of Part II, gives you a fast, simple way of getting to cash management data. But there is more to being successful than simply getting to the data. The specific reason your particular business might fail is constantly changing. As a business moves from one year to the next and from one stage to the next, new cash management problems appear. First, there are the startup cash problems. Next come the cash problems dealing with a rolling cash fund. Third come the seasons. Fourth, the cash problems associated with a successful, taxpaying business appear. A fifth, all-inclusive, set of cash problems can develop if an owner decides to expand the business too quickly or becomes involved in dynamic growth.

The common denominator in the control of these various problems is an understanding of accounting data. To avoid failure, the data must be compiled monthly, it must be accurate, and the data must be used objectively to avoid emotional, uninformed decisions.

Why Businesses Fail

So what about business failure? A study of the factors that cause businesses to fail will shed light on the need to understand accounting. Explore, then, what is already known.

What Makes A Business Successful

Two Small Business Administration officials wrote a definitive article on business failure.[1] They say that "the most staggering cause for failure is a general lack of managerial skills." Because most entrepreneurs lack managerial skills, they essentially begin in a "sink-or-swim" environment. Consider this list of reasons for failure, which have been extracted from the article.

- Poor site selection.
- No financial projections.
- Lack of established financial relations.
- Offering long-term credit to new customers.
- No budget for the first few difficult months.
- Relative ignorance in handling financial matters.
- Laxity in submitting financial statements to banks.
- Uncontrollable urge to invest in long-term commitments.

Each of these points is either a direct cash management problem or a problem that has its roots in poor cash management. The reasons for failure are discussed here in turn, with tips on how to avoid them.

Choosing a Low-Traffic Site

Poor site selection, for example, has its roots in poor cash management. Inherent in the poor site decision is the knowledge that a particular site is not "the best." Poor sites are virtually always selected because they were all their owners could afford. The entrepreneurial zeal that drives individuals to try their hand at ownership is so strong that they will try, regardless of site.

A typical site decision is based on the amount of available cash the entrepreneur has to invest in a building or a lease. The owner asks "How much good location can I afford?" rather than "How much cash is required to obtain a site that can generate sufficient traffic?" If the required cash turns out to be more than the owner has available, moving ahead is a poor cash management decision. Why risk it all when the first decision is knowingly a bad one?

Omitting Financial Forecasts

Lack of financial projections is a very direct cash management problem. A bank loan officer tells of a loan applicant's request that illustrates this point. An individual in a Midwest town of approximately 14,000 people wanted to borrow money to start a videocassette rental store. He wanted to know how much money he could borrow to get started.

Had this entrepreneur done even a simple preliminary projection, he would not have gotten as far as the bank! The town already had six video stores. If you assume the average family has four people, there are approximately 3,500 households. Today 68 percent of U.S. households own a video player, so apply that average to this town. This leaves 2,380 households. If we optimistically assume that

---

[1]"Why So Many Small Businesses Flop," in *Across the Board* (February 1979). Pat L. Burr, Assistant Administrator for Management Assistance, and Richard S. Heckmann, Entrepreneur in Residence, Small Business Administration, Washington, D.C.

the new business could immediately grab 30 percent of the market, the entrepreneur would be left with 714 prospective clients. Many VCR owners rent fewer than two videos per month. But assume the store did rent two each month to all the 714 prospective clients; 1428 videos would be rented monthly. At an average of $2 per video, monthly revenue would come to $2,856.

A video store would likely need to be open 10 hours per day, 7 days a week, or 70 hours weekly. At $4.25 per hour, the wages per week for a single employee without overtime total $297.50. Multiplied times 4.3 weeks per month, this minimal amount of labor would cost $1,279.25. Add $800 for rent. Then the costs for the phone, lights, heat, insurance, a decent wage, FICA, paying back a loan, and so on, are factored in.

It becomes perfectly clear that probably five of the six video stores already must be operating at a loss. What if only half of the households have a VCR? What if our investor succeeds in winning only 20 percent of the market? Clearly, this is not the kind of situation from which a successful business venture is made. If the entrepreneur in this example had the money to begin this venture on his own, he surely would have lost it all.

Lacking Firm Outside Financial Contacts

The absence of established financial relations is another direct cash management problem. Every business needs to borrow money at one time or another. Omitting the establishment of banking relations can make the financing of a new business difficult.

Banks need to be provided an individual's credit record in order to make a favorable judgment on a loan application. In the absence of such a record, you need extra collateral or cosigners in order to get a loan. Both are hard to come by, especially at the last minute. The financial relationship most required is proof that your debts are paid on time. The record of a personal bank account, car payments, or a rental record may suffice. But these indications are "level sensitive." That is, a borrower's good rental record at $400 per month is only a partial indicator that he could be trusted at the $1,000-per-month level. A borrower may still be able to obtain financing, but only with an unreasonable amount of collateral.

Collateral is an important part of arranging financing. As described in Chapter 1, many small business owners use the collateral built up in their home. Once you have borrowed money on the order of a home loan, you have an established financial relationship. An established payment record with a mortgage and a willingness to use your most prized possession as collateral are two important ingredients in developing a financial relationship. The mortgage shows that you are capable of carrying a large loan. The willingness to use the equity in that home is proof that you are willing to risk personal assets before you ask a bank to risk its assets.

Offering Long-Term Credit

Another direct cash management problem is offering long-term credit to customers. In fact, offering credit of any term to any customer is a cash management problem, with one exception: credit card sales. The risk associated with credit card customers is carried by the credit card company. Once a legal purchase is made with a credit card, it is the credit card company's responsibility to collect the amount due.

Consider that a credit sale cannot take place until all the regular business expenses have been incurred. A building, inventory, and utilities must be in place and labor must be performed. To come this far and let the product walk out the door as an account receivable requires more cash to carry the business until the receivable is finally paid.

Sometimes accounts receivable will equal several months' worth of sales. This means a business must have enough cash in hand to pay for the expenses and purchases it generates during this period. If the business does not, it may fail before the receivables come in. Also, there is always the problem of accounts receivable that cannot be collected within 90 days—and some invoices that never get collected. Effective management of accounts receivable is one of the most difficult cash management problems. Only a handful of companies I have dealt with have been able to consistently manage accounts receivable. A business that must use accounts receivable is a business that must have more cash in hand in order to succeed.

Lacking an Initial Budget

Not creating a realistic budget for the first few difficult months is of course a direct cash management problem. Consider this problem from the perspective of the entrepreneur described earlier who wanted to own a video store. He had no financial projections. Neglecting to prepare a budget is essentially the same as omitting a projection. Both are defined as a plan. The video store situation clearly points out that the lack of a plan, in whatever form, can directly contribute to business failure. More probably, the lack of a plan *ensures* failure rather than merely contributing to it.

Lacking Expertise in Finance

Relative ignorance in handling financial matters is a very general condition. But consider some examples. You could be considered ignorant in financial matters if you are not able to prepare a cash analysis, a balance sheet, or a profit and loss statement. Or you may not know the difference between cash and accrual accounting. Many entrepreneurs know nothing about social security and self-employment taxes, workmen's compensation, and unemployment insurance. The difference in costs and obligations between the various methods used to compute interest is often unknown.

Only a few entrepreneurs know how to make an appropriate loan application or a good business plan. Some cannot even balance a checkbook. A complete list may go on forever. The typical entrepreneurial venture, however, seldom sinks from a single bit of ignorance. It is the gradual, or sometimes not so gradual, cumulative effect of many small missing pieces that takes its toll.

Omitting Submission of Financial Statements

The laxity in submitting financial statements to banks is another direct cash management problem. This seems to stem from the entrepreneur's belief that the financial institution is the one shortchanged by the lack of statements. The entrepreneur might think that his or her own problems come first, the bank can wait.

In one of my seminars for banking industry employees, this very topic was covered in depth. The president of the bank pointed out that federal regulations required him to keep certain supporting documentation on file for each loan customer. One minimum requirement was semiannual statements. A bank is visited by bank examiners frequently. If during these periodic visits the examiners discover loan files with missing or outdated information, the bank is subject to disciplinary action and, ultimately, the loss of its charter to operate. An entrepreneur's laxity in supplying statements, then, can make the banker look less than professional to those to whom he or she reports.

The real problem, however, is this. Both the banker and the examiners know that loaning money to a business that cannot find time to perform timely, monthly accounting is risky business. They know from many years of experience that a business that does not develop monthly statements is one that is being followed by the investor, rather than one that is being guided by the investor. Constant monitoring through monthly financial statements is thought to keep the entrepreneur in a guiding posture rather than a following posture. This is the reason a bank will sometimes require monthly statements. The loan officers want to make loans to as many marginal customers as is prudent, but— especially in our country's current banking atmosphere—the officers must be able to demonstrate to the examiners' satisfaction that every effort has been made to ensure collectability.

So it is the entrepreneur who is short-changed if the business is not monitored monthly. In the absence of such monitoring, the chance for success declines considerably. The bank will be covered, however, because it would have taken sufficient collateral to ensure that any loan would be paid off.

Warning: The simple process of having monthly statements prepared by a bookkeeper or accountant is not enough to protect you. As the chief decision maker, you must be personally involved.

Locking Money Up in Long-Term Commitments

The uncontrollable urge to invest in long-term commitments is another direct cash management problem. A typical example is a local restaurant that has had several owners over the past few years. Each one begins operations by rebuilding or redecorating a significant portion of the facility. Each dollar so spent becomes locked into the "value of the business." As such, these dollars are still with the entrepreneur but have been converted from cash to equity.

This cash can only be recovered in two ways. One way is to obtain 20 to 80 cents on the dollar by using any restaurant equity as collateral on a loan. The other way is to sell the business. The sale may also return some fraction of the dollar invested. And so it goes. Neither method is an efficient use of cash. The result is that when cash is needed to deal with a problem it is not available.

The problem of money locked up in long-term commitments is described well in an article entitled, "Why Businesses Fail," which appeared in the January 1982 issue of *Hardware Age.* "Most businesses that fail don't have a strong cash flow and cash forecasting. Everything revolves around one basic concept, recordkeeping." In my

15

experience, these statements are 100 percent true. Whenever a particular business problem surfaces, it seems to somehow stem from poor cash management. The full recognition of that particular problem must come from the records that were kept. The solution to that problem inevitably requires better recordkeeping in the future.

For example, Jim has been operating a new business for three months. Things have been going well. Jim opens his mail one morning and discovers that his accountant has notified him of a quarterly payroll deposit. Now $800 is due within five days. The problem is that Jim does not have $800 in his checking account. This problem should have been recognized from Jim's records. A running total of the tax obligation from each payday should have been recorded on the 941 tax reporting form, but that form is with the accountant. To solve the problem, Jim will have to see the bank for a short-term loan. To get the loan, Jim will have to provide financial statements, which brings him right back to recordkeeping.

The great cost of ignoring this data is reflected in two ways. First, Jim's accounting bill will be larger because he's asking a professional accountant to do work outside that could easily be done in-house. More importantly, Jim will soon make an uninformed business decision. Its cost will be greater than the excessive accounting bill. Gradually these mistakes accumulate until the Cycle of Demise is triggered. The Cycle of Demise is discussed in detail shortly.

The long-term solution is to forecast this requirement. The running total of the amount due will have to be accounted for on the Internal Revenue Service's 941 form as it should have been. Other cash outlays will have to be structured so that they do not coincide with the quarterly deposit, and so on. This "structuring" and "forecasting" can only come from good, complete records. There is simply no way to avoid recordkeeping. The less distant you remain from recordkeeping, the lower the cost and the fewer the surprises.

A review of Kenneth J. Albert's *Straight Talk About Small Business* (McGraw-Hill, 1981) also confirms poor cash management as the culprit.

Albert says, "Most owners of successful small businesses feel that the prime reason for small business failure is inadequate capital." The term often used in the accounting profession to describe the poor cash management syndrome is being *undercapitalized*. Almost by definition, small businesses are chronically undercapitalized.

This constant cash shortage seems to relate to the example used in the discussion of poor site selection. If entrepreneurs have $30,000 to invest, they will invariably seek to leverage that investment completely. This means the entrepreneurs will attempt to buy a business, property, equipment, and so on, such that the $30,000 represents a minimum down payment of 10 or 20 percent. A purchase price of $300,000 may result. The resulting periodic interest and principal reductions effectively handcuff the new venture. This "shackling" locks future profits to the repayment of borrowed capital.

It is important to know that *debt can only be retired from profit*. If it turns out that this is the same profit the entrepreneur had hoped to live on, one (the repayment of debt) or the other (living) must suffer. Therefore, a startup decision that leaves no room for error in the management of cash is a direct cash management problem. Cash management is the single most important tool an entrepreneur can use to avoid business failure.

The Professions and Failure

There is a certain irony about the professions and small business failure. That is, the very help and guidance the small investor is willing to seek and pay for might be the guidance and expense that causes the business to fail.

I can recall the days just before my first entrepreneurial venture, The Old Church Inn. Friends and strangers alike felt compelled to offer the advice they thought made the difference between success and failure. Two of the more common bits of advice were: "If you're going to make it, you've got to use other people's money" and "The first thing you have to do is get yourself a good attorney and a good accountant." Presumably, "good" means one who is more expensive. I am quite certain now that all this advice was wrong. Why? I now believe that every entrepreneur must begin by learning some entrepreneurial navigation skills. In the introduction, I defined learning these skills as learning to do one's own accounting. Business owners should do their own accounting at least until they become thoroughly familiar with the entire process. An acceptable level of familiarity should include the ability to generate a cash analysis monthly, the ability to prepare a monthly profit and loss statement, the ability to maintain the balance sheet, and a thorough understanding of the company's record system. The time and expertise required to do these tasks is dramatically reduced by using No-Entry Accounting, the subject of Part II of this book.

The Bankers
Using other people's money is an absolute necessity to most businesses. The degree to which it is used and under what conditions compose the difference between healthy businesses and failed ones. The more that a business is leveraged (in debt), the more important accurate and timely accounting data becomes. The greater the need for accounting data, the greater the need for the entrepreneur to understand that data in detail and to be personally involved in its accurate preparation.

In my experience, banks offered more credit than I could handle. Later, the loans were very difficult to repay. One bank officer actually admitted to making heavily collateralized loans to individuals the bank knew would have extreme difficulty repaying. If the collateral was sufficient, the banker was willing to let the borrower worry about how it was to be repaid. A loan collateralized at four or five times the amount of the loan might be the result.

This problem affects the small business borrower in two ways.
- If an individual cannot clearly define a repayment plan, a loan should not be requested. The repayment of the principal and interest will eventually squeeze some other critical need for cash. The squeeze will always occur at precisely the wrong time and in precisely the wrong way. A small business loan based on collateral and no cash flow is a no-no!

- To take a loan in the absence of a clear method of repayment inefficiently ties up collateral that might be needed later.

Banks make loans on a cash flow basis and on a collateral basis. If the cash flow is weak, the loan officer will go double or triple on the collateral requirement. The result could be a $10,000 second mortgage collateralized with $80,000 in home equity. This mortgage may have cost several front-end points (1, 2, or even 3 percent of the loan amount to be paid in the beginning), an appraisal fee, and closing costs. The resulting effective interest rate will likely be higher than a typical commercial loan. It causes the borrower to pay too much for too little, while giving up too much in the way of collateral reserve.

Taking a loan on this basis is, therefore, poor cash management. It can contribute directly to failure several months down the road when another $40,000 in collateral might mean the difference between success and failure.

Another way the small business owner can get in trouble is to obtain a loan for which the repayment schedule is too fast. The bank is necessarily required to keep its interest first and the borrower's interests second. When a loan is granted, it is sometimes to the bank's advantage to keep the repayment period as short as possible. So if the borrower does not make his or her needs clear, not only in amount but in time, the result is often a repayment schedule that triggers a real cash crunch.

Banks are meant to loan money only to well-qualified borrowers. This situation is recognized by the commonly used expression, "Banks only loan money to people who don't need it." The typical small business owner does not realize that a bank becomes suspect when bad loans reach 1.5 percent of its total portfolio. Compare the 1.5 percent failure rate banks are required to work with against the 80 percent failure rate of small business. It becomes clear why small businesses and banks sometimes seem worlds apart.

The Lawyers

The advice about getting a good attorney may be sound in certain situations. One such situation is if an entrepreneur has substantial "net" personal holdings to protect. ("Net" means the amount of assets left after mortgages and other contractual considerations have been subtracted.) The laws involving business transactions deal with civil laws rather than criminal laws. Stealing or fraud, of course, is criminal. But if someone does not repay a loan or makes a mistake that costs someone else money, that is a civil matter. Civil matters are satisfied with cash, not jail. The borrower who does not repay a loan can be required to make payment by a court from whatever other source that individual may have. If there is no such source, the delinquent borrower walks away with nothing more than a bad credit reference. The lender must eat the bad loan.

The individual who makes a costly mistake can only be pursued to the limit of his or her net assets. Consequently, if there is no net monetary target, there is no reason to pursue these matters through the court system except as a matter of principle. Small businesses, however, cannot afford to be in court over matters of principle!

Small businesses need to avoid high legal bills, hollow victories, and the time and money spent in nonproductive ways. Legal problems can cause uncontrollable cash management problems and give little satisfaction. If you become involved in a venture that routinely involves legal matters, such as all of the construction industry, keep extra cash in hand and add to your markup. Take whatever courses might be available. Attend industry association meetings where pertinent legal concepts can be learned. Attend association functions and network with your counterparts in other companies. Most small business owners are eager to share what they know when be approached in a relaxed environment. Remember, the most expensive way to learn about the law is by watching an attorney work while the clock is running.

The legal expense of incorporating should also be avoided until a business's annual profit is regularly at least $45,000. Recent changes in the tax law may push the profit level even higher. This consideration and liability protection (employees and stockholders are not liable for actions of the corporation) formerly were common arguments for incorporation. The liability protection a corporation is thought to provide is of limited use, however. There are many ways to penetrate the liability protection, and a company must waive liability protection to obtain large loans or deal with major vendors. A good liability insurance policy may be a better bet at the outset.

A quirk involving the tax system and accounting rules for corporations is another reason not to incorporate early. Certain types of small corporations are often advised to show no profit at year end. Considerable time and money can be spent with the professionals trying to find loopholes that permit the extraction of profit without paying tax. This is particularly important to small corporations, because the owner of a small corporation may be double taxed. A corporation pays income tax on its profit, and its rate is usually higher than an individual's. Such profits are occasionally distributed to the stockholders of that corporation. These "dividends" to the stockholder become dividends and interest income to the individual and are taxed as regular income. Because the income was first taxed through corporate profits, and again at the individual level, the small corporation owner is taxed twice on the same income.

In summary, the following reasons make it advisable to hold off incorporating your company:

- Some companies incorporate to enable owners to generate capital for which no monthly payment is required, for which no interest is due, and that never has to be paid back. Small businesses, however, seldom have a track record sufficient to attract investors for such capital generation.

- Tax deductions and the "liability protection canopy" are not economically advantageous to an individual until proprietorship net profit reaches a stable level annually of about $45,000.

- Starting a corporation and meeting its additional accounting and tax-reporting requirements all cost more money than starting a proprietorship.

- Corporate owners may be taxed twice on the same income.

- The corporate tax rate may be higher than an individual's tax rate.
- The corporate entity is much less flexible to manage than is a proprietorship or partnership, because a corporation cannot intermingle personal and company funds and because a corporation must have officers, annual meetings, and so on.

So, use common sense. Write down business agreements and get them signed. Learn to compromise before going to court rather than being forced to pay for legal fees as well as a court-imposed compromise. Remember, all the legal protection in the world is useless if all it does is keep the attorney in business while putting the entrepreneur out of business.

The Accountants

The *United States Statistical Abstract*, published annually by the U.S. government, tabulates the year-end results of some 16 million nonfarm businesses. As mentioned earlier, these results show that 98 percent of these businesses have annual revenue under $1 million, and 84 percent have annual revenue under $100,000.

A typical practicing CPA needs to set the bottom of his or her client marketplace (business that he or she can economically pursue) at firms where annual gross revenue is in the $500,000 range. A nationally known accounting firm that employs practitioners who are mostly not CPAs finds that the practitioners need an average monthly fee of $100 plus per client to make ends meet. A year-end fee is several hundred dollars more. Thus, the bottom of this company's client market goes well below the $100,000 annual revenue level and is based on a transaction count. Clients for whom a monthly fee would be less than $50 (for fewer than 10 transactions per month) are not considered economically viable. Economic viability for a full-time practicing accountant, therefore, begins at $750 in annual accounting fees. ($50 times 12 months equals $600, plus $150 year-end fee equals $750.)

So here is the problem. A typical operating business, from which an owner is generating the largest portion of his or her income, will generate a transaction count on the order of 30 per month, I would guess. Transaction count includes items such as checks written, charge card and cash receipts, transfers between business and personal accounts, and bank deposits. This level of business activity will be charged fees on the $130-per-month level. Annually, this business activity typically represents a $1,500 accounting bill.[2] If a business had a 5 percent net profit—and recall that most average less than 5 percent—then $30,000 in sales must be generated to pay for the accountant without a decline in profit (0.05 divided into $1,500 equals $30,000). To the small business owner, even this entry-level price is unaffordable. It translates into the cost of a simple vacation, perhaps some new tools, or perhaps a major repair.

A business in this situation generates the same net profit if its owner does the accounting as if sales increased by $30,000. In most cases, an extra workload of an hour a month is all that is required to prepare the monthly statement. A business owner may already be spending that much time just getting everything ready for the accountant. I have never known a small business operator who could generate an

---

[2] Sole proprietor accounting does not provide for an owner's wage. Therefore, an appropriate wage for the work that a proprietor performs must be subtracted from proprietorship net profit in order to make this comparison.

extra $30,000 in sales for the business in just 12 to 15 hours per year. On the other hand, I know of many owners who now do their own accounting and save that $100 per hour for themselves.

In one instance I am familiar with, accounting fees had reached 35 percent of annual revenue. It was being paid by a freelance photographer who not only loathed numbers but would not find the time to shop around for a more reasonable price. He probably would have fought anyone who threatened his camera and equipment, but he permitted himself to be victimized from within by silently paying exorbitant rates to his accountant. In comparison, a typical Fortune 500 Company spends less than one-half of one percent of gross annual revenue for accounting.

The Accountant/Client Gap

The accountant/client gap is the perceptual difference between what the small business owners think they are buying in accounting services and what the accountant is trained to provide. The gap can be seen from a variety of accountant/client situations. It is dealt with here from the perspective of a new business whose owner is deciding which method to use to value inventory. Most entrepreneurs have no idea what methods may be used to value inventory. Most have no idea what record keeping is required to make a particular method work. Nor do the owners understand the impact of not performing a monthly physical inventory and determining its value by the chosen method.

Assume that a business has just begun operation and has hired an accountant. The first session may proceed as follows:

1. The new accountant will explain to the business owner that he or she needs to perform a regular inventory. Each in-house item must be counted and multiplied by the cost price. This cost price is determined by the math used in the valuation method chosen.

2. The typical business owner will respond, "That's a lot of work. How am I going to get it done every month? There has to be another way."

3. The new accountant usually agrees that a once-a-year inventory is easier. The accountant may add that most small businesses only do inventory once a year for just that reason. The accountant will explain that tax law requires an annual physical inventory, but once a year really isn't good enough.

4. Anxious to save time and deal with more important and immediate problems, the business owner takes up on the once-a-year idea. The business owner says, "If once a year is good enough for Uncle Sam, once a year is good enough for me." Because the accountant's viability is based upon obtaining new clients, he or she feels compelled not to press the matter further.

The accountant has thus provided defense against the claim that proper advice was not provided. The need for taking inventory more frequently has been pointed out. The client, however, is free to exercise ignorance. As this scenario transpires, another new business takes its first giant step toward failure. The very ignorance that business owners hope to protect themselves against by hiring an accountant can overpower the accountant's will to get the job done right. The accountant takes the position that it is often easier to give a new client what is wanted than to sell the client on what is needed. A loss of inventory control will certainly result. Loss of inventory control leads to loss of cash control. Loss of cash control triggers the Cycle of Demise, which results in business failure.

The underlying problematic result is this: The uninformed business owner perceives hiring an accountant as paying for protection from accounting ignorance. Sometimes a client believes he or she is being protected from the IRS or the state tax collector. Of course, neither situation is true. The business owner anticipates being led by the hand and forewarned of any impending "accounting problem." This example shows that the business owner's ignorance can overpower the forewarning.

In some small businesses, months of monthly financial statements lie stacked in a dirty corner, unopened. When asked why the business owner has not even opened the statements, the answer is, "My accountant takes care of all that. What do you think I pay him for?". The fact that the statements may be worthless because of insufficient data or lack of timeliness, or that the inventory figure used for cost of sales may be grossly in error, or any other malady, is unimportant because the accountant is taking care of it. The client essentially believes that in hiring an outside accountant a phantom manager is being paid for, one who will provide guidance and protection.

The owner may think, "If the accountant needs something, it will be asked for," or, "If I (the client) am doing something wrong, the accountant will point it out."

Meanwhile, the accountant is operating on a different premise. The monthly fee is earned by performing the work necessary to provide proper statements. The accuracy of the statements depends on the data the client provides and on mathematically correct calculations in generating the statements. The accountant assumes responsibility *only* for mathematical correctness. If the statements are in error, the accountant heard nothing about it. The accountant has been available for answering questions, but none were asked. If the client is doing something wrong that shows up in the statements, the accountant will call it to the client's attention. It is the client's obligation to take appropriate action.

Then there is tax advice, which is available to the client if the client will only ask. Furthermore, the accountant has to get the client's job done with tardy, partial, sometimes intentionally misleading data. Some accountants feel a portion of their fee is earned by having to provide constant follow-up to obtain the data in usable form. Another part of the fee is earned for providing on-the-job training in accounting and finance. Internal considerations such as cash management or inventory control simply must be the responsibility of the business owner and are not included as part of the monthly fee.

The two perceptions are quite distinct. This client/accountant gap in expectations is a fundamental contributor to the high level of startup business failures. This is because 9 of the top 10 reasons for business failure have their roots in poor cash management. Neither the information provided by the accountant nor the information asked for by the business owner provides a direct look at cash position. By the time a cash problem becomes apparent in the typical monthly profit and loss statement and balance sheet, it is usually too late to save the company.

A complicating factor is that small business owners are often advised to use accrual accounting. This practice results in statements that completely mask the cash position data. I have never seen an accountant who provides either a periodic cash analysis or the training for clients to prepare one. And yet, an accurate cash requirements forecast is the *single most valuable document* to any business. Ironically, the cash a small business person spends for accounting statements and advice may be the very cash expenditure that triggers the company's Cycle of Demise. (The Cycle of Demise is the process of business failure that is discussed at the end of this chapter.)

The bottom line is that if a small business owner needs to lean heavily on professionals and/or banks to get started, the business's chances for success are considerably diminished.

The Entrepreneurial Trojan Horse

A review of the Trojan Horse story from Greek mythology is appropriate for the small business owner. The Greeks had been locked in war for years attempting to conquer the city of Troy. The Greeks eventually realized that the only way they could conquer Troy was from the inside. The way in, they decided, was to build a monument that could harbor soldiers and get the Trojans to accept the monument within their city gate. The Trojan Horse was built and left at the gate. The Greeks then sailed into the sunset in apparent retreat. In the meantime, a captured Greek had convinced some of the Trojan hierarchy that the Trojan Horse was a sacred symbol that would bring the protection of the gods to its owner. The Trojans believed the story, so they pulled the horse inside the gate. That night, as the Greek army sailed back to Troy under the cover of darkness, the soldiers hidden in the horse slipped out and opened the gates from inside. The Greek army was then able to enter the city fortress unchallenged and easily conquer Troy.

Businesses have their Trojan Horse in the form of common misconceptions. Once an owner permits these misconceptions inside a business, they defeat the business from within. These misconceptions lie with the owner as well as the employees.

The Fallacy of Wealthy Business Owners

A basic employee misconception is that anyone who is in business must have a lot of money. The employees often believe that the owner is making much more than is ever the case. The unscientific research I have conducted underscores this belief. Several high school classes and numerous employees of various companies were asked what they believe to be a typical profit margin. (The query was how many cents of each dollar in sales they believe a company earns as profit.) The answers typically centered around 25 cents of each dollar in sales, with a high of 75 cents. A correct answer is less than 5 cents on the dollar. The common belief that profits are much higher than is actually the case and that owner earnings are much higher than is the case sometimes leads employees to

- Lackadaisical work habits.
- Carelessness with company property.
- Unreasonable demands for wage increases with no thought of increased productivity.
- Theft.

Why do employees develop such bad attitudes? They believe the company has lots of money and can write off losses. "Why work any harder than necessary when it just puts more money in the boss's bank account?"

The owners of small businesses do little to dispel these beliefs. Many of them have come to their entrepreneurial adventure with dollar signs in their eyes. People come to believe that owning a business means living the high life shown on TV and in the movies. Many new business owners believe that to be in business one needs to act like a successful business owner. Buying a new car or new equipment, moving to a plush office, or obtaining a prestigious address are only a few of the ways in which the role of a successful business owner may be played out. Employees pick up on these "signs of success" and may think nothing of wasting company materials or working four hours for eight hours' pay.

Any of these "impression" acts may also cause a new business to become locked into a course to failure before its doors even open. Failure comes from uninformed decisions that tie up cash on "impressions." Owners never learn that cash should only be used for expenditures that will generate more revenue or lower operating costs until the business can genuinely afford luxuries.

The Closed-Minded Owner

Another common owner misconception is the belief that employees are paid to do as they are told, like it or not. Whether they are right or wrong makes no difference either, because the person who signs the check is always right. This managerial attitude invariably turns on the owner and costs him or her the business, for the following reasons:

- Employees who stay on the job under such conditions learn to withhold their opinion. Perhaps an employee opinion or observation was wrong or unnecessary on one day, but the next day the same employee may save the owner embarrassment and the cost of a major mistake.

- This managerial attitude leaves the employee with bitterness or a feeling of being always put down. When an employee develops this feeling, it can become a cash problem. The employee will feel essentially relieved of any obligation to put in his or her best effort every day. The cash impact on the business comes in the form of theft or "working to rule" (doing precisely as directed, paying attention to every detail, but volunteering nothing and taking no initiative).

The usual effect is to bring an operation to an unprofitable slowdown or perhaps even to a standstill. The employees remain on the payroll without just cause for dismissal.

A true story will help to illustrate these points. A national chain of nursing homes had just purchased a small-town nursing home that had been up for sale. The firm sent in its representatives to provide an overview of life under the corporation's system. The home office's existing supervisors were sent off to corporate training facilities to learn the new owner's methods and procedures. A visit was planned by the president of the corporation to mark the entry of the new facility into the national family of nursing homes. It was no ordinary visit.

The employees were assembled as the president's helicopter settled into the nursing home parking lot. The president gave a speech about the advantages of being part of a big operation. The president stressed how supplies and equipment could be purchased more cheaply, well-documented procedures would aid in making a profit, and so on. He summarized by asking for the total cooperation of all the employees. Cooperation was a must, he said, because profits for this national operation were averaging around one cent on the dollar. There was, therefore, no room for error.

An employee (one of the supervisors) was very impressed. She said, "This company really has the money! It can afford to send all the supervisors off for weeks at the company's expense. Old, inadequate facilities at the nursing home are going to be completely redone. The president even flies around in his own helicopter! Now maybe I'll get a good raise." The Trojan Horse had arrived. The president's arrival in a helicopter set the stage for high expectations, whereas his 1 percent profit margin speech fell on deaf ears. Almost no one believes that a national corporation makes only one cent on the dollar. A common belief is that corporations have ways of taking writeoffs and hiding income in tax laws, so that the net profit is really a lot more. In fact, a 1 percent profit is very believable.

The favorable impression quickly wore away as the corporate team moved in with its rigid procedures and even more rigid changeover managers. The cold, hard, take-it-or-leave-it approach resulted in the disgruntled departure of some employees. Employee departure under such conditions is usually calculated to maximize misery and cost to the employer. Theft and failure to report for a weekend shift are just two methods. Other employees were fired. Some replacements were hired at higher rates of pay than those who had been chased away, so the payroll went up. The new people had to be trained, which was an additional cost. The excitement over facilities improvement faded as time passed by with no change. And so it went.

About a year later, the facility was sold again. Costs had risen so much that there was no chance the facility would be able to earn its 1 cent on the dollar. The corporation had lost stockholders' money, and the training and jobs of several qualified, loyal, former employees had been sacrificed. Most importantly, however, an employee/management friction had developed that left the facility with a caustic atmosphere.

The hope for profit in such an operation becomes more distant. Employees are less likely to volunteer their help if someone else drops the ball. Some employees will work to the rule, doing exactly as they are told and absolutely nothing more. They may withhold their cooperation and initiative in defining and solving company problems. They may take what they believe they have coming by stealing or filing false injury claims. They may chase customers away with intentional blunders or rude treatment. Each small contributor to operating cost pushes profitability into the future.

The bottom line to the concept of the Entrepreneurial Trojan Horse is this: Employee and owner misconceptions translate directly to cash problems that can cause a business to fail from within. Because business owners don't know what they don't know, additional cash must be kept aside to provide for the unseen. It will surely be needed before an entrepreneurial venture reaches its first anniversary.

The Cycle of Demise

The Cycle of Demise is my name for the process and mechanics of business failure. The trigger point for the Cycle of Demise differs for each business. This point also changes regularly within a given business. Despite this elusive quality, the trigger point is actually very simple to compute.

The trigger point in each business is that dollar amount where:

Business sources of cash = Business uses of cash

Many of the sources and uses of cash are listed on the cash analysis form, Figure 13.1. This form is designed to help the business owner quickly compute the company's position with regard to the Cycle of Demise. A cash shortfall computed indicates that the Cycle of Demise has been triggered. A cash surplus indicates that a business is operating safely above the trigger point.

To use the cash analysis form to calculate the trigger point, you need to know a specific date through which cash will be analyzed. Enter some cutoff date in the "Cash Requirements Through" notation. Enter and add the amounts of all the sources and all the uses of cash within this time period. The sources of cash should include, for example, accounts receivable in the period. The use of cash should include debt commitments that fall due in that period, and so on.

The same form can be used to analyze cash as it was used. For example, you could analyze all the cash that flowed through your business in a prior year. Where did cash come from and where did it go? You *must* prepare such a "lookback" document before you visit a bank for a loan. It shows the banker that you are really on top of your business, especially if you can demonstrate that you arrived at the information without preparation by an accountant. This form can also reveal beforehand whether your loan application has a chance of being accepted.

All businesses operate for varying lengths of time and at varying dollar amounts below the trigger point. A ski lodge, for example, very likely triggers the cycle each summer. If the business is a viable one, however, it quickly recovers the next season and continues. Some businesses go so far below the trigger point that they must file for bankruptcy in order to recover. Once a business has gone this far, however, it seldom recovers.

The Cycle of Demise is pictured graphically in Figure 2.1. Scene one depicts the hometown optician's business operating above the trigger point. At this level a business has sufficient cash to meet the prompt payment requirements of vendors who offer credit and a living wage for the owner. Below the trigger point it does not.

Scene two depicts the optician's first outright sign that the Cycle of Demise has been triggered. A major vendor has placed the optician's business on C.O.D., so no further deliveries will be made until all unpaid items are settled. This action causes the business that is already strapped for cash to require even more funds, immediately!

Scene three depicts the optician's first effort to meet the shortfall. The typical business owner, like this optician, extends his or her own 30-day credit with vendors whose credit collections are lax. The owner does this by simply not paying in 30 days.

Scene four depicts the optician using the next technique for dealing with a cash shortfall. He begins to cut corners by carrying fewer inventory items; trying to get the job done with too little help; and by cutting back on cleaning, maintenance, or other nonessential expenses.

In scene five, the secondary vendors, who have been extended by 30 days to provide cash for the optician's C.O.D. purchases, themselves go C.O.D. The cash squeeze gets tighter.

Scene six depicts business clientele beginning to notice the shortcuts and deciding to take their business elsewhere. This causes sales to drop, which provides even less cash with which to run the business. At this point, it is common for the business owner to run to the bank in hopes of getting "a little cash to tide me over." The banker, of course, requires a set of financial statements, which most small businesses do not have. The optician hires an accountant with his last available cash to prepare a proper statement.

Scene seven depicts the result of reviewing the optician's financial statement. The statement appropriately shows that the business is in dire straits. The banker is further deterred by the discovery that the optician has arrived at such a predicament and appears to be completely unaware of it. Naturally, the banker must refuse the loan. Ignorance has prevailed and the business has failed.

Scene eight depicts the optician's empty contemplation of bankruptcy.

Mismanagement of cash is not the only factor that can trigger the Cycle of Demise. The national economy can trigger it as well. If the economy reaches a point where sales peak but costs continue to climb, the net effect is to reduce the size of a business cash fund. If the business is operating too close to the trigger point when this happens, it can cause a shortfall of cash. For example, assume that a business has a cash fund of $12,000 and is operating monthly within $500 of this limit. Should the economy require the replacement of inventory at a cost significantly higher than the cost of the inventory sold, the business can easily slip from $500 above the trigger point to $500 below it. This is especially true if the increased replacement cost should happen in a one- or two-month period when other large cash outlays are due, such as a note payment or an annual insurance premium.

Figure 2.1. The Cycle of Demise: The Mechanics of Business Failure

Another often-encountered trigger mechanism is new competition. If a business continually operates near the limit of its total potential cash fund and a new competitor drains even as little as 10 percent of that business's gross revenue, the impact can be overwhelming. The underlying problem is that *any* given percent change in sales typically results in a net profit change several times as dramatic. Table 2.1 summarizes this effect.

Table 2.1. How a Decline in Sales Magnifies a Decline in Available Cash

Record Item	Before Competition	After Competition	Effect
Sales	$10,000	$9,000	10% decline
Cost of Sales	4,500	4,000	Still 45%
Wages	2,000	2,000	
Rent	1,000	1,000	
Expenses	1,500	1,500	
Net Profit	$ 1,000	$ 500	50% decline in available cash

This simple but realistic example illustrates an impact on cash that is five times greater than the impact on gross sales. Any mechanism that causes sales to decline will have the same effect. Some other factors might be a decline in customer service, poor weather, or a diminishing market. Perhaps the most common victim of the Cycle of Demise is the business that, from its inception, is never able to operate above the trigger level. That is to say, it was never able to pay its vendors within the credit cycle allowed, and provide sufficient cash flow for an owner to meet personal obligations.

The cash fund of last resort is the trade-off the owner is willing to make with regard to his or her lifestyle. If you have a very strong desire to make a business work, the sacrifice of a comfortable lifestyle can sometimes make the difference. The sports car might be traded in for basic transportation. Perhaps you move out of a nice home or apartment and into the basement of the store. Giving up a vacation, paid or otherwise, for several years provides cash. Some entrepreneurs give up all of these luxuries. When failure arrives for this type of business owner, there is nothing left. Failure is total. But if success prevails, it can be euphoric. It can result in living the American Dream.

Summary

Small business survival, then, depends to a considerable degree on the entrepreneur's ability and desire to become and remain an informed decision maker. A thorough understanding of the concepts in this chapter and an application of these concepts within your enterprise goes a long way toward helping you become that informed decision maker.

Chapter 3

Some Key Points
Small Business Owners
Need to Know

Over my years of giving No-Entry Accounting seminars, I've found a series of questions recurring. These questions have centered around the concepts covered in this chapter. As an entrepreneur you need to understand each of them in order to optimize the return from your business.

Proprietorship Versus a Corporation

In addition to some legal differences between a proprietorship and the corporation, there are some accounting differences as well. A primary difference is in the manner by which the owners of small corporations or proprietorships take their income from the business. Look at the simplified income statement for Joe's Bar & Grill in Figure 3.1. It compares the net profit of the same business as a proprietorship and as a corporation. The manners in which sales, cost of sales, and operating expenses are treated are the same, but the treatment of wages is different. (Partnership rules in this case are the same as proprietorship rules.)

Profit Versus Wages

Under an identical operation to Joe's Bar & Grill, the corporate owner shows $45,000 in *wages*, whereas the proprietor shows only $15,000 in wages. This difference causes a dramatic change in the net profit percentage: only 10 percent for the corporation and 40 percent for the proprietorship. The proprietorship reflects the entire earnings of the owner as *profit*, and no owner wage is taken. The $15,000 shown as proprietorship wages are the wages paid to employees only. Corporation accounting distributes earnings as an executive salary and dividends. The owner is not permitted to simply remove profit, even if he or she is the sole owner of all the stock. Money can be removed from the corporation only as a paycheck to an employee, or a dividend declared by the board of directors for its stockholders.

Joe's Bar and Grill:

	Corporation	Proprietorship
Sales	$100,000	$100,000
Cost of Sales	–35,000	–35,000
Wages	–45,000	–15,000
Operating Expenses	–10,000	–10,000
Net Profit	$10,000	$40,000
	10% Net	**40% Net**

Figure 3.1. Wages and Net Profit of a Corporation Versus a Proprietorship

The difference is simply a matter of accounting rules. Proprietors do not take a paycheck from their business, because tax laws do not permit the owner to write off his or her wages against profit. A proprietor's income is taken by simply removing money from the business as draw, which is not deductible. A recent change permits sole proprietors to deduct a portion of self employment tax on their 1040 (personal) tax form.

Another difference is that self-employment tax has greater flexibility in terms of when it must be submitted to the government, which can aid in dealing with cash flow problems.

If a company's total withholding is high enough (currently $3,000) the with-held tax must be deposited within three working days. Self-employment taxes need only be deposited if a profit is made and then only quarterly. This is a considerable cash management advantage, because almost every business has an unprofitable quarter or two each year.

If there is profit, the proprietor may take it as he or she sees fit. No taxes are immediately withheld, because draw is not a paycheck. In fact, a proprietor need not have profit to take a draw. The business owner can draw from the business at any time and in any way:

- The draw may come as cash taken from the cash register.

- It may come as a check made payable to the proprietor with no taxes withheld.

- It may be taken by using company goods for personal reasons or company money to pay personal bills. (Note: goods, services, and money so taken must be separated from company accounting and not deducted as a business expense.)

Any one of these methods may be used, regardless of whether the business is earning a profit. If there is no profit, however, the proprietor is simply drawing off the life blood of the business—cash. If too much is taken in the absence of profit, the Cycle of Demise will be triggered and the business may fail.

Tax Payments
If a profit is being earned, the proprietor must be aware of it and make accurate and timely estimated tax payments to the Internal Revenue Service (IRS). These deposits

have a way of catching the small business operator off balance. The problem seems to stem from being able to take cash from the business without having to write a paycheck and withhold taxes immediately. The problem can also stem from a lack of monthly statements showing the proprietor the profit that is being earned. Because there never seems to be any cash left over, the proprietor typically assumes that there is no profit. The problem is often not the absence of profit, but rather the debt-to-equity transfer, or the building of inventory or accounts receivable, which consumes the cash.

There is a major problem in running a business by the checkbook balance and assuming no cash means no profit: If you do not know you have made a profit, why worry about taxes? All too often the proprietor comes to know of the taxes that are due only after the year-end visit to the accountant. The accountant discovers a healthy profit but no deposit of estimated taxes. By this time it may be too late. Penalties and interest for Uncle Sam and an inflated accounting bill will unproductively add to the mismanagement of cash. Often the proprietor has insufficient cash to pay the accountant, pay the taxes due, and also pay the penalties and interest due on the delinquent tax deposit. The Cycle of Demise is triggered, and the problems intensify.

The proprietor's tax takes two forms. First is self-employment tax, the social security payment for self-employed people. This tax is based on raw profit from the very first dollar that is earned. The current rate nets out to 13.2 percent of the first $53,400 in proprietorship profit for a given year. A proprietorship income of $53,400, then, represents $7,048.80 in self-employment taxes (13.2 percent of $53,400). The IRS assumes that this amount will be submitted as part of the owner's federal income tax payments in four equal quarterly deposits. If it was not earned equally through the four quarters, Form 2210 can be filed with the Form 1040 at the end of the year. This form permits you to deposit tax as you earn the income rather than in four equal payments. It is a significant cash management advantage. Proprietorships and partnerships can use this form. Corporations use form #2220. It is the owner's obligation to estimate the taxes due within 5 percent and make the appropriate deposit on a timely basis. Otherwise, fines and penalties will be incurred as well.

The second tax is federal income tax. The amount of this tax depends on the personal deductions and other adjustments an individual or married couple may have. Expenses such as home mortgage interest, dependent exemptions, casualty losses, and prior business losses may be deducted. These deductions are subtracted from the proprietor's total income figure to arrive at an adjusted taxable amount. It is possible for a proprietor with a large family, living in a large house, with large medical bills, and perhaps some prior losses to owe the full amount of self-employment tax but no income tax. That is, the business owner may have earned a $45,000 profit, on which the self-employment tax is due, but adjustments may reduce the earnings back to no taxable net income for withholding tax purposes. Most small business owners pay more in self-employment tax than in income tax.

Important Note: Taking any type of unrecorded draw for the purpose of reducing profits, and therefore taxes, represents tax fraud, which is punishable by fines and imprisonment. Any removal of cash, goods, or services from a proprietorship is considered draw. Any such amount must be duly separated in the accounting record and not treated as a business expense or reduction in revenue.

A regular corporation—as opposed to a Subchapter-S corporation—is different. It is a separate entity from its owner and requires separate tax filings from its owner's Form 1040. The stockholders of small corporations are *employees* of this separate entity, even when the owner is the sole stockholder/employee. The paycheck is the usual manner by which the working stockholder takes money from the corporation. Because the method of payment is defined as a paycheck, taxes must be withheld at the time the check is written, and these taxes must be deposited with the IRS per the Internal Revenue Code.

One other method by which the stockholder may remove cash from the corporation is to declare a *dividend*. The board of directors must declare a dividend of so many dollars per share. Checks are then written to all shareholders based on the number of shares they hold. If one holder owns all the shares, one check is written. The problem here is that this dividend would only come from the corporation's profit. Because the corporation is a separate entity, it must pay income tax on its profits. Once the *tax is paid* and there is still cash available to pay a dividend, then the stockholders can receive their dividend checks.

Dividends are not income to the corporation and are, therefore, not taxable to the corporation. Dividends are taxable to the recipient for whom they represent income.

So what happens, and what does this mean? Profit from the corporate entity is first taxed as corporate income. Then, if cash remains, a dividend is declared. The recipient of the dividend must pay income tax on the amount through his or her own personal income tax filing. The corporate owner (the stockholder) and the dividend recipient are the same person, so tax is paid *twice on the same income*—first as income from the company owned, second as personal income tax on dividends received.

Another difference is that a corporation cannot be used like a proprietorship. Personal bills cannot be paid with company money. Company goods cannot be used for personal reasons. All such transactions must be made at arm's length, that is, as though the corporate owner were one of its customers or other outsider. To mingle personal and corporate uses puts the incorporation at risk. A tax court has held that when a corporation operates as a proprietorship, its incorporation can be considered null and void. It can lose its liability canopy and certainly its tax status as a corporation.

I have seen corporations where the owners had no idea what incorporation meant. They had been advised to incorporate by their accountant or attorney. It was perfectly obvious, however, that these businesses were being operated as proprietorships. The owners would use the corporate checkbook for a variety of personal reasons. Rather than stop the owners from continuing this way, the accountant would attempt to cover this misuse. This can be done by running personal expenditures through the payroll register as though the owner were actually being paid this amount with a paycheck. During an audit, or in a tax court or a court of law, this kind of practice sticks out like a sore thumb.

No auditor or attorney would have any trouble at all determining which came first—the payment of the corporate money for personal use or the kludged up payroll journal to disguise it.

Some small corporations have never had the required annual meeting of the officers and sometimes do not even know who the officers are. Many have not produced the minutes of the annual meeting and have not filed these minutes with the government, as required by law. Certainly the incorporation of these businesses is suspect as well.

So, why incorporate and spend the extra time and money necessary if subsequent actions or knowledge—or the lack of either—may deprive you of the benefits intended?

The Balance Sheet

The balance sheet is essentially a list of what a business or an individual owns and what is owed. If more is owned than is owed, the favorable balance is considered to be the equity the owner holds. The balance sheet's use for the small business person in the conventional double entry form is rather limited. If a small business is a corporation, it is a mandatory part of the annual tax filing.

The first balance sheet restriction deals with corporations. A balance sheet must contain business items only, which must be used as conventional accounting dictates. It is also restricted by double-entry considerations such as book value. *Book value* is the purchase price of an asset, minus any amount that may have been written off as depreciation.

The book value is only of value in filing taxes. The *street value* of the same asset—the price the asset would fetch if sold—is of more interest to the small business owner (whether a proprietorship, partnership, or corporation), but this value is not maintained in conventional accounting. The street value is needed to compute the equity or net worth of the entrepreneur. It is also an important part of the calculation used to arrive at the value of collateral that might be used for a loan.

The No-Entry Accounting balance sheet is designed to meet the most frequent needs of the small business owner. It is a statement of personal position that combines both personal and business financial matters. This is the format required for a loan application. It is also helpful in determining whether a self-employed person is gaining or losing the entrepreneurial battle by making it easier to arrive at an individual's total real net worth.

Both a bank loan application and the net worth calculation require that business and personal matters be considered as one. This is because they are often indistinguishable for the small business owner. A personal residence is often the collateral on a business loan, and the home phone may be the business phone as well, for example. For a loan application, the book value of an asset shown in a conventional balance sheet is of no use. The market value of an asset must be known in order to determine the collateral value. The *equity value* or the *collateral value* of an asset is what is important to the small business owner. The No-Entry Accounting system's balance sheet, then, includes business and personal items, so total growth can be easily monitored. A copy of the document is shown as Figure 3.2. Follow along with the form as you read this section.

The balance sheet is divided into assets—what one owns—and liabilities—what one owes. The equity or net worth is computed using the math shown in the bottom right-hand corner of the figure. If the lines presented on the form do not relate directly to one's own assets, the form can be changed until it is appropriate. Let's begin with the assets.

Assets

The most desirable asset is, of course, cash. To complete the Assets half of the form, begin by listing the various sources and amounts of cash at your disposal. Personal checking and savings accounts and a business checking account are the most common sources. The important difference here is not whether the Assets items are business or personal but that both business and personal items are combined for an unobstructed view.

The next several items deal with the various stocks or bonds the entrepreneur may own, be they purchased in the company's name or the individual's. List them and enter their market value. Stocks and bonds have less collateral value than other types of assets, because their value can change rapidly.

Real estate owned includes both business and personal real estate. Again, list each and enter its market value. Accuracy is important. The assessed property tax value is a place to begin in searching for an accurate number. If a major loan application is coming up, it may be worth paying for an appraisal. If an appraisal is obtained from a licensed appraiser who is employed by a savings and loan association, it will tend to be very conservative and list only enough collateral to cover a prospective loan. If an appraisal from a Realtor is obtained, it will reflect more optimism and not be constrained by the appraiser's desire to keep its client's best interest in mind. The Realtor's value is more likely to reflect a hopeful "market value." An amount somewhere in between is usually reasonable.

Have you loaned any money that is now outstanding? If so, list to whom you loaned it and in what amount. Comment on collectibility.

What is the value of your personal property, such as furniture and automobiles? A collection of some sort, such as jewelry, artwork, or baseball cards, may be of value.

The final consideration is the value of any business or other asset. Inventory, accounts receivable, tools, office equipment, and so on, are just a few. Some banks will set up an open line of credit using inventory, receivables, and equipment as collateral. A reasonable estimated value of a copyright, patent, or long-term contract may be a part of assets that can contribute to a collateral base. The sum of all the listed assets should be entered on line A.

Liabilities

The other side of the balance sheet is for listing your liabilities, or the amounts you owe. Complete this side following the same process as for assets, listing each amount

Some Key Points Small Business Owners Need to Know

Balance Sheet

Date_____

Assets	Liabilities
Cash on Hand and in Banks	**Notes Payable to Banks (Secured)**
_____ _____	_____ _____
_____ _____	_____ _____
_____ _____	_____ _____
U.S. Gov't & Marketable Securities	**Notes Payable to Banks (Unsecured)**
_____ _____	_____ _____
_____ _____	_____ _____
Nonmarketable Securities	_____ _____
_____ _____	**Due to Brokers**
_____ _____	_____ _____
Securities Held by Broker in Margin Accounts	_____ _____
_____ _____	**Amts. Payable Others (Secured)**
Restricted or Control Stocks	_____ _____
_____ _____	_____ _____
Partial Interest	_____ _____
Real Estate Equities	**Amts. Payable Others (Unsecured)**
_____ _____	_____ _____
Real Estate Owned	_____ _____
_____ _____	_____ _____
_____ _____	**Accounts and Bills Due**
_____ _____	_____ _____
Loans Receivable	_____ _____
_____ _____	**Unpaid Income Tax**
_____ _____	_____ _____
Automobile and Other Personal Property	_____ _____
_____ _____	**Other Unpaid Taxes and Interest**
_____ _____	_____ _____
_____ _____	**Real Estate Mortgages Payable**
Cash Value of Life Ins.	_____ _____
_____ _____	**Other Debts - Itemize**
Business, Other Assets	_____ _____
_____ _____	_____ _____
_____ _____	_____ _____
_____ _____	_____ _____
_____ _____	
_____ _____	**Total Liabilities (B)** _____
	Net Worth (A) – (B) _____
Total Assets (A) _____	**Total Liabilities and Net Worth** _____

Figure 3.2. Blank No-Entry Accounting Balance Sheet

outstanding. Be sure to include the liability of your spouse. Anything for which you or your spouse have cosigned and that may have some subsequent liability must be listed. A lawsuit for which either spouse may be held liable should also be listed. *Secured loans* are those for which collateral has been provided. *Unsecured loans* are those that have been granted on a signature or your word alone.

Enter the total of all liabilities on line B. To determine your net worth, subtract line B (what you owe) from line A (what you own). The result is the net worth or equity.

Evolution of the Balance Sheet as Your Business Matures

A common occurrence when a new business is started is for personal equity to become transformed into business equity. This is evidence for the inseparability of business and personal finance for small business operators. Total equity usually declines somewhat as business financing is obtained using personal assets as collateral. This decline results from the proceeds of early loans being used in some part as the entrepreneur's living wage.

After the first year or two, a periodic review should show net equity at first holding its own, then beginning a slow rise. This rise is the result of debt being retired and business and personal assets beginning to appreciate. It is this equity or net worth that is referred to when someone achieves the title of "millionaire." Statistical research has shown that most millionaires—65 percent—are made by 30 years of long hours of self-employment. Years of small business profits, the debt- and labor-to-equity transfers, and appreciation of assets are the primary contributors to one's becoming wealthy.

In the beginning, the value a business contributes to equity is limited to the value of its assets, less any amount that is owed on those assets. This condition persists until the business becomes profitable. Once a record of consistent profit has been established several years running, an operating business can become more valuable than the value of its assets. This situation is discussed in more detail in the discussion of buying and selling a small business in Chapter 11.

The balance sheet changes slowly over time and therefore does not require the monthly attention that cash and profit require. It is important just the same. For example, my trucking business has brought me close to several repair shop operations. The repair of cars and heavy equipment requires an almost unimaginable array of special tools and equipment. Over the years I have noticed that these mechanical entrepreneurs are—almost by definition—chronically cash short. I finally got close enough to two of them to understand their plight. Their situation is a result of fascination with specialized equipment to some extent, and need to a lesser extent. Both the need and the fascination are so great that several successful large businesses have been developed to provide such mechanic's tools; Mac Tools and Snap On Tools are good examples.

The mechanics are called on weekly by salespeople driving expensive custom vans that have walls, ceiling, and many shelves covered with tools. The desire to own such a complete set of tools becomes overwhelming. Imagine an entrepreneur who has spent the day crawling under a truck trying to get a repair job done with a tool that is not just right. If the tool salesperson shows up at just the right moment, the mechanic becomes a buyer. There is no need for the salesperson to become a seller.

The tool salesperson quickly discovers the monthly limit of the mechanic's cash flow and makes every effort to secure that amount in installment payments for tools. The mechanic adopts a Spartan lifestyle as a result. There is enough income to live on, but not much left over.

If the mechanic prepared a balance sheet (Figure 3.2) and the minimal updates each quarter as described in the accounting and tax cycle flow chart (Chapter 18), he would see what is happening to his lifestyle. He would discover that the item of greatest change each quarter would be the value of his tool collection. With the balance sheet and the monthly cash analysis together, he would be able to see his discretionary cash being consumed by tool purchases, and the extent to which these purchases had accumulated.

Some relief from the Spartan lifestyle may come from the knowledge that family assets have increased by thousands of dollars a year in tool purchases. This may not be the form in which one might like to see the family assets, but they are there just the same.

Unfortunately, none of the dozen or so mechanics I have hired or consulted has an inventory list of the tools they have purchased. Each has just a guess as to the total value his tools have reached. No one seems to have an idea of the impact tool purchases have on his or her lifestyle. Instead of planning the growth of the business into areas that require different tools, he simply responds to the next job that arrives at the doorstep. The result is a business in which tens of thousands of dollars must be pumped into equity in the form of tool purchases. These dollars become locked into the equity of the business and are only available as collateral on a loan or if the business is sold.

The blindness caused by this lack of accounting control leads the mechanic to never gain a perspective on what's happening behind the scenes. He never comes to know that he is buying the tools the most expensive way possible. The use of this personal service method of marketing requires high product markup, often more than twice as high as other quality tools. The markup must be high enough to cover the cost of the expensive van and its operation, and a good commission structure for the salesperson. A high rate of interest to carry the installment payments may also be buried in the price. If the mechanic were a business owner instead of just a mechanic, he would buy his tools when they are on sale from low-markup retailers who offer quality tools and a lifetime guarantee with nothing buried in the price.

A mechanic might free up several thousand dollars a year in cash flow by simply planning his or her tool purchases. The mechanic would be better off to go to the bank and borrow the money to pay cash for a full set of tools than to be strung along monthly at high prices, high commission rates, and much higher-than-bank interest rates.

Convenience is the force that drives the high-priced purchase. It is more convenient to buy on the job than to shop around. It is easier to just pay monthly than to plan cash flow or turn down a job for which the proper tools are not in hand.

Ignorance is the condition that makes this waste possible. Business knowledge acquired by keeping one's own balance sheet can head off such predicaments. The lack of such involvement, however, keeps the entrepreneur from ever being aware of this entrepreneurial bleeding ulcer. The difference between remaining a mechanic and becoming a repair shop owner deals with convenience and ignorance. The degree to which an entrepreneur can deal with these forces is a measure of his or her ability to succeed.

Return on Investment

Return on investment (ROI) is a simple concept that many small business people know nothing about. ROI refers to the earnings any particular investment yields to the investor. It is calculated by dividing the cash that is invested in a business into its annual profit. ROI includes all the cash that an owner has invested for equipment, buildings, inventory, operating expenses, and other items but has not taken back out of the business. In the following example, the owner has put $100,000 into a business that has earned a $10,000 profit in one year:

$$\frac{\text{Annual Profit}}{\text{Total Cash Invested}} \quad \frac{10,000}{100,000} = 10\%$$

A 10 percent return on invested capital can be an elusive goal. History has shown that as the hoped-for percent return rises, so does the risk that the hoped-for return may never materialize. In fact, few investors over any number of years consistently obtain a true net of 10 percent. Inflation may push the figure up for a year or two, but recession and an occasional bad investment loss will push it right back down.

A knowledge of how ROI affects a business becomes important when the business owner attempts to cash in. The owner must be able to show with valid accounting records (filed tax forms, Schedule C, and the Form 1040 are considered valid) what return the business can provide to a prospective investor. For example, if an investor were to buy a small business that required $50,000 in cash, either as a down payment or a payment in total, the investor would have to be shown how the business generates enough cash so that when all the bills are paid, including a decent salary for the owner, there should be $5,000 left over. If so, the business would have provided a 10 percent return on investment.

$$\frac{\text{Returned}}{\text{Invested}} \quad \frac{\$5,000}{\$50,000} = 10\%$$

For the sole proprietorship and partnership, the accounting method used to arrive at net profit percent does not subtract a reasonable wage for that proprietor. To calculate ROI, then, *a reasonable wage* for the work that the proprietor or partner does must first be subtracted. The ROI calculation may then be done with meaningful results. In the absence of good, regular accounting, ROI cannot be computed.

Misunderstanding the Writeoff

The concept of "writing something off" is grossly misunderstood. It deals directly with the adjusted taxable amount computed with the 1040 income tax packet. Two different types of writeoffs are involved: ones the owner initiates with purchases, as in "Don't worry what this costs—I can write it off," and ones thrust upon the owner, such as bad debts. Bad-debt writeoffs are also called *operating writeoffs* or *accounts receivable bad debt*.

Owners who indulge in the first type of writeoff don't realize that by "writing something off" their tax break equals only a *fraction* of the expenditure. The amount of this fraction is determined by the income tax bracket percent into which the individual, the couple filing jointly, and/or the business falls. (The current rate for most individuals is from 15 to 28 percent. Under certain conditions the rate is as much as 33 percent. For corporations the rates are 15, 25, and 33 percent.

To determine the percentage, the adjusted taxable amount of an individual or business must be computed using the tax rules and the IRS Form 1040 package. That taxable amount is looked up in the 1040 tax table to determine the amount of tax from which a percentage can be computed. If the tax amount is 15 percent ($35,000 earned, $5,250 taxes paid) then the benefit of "writing something off" is equal to 15 cents per dollar spent. In other words, if you are in the 15 percent tax bracket and spend $1 for a donation you will receive a 15 cent break on income tax due at year end. If you are a wage earner in the 34 percent tax bracket you will receive a 34 cents per dollar tax break when taxes are due at year end. A business or an individual that earns no profit or a family in which adjusted income is under $10,000 gets no benefit at all. Since the 1987 tax change, the arguments for writing something off have become much less appropriate, because most everyone is in a lower tax bracket, and many loopholes have been closed.

An operating writeoff such as a bad debt is quite a different situation. A direct cash management problem is the accounts receivable bad debt. If a business uses the accrual accounting system, a variety of taxes would have been paid on the accrued sales amount in anticipation of the account receivable being collected. The accrual system counts the sale when it is made rather than when it is collected. Should the tax deadline pass between the sale and the writeoff, the loss is greater than the cost of the item sold.

Here is why. The accrual sale would have increased profits and therefore taxes. Benefits received from writing off the bad debt will have to wait until the next tax filing. Its benefit at that point is to reduce total sales and therefore profit. Less profit results in less tax. Only the amount of the sale is written off. The writeoff does not include any income or self-employment tax that might have been paid because of counting the sale in the prior year. When the writeoff passes through the records a year later, it may be at a lower tax rate. So the cost of goods sold is lost, attempted recovery costs are lost, interest for temporary financing may have been incurred, and when the whole thing is finally written off the business may be out some tax dollars as well. It may have paid 25 percent in taxes during the year in which the bad debt was counted as a sale but only 15 percent in the year in which it was written off.

In summary, there is very little redeeming value—other than charity—to writing something off, which is contrary to common belief.

Skimming: It's a Mirage

Skimming is the act of removing unrecorded cash from a business for the purpose of avoiding taxes. The lack of documented proof of profitability, however, is one of the reasons the practice of skimming is always counterproductive. Business owners who skim can only sell their business by convincing the buyer that they really are taking out more from the business than they have claimed to in their accounting records. The buyer is required to accept this representation in the absence of any proof.

In one really sad example, a franchisor had convinced a franchisee that the only way to succeed in a beauty salon was to skim. The lady had invested the family retirement fund in a beauty salon franchise. She was violating all the tax laws at the direction of the franchisor, and was still losing money. She had been advised that profits came from skimming. Her accounting records were being deliberately withheld by the franchisor's accountant, because a profit and loss statement would have shown a substantial loss.

Just imagine! Here was an innocent woman becoming a criminal through tax fraud on the advice of her franchisor. She was essentially paying for the opportunity to lose a life's savings. Can ignorance be any more costly?

Most skimming is done in businesses such as this beauty salon, where little or no tax is due in the first place. Most businesses do not make sufficient profit long enough to legally be required to pay taxes. This is one of the reasons why it is so important for the entrepreneur to understand accounting and taxes. You should arm yourself with such knowledge to prevent the possibility of an unknowing error that may even be illegal. Some business owners reply, "That's what my accountant is paid for, to take care of all of that." Be warned that no accountant considers the fee to have been earned by covering up skimming in the records. If an audit should occur, expect that the accountant has taken steps to ensure being insulated from any implication of wrong doing.

The picture that comes to mind is of an entrepreneur out clinging to the end of a skinny limb, high in a tree. The entrepreneur's accountant stands watching as an IRS agent on the trunk of that tree with a saw in his hands contemplates his next act. Consider these facts.

A direct loss to the skimmer is loss of social security benefits. The average social security beneficiary receives back 2.5 times the amount he or she has contributed. The monthly retirement benefit received is based on annual contributions an individual has made over the years. For the small business owner, the annual contribution is based on annual "reported" earnings. (Recall that approximately 13.2 percent of the first $53,400 in profit shown on the annual Schedule C is the contribution a sole proprietor must make. The corporate employee deposits 15 percent of gross wages to the first $53,400, half of which is deposited by the employer.) The skimmer, then, is actually stealing from his or her own retirement benefits. Each $1 so stolen ultimately costs the thief $2.50.

The same scenario is true when it comes time to sell the business. The only way to sell a business for more than the value of its net assets is to make a profit and authenticate that profit by paying tax. The value of a building brings a one-to-one exchange. That is, $1 in actual value typically brings $1 in sales value. The value of $1 in profit, however, may have a heavily leveraged value. Some profitable businesses bring over 10 times their annual profit when sold. Therefore, the act of skimming reduces the verifiable value of a business by understating its profitability. In this case, each $1 stolen may ultimately cost the owner $10.

The fact is, most skimmers are ignorantly drawing out of their business its life blood—cash. The skimming begins when the business generates insufficient profit for the personal needs of the owner. By skimming, the business owner hopes to reduce his or her tax liability enough to make it worthwhile to remain in business. The owner may be paying employees in cash to avoid matching social security contributions and unemployment insurance. The company is typically operating without workmen's compensation insurance as well. These conditions can be compared to buying a job with no benefits rather than owning a business.

Skimming is a major indicator that a business is not a viable one. If a business cannot operate within the law and generate sufficient profit to provide unemployment insurance and workmen's compensation, and pay taxes, it is not viable. Its return on investment is zero.

Renting Versus Buying

The primary consideration in this decision is which one cash flow will permit. If a business has sufficient cash to permit the purchase of equipment and fixtures, land and a building, and so on, it is almost always wise to do so. The primary advantage to renting a building is that the commitment is limited to the term of the lease, and cash flow is impacted only in small monthly pieces.

Buying a building, however, requires a down payment, closing costs, a long-term commitment, interest expense, property taxes, and the monthly principal and interest payment. You can plainly see that both the cash drain and the commitment are significantly greater with the buying option.

An argument for the buying side of the decision is the fact that much of the long-term gain to be had from owning a business is from the appreciation of business assets. If renting is your only option in the beginning, bear in mind that renting permits a significant portion of the entrepreneur's potential gain to pass to the landlord. The same is true for equipment and company cars, but to a lesser degree, because equipment seldom appreciates in value after some years in use. New cars and equipment experience a greater decline in market value once purchased than do used cars and equipment. The trucks and tractor I have owned for 10 years, for example, can still be sold for what I paid for them. My new car, however, is now only worth 30 percent of what I paid. The only thing I own that has gained in value is my personal residence. In 13 years the house and property have increased by more than 300 percent.

In summary, rent when you must, buy when you can.

New Versus Used

An uncontrollable urge to invest in long-term commitments was shown to be one of the more common root cash management causes for business failure. The actual impact a long-term commitment makes on cash is felt in three different ways:

- The long-term commitment usually consumes a significant portion of cash-in-hand by way of a down payment.
- Future profits are reduced by the debt service (interest charges) that accompanies these commitments.
- The long-term commitment ties up these reduced future profits, by virtue of mandatory principal reductions. The borrowed money can only be repaid from operating profits.

So what's the point? Long-term commitments can often be reduced dramatically by beginning with used equipment rather than new equipment. Good used equipment and facilities can often be obtained for less than half the cost of new items.

My trucking business is a case in point. Over the years I have been repeatedly teased, ridiculed, scolded, mocked, and so on, for trying to run a business with used equipment, especially when it breaks down. Only the intimate financial knowledge I have of the business keeps me from giving in to my desire and the pressure of associates to buy new, "trouble-free" equipment. I know that the moment I try to run my trucking business with new equipment, will be the moment the business will fail.

Nine years of business have shown that only the best year would have carried the debt load the purchase of new equipment would have required. In each of the other eight years the large, long-term commitment for new equipment would have resulted in bankruptcy. The extra annual interest expense on the order of $10,000 the first couple of years, plus the annual principal reductions, would have severely reduced the available cash. My family would not have been able to live on the remainder. So it is with a large number of entrepreneurial attempts.

Each business can support only a certain level of investment. It is always best to begin with the least possible cash commitment as a hedge against failure. My trucking business has provided a good living, and paid for college for two children. It has also provided time for the development of No-Entry Accounting and the writing of this book. None of this would have been possible had I given in to the taunts and jeers of the uninformed.

Don't let the impression you hope to project by being in business become more important in the new versus used decision than bottomline cash flow considerations. Should it turn out that a business can carry the cost of new equipment, then go ahead. But remember, new may be less troublesome but is seldom less costly.

Interest: It Can Cost More Than You Think

Surprisingly few small business owners understand the difference between the various methods used to compute interest. The method used can have a significant impact on cash flow and long range planning. The two most commonly used methods are simple interest and, for installment loans, the Rule of 78s or sum of the years' digits method.

Simple Interest

Simple interest is the best from the business owner's point of view. It represents straightforward interest, principal times rate times time:

$$\$5,000 \times 10\% \times 1 \text{ year}$$

$$\$5,000 \times 0.1 \times 1 = \$500$$

Most loans using this method have no prepayment penalty. This means that the principal amount can be paid in full at an early date and the borrower will be charged only the interest earned through the period of time the money was used. Most business loans that use this method have lump sum payments. They can often be renewed at the expiration date, however, if some portion of the principal has been paid. In the previous example, $5,500 would be due at year end.

Most home mortgages are also based on simple interest with no prepayment penalty. The borrower must be certain that any loan papers signed permit prepayment without penalty.

Rule of 78s or Sum of the Years' Digits

Rule of 78s interest is very different. This method is widely used for installment loans of all sorts and for most leases. This method of calculation loads the bulk of the interest charged at the front end of the loan. The justification for this practice is that the lender experiences the greatest risk of not being repaid at the beginning of the loan. Therefore, the effective interest rate for the first part of the loan should be higher than the effective rate for the latter part of the loan.

This is how it works. First, add the months over which installment payments must be made. A one-year installment loan would consist of 12 payments. So:

$$1 + 2 + 3 + 4 + 5 + 6 + 7 + 8 + 9 + 10 + 11 + 12 = 78$$

The first payment is calculated by finding 12/78 of the total amount of interest to be charged. The second payment equals 11/78 of the total interest, and so forth. Using the same figures as for simple interest, a $5,000 installment loan at 10 percent for one year would cost $500 in interest. Of that $500 in interest, 12/78 is due on the first payment. 12/78 converts to 15.3 percent of the total. Therefore, 15.3 percent of $500 is earned by the lender on the first payment coming due.

$$
\begin{array}{r}
\$500 \\
\times\ 0.153 \\
\hline
\$76.50
\end{array}
$$

If the loan or lease goes to full term, no one is out anything, because the interest rate declines. For the last payment, 1/78, the rate is just 1.2 percent. The high and the low balance out to the 10 percent charged at the onset. The problem is that things often change before the loan is paid off and the borrower may want out early for some reason.

During my years of selling computers it was common to see equipment leased for a five-year period. It was also common that halfway through the lease, either the job requirements would change or the customer wanted some type of system change. The buyout figure halfway through the five-year lease would leave most of the purchase price still due with the trade-in value substantially reduced. Needless to say, few changes were ever made because of the high cost to buy out.

Look at the effect in the previous example. The interest paid through the first six months, halfway through the one-year loan, would equal

$$12 + 11 + 10 + 9 + 8 + 7 = 57/78 \text{ or } 73\%$$

That is 73 percent of the interest due when the money was used for just 50 percent of the time.

$$\begin{array}{r} \$500 \\ \underline{\times \ 0.73} \\ \$365 \end{array}$$

If $365 is subtracted from the $500 total due, the borrower will save $135, perhaps even less if a prepayment penalty is involved. To see the true effect of this change, the $365 paid for the use of $5,000 for one half of a year can be doubled as though it were used for a full year. Add $365 for the first six together with $365 for the second six months. This calculation results in annualized interest of $730.

$$\$730 \div \$5,000 = 0.146 \text{ or } 14.6\% \text{ of } \$5,000$$

The cost of borrowing money thus increases by nearly 50 percent, from 10 percent to just under 15 percent. Decisions that result in a 50 percent increase in the cost incurred, must be avoided if at all possible. New cars are commonly financed over five years to keep the payments down. Another common practice is to trade that car in for still another new car in just two and a half years, for a variety of reasons. However:

- You can see from the previous example that this practice increases the effective interest rate significantly.
- The most rapid depreciation of a car is during its first two years. The computed trade-in value will reflect this rapid decline in value.
- The practice of absorbing extra interest by changing a Rule of 78s loan early, together with absorbing most of new car depreciation in the first two years, is financially ruinous. The effective first-year cost of buying anything under such conditions can easily reach 45 percent (15 percent interest plus 30 percent first year depreciation).

One of the mechanics discussed earlier made it a practice to buy new cars just this way. He was also one who bought all of his tools using high-interest-rate installment loans from the mobile tool vendor. He took every opportunity to make bad business decisions involving interest expense. He had reasons for each decision. But the reasons were based on convenience or appearances and not on sound cash management. He complained that he could make ends meet with his business, but nothing more. There was never anything left over.

The fact is that there was plenty left over. The problem was that he continually decided to spend the left-over cash on interest and depreciation instead of paying off debt or purchasing some productive new asset. Whether the practice is used in the entrepreneur's personal affairs or business affairs makes no difference, because the cash comes out of the same pocket. Financing business assets with Rule of 78s installment loans or leases usually results in postponing the day on which success arrives. Sometimes it is postponed indefinitely.

Summary

Overcoming the gaps in understanding that have been described in this chapter can provide you with more cash. Essentially, each new piece of knowledge permits you to plug another hole in the dike until one day there are no more cash leaks.

Chapter 4

Priority One—Cash Management

The strongest point I hope to make in this entire book is that nothing is so important to the small business owner as precise, total control of cash. Cash is the life blood of a business. Profitable or not, new or old, well managed or poorly managed, once the cash runs out a business goes on the endangered species list. It can recover, but diligent, educated, long-term effort will be required to bring it back. Cash management concerns come well before profit and leagues ahead of taxes in terms of where to focus your small business thinking.

Unfortunately, accounting services seem mostly geared toward the preparation and filing of taxes. Make no mistake, taxes must be done. But no tax is due until there is profit, and profit in the absence of available cash will not keep the best operation afloat. Proficient cash management is where every business owner must begin if there is any hope for success.

The Life Cycle of Cash Management Problems

Cash management problems have a life cycle of their own. They stem from the following five periods or situations in which a business may find itself:

1. Startup cash problems.
2. The rolling cash fund.
3. Seasonal fluctuations.
4. The arrival of success.
5. Dynamic growth.

Startup Cash Problems

Startup cash management problems are those that emerge from a business venture that has just begun. Virtually every business I have studied has insufficient cash to accomplish all that its owner desires at the outset. The specific cash management problem associated with a startup is essentially deciding where first to put limited resources to work.

Consider the case of four salespeople from the stone industry who decide to start a crushing operation. The men decided to pool their resources, buy some used equipment, and secure the mineral rights to an available piece of property. Each one, having worked on an expense account for years, had the opinion that the owners of such a business should travel first class and at company expense. They promptly leased four new luxury cars. Their next decision was to pay themselves an owner's salary—or at least what they thought was an owner's salary. By virtue of these two decisions they ran their new business out of cash before the first year ended. They had to abandon the operation as a total loss.

Every effort must be made to keep a supply of cash available during the early days of your business. These men should have kept their family cars, paid their expenses from their own pockets, and not drawn a paycheck until company finances would permit. Had they done so, their business would have had a good chance for success, because their sales efforts were generating increasing amounts of revenue.

The Rolling Cash Fund

The rolling cash fund is the cash available on a month-to-month basis. It is in a constant state of flux, because of the time that elapses between incurring expenses and being paid for accounts receivable. For example, when does the annual insurance premium come due? Is it during a high revenue month or a low revenue month? Can insurance perhaps be paid monthly or quarterly? How does the quarterly tax deposit coincide with the trend of available cash? Does an owner's personal need for cash fit the peaks and valleys of the business's income? If not, how can the difference be managed?

I once encountered an example of the extreme demands that a rolling cash fund can place on a business. The business supplied the stock for junior high and senior high school shop classes. Steel bars would be cut into 6-inch pieces from which a student could make a chisel; 4-foot by 8-foot plastic sheets would be cut into pieces just large enough to make a letter opener; and so on. Some 95 percent of the company's revenue came in during the month and a half before school started.

At the time, it seemed like such a simple business to me. Here was a man who obviously had a very good business. Over eight years the business had grown to the point where the owner was discussing the purchase of a $65,000 computer system.

What struck me the most about his business was that he had little or no competition. How could a business as simple as cutting big pieces into little pieces have no competition? It took the experience of writing this book for me to understand what happened to the competition: They couldn't make it. This business owner is probably the only entrepreneur in the area who could manage a no-cash-in situation for more than 10 months a year.

Less than a handful of entrepreneurs I have worked with have had the ability to manage available cash through such a long income valley with just a single peak.

50

Seasonal Fluctuations

Seasonal fluctuations are usually not as severe as the school supplies business just described. A more typical example is the golf course in a northern state or a ski lodge in the mountains. The problem is severe nonetheless. As the bills for the peak half of the cycle come due, income is in a state of decline. If cash is not spent correctly during the peak period, some obligations may be left unsettled as cash runs out at season's end. Businesses involved in this type of annual cycle trigger the Cycle of Demise every year. Only those businesses that are managed by cash-minded owners have the hope of surviving a six month peak to valley cycle.

One common method used to cope with this seasonal cycle is operating two complementary cyclical businesses, such as a bicycle shop during the summer and a cross-country ski shop during the winter. There are still peaks and valleys—spring and fall—but the valleys can usually be kept shorter in duration than 90 days. What is magic about 90 days? It is the time well-run businesses let customers slide on outstanding credit before the cash on delivery (C.O.D.) ax falls. If cash can be managed sufficiently to avoid being placed on C.O.D., a business has a good chance for success. The Cycle of Demise is never triggered.

The Arrival of Success

The arrival of success is characterized by earning the right to pay income taxes as a going concern. To keep the arrival at this juncture from capsizing the boat, it must be foreseen. This major cause for business failure stems from the arrival at genuine profitability. It is the focal point of Chapter 5.

Dynamic Growth

Dynamic growth presents uncontrollable cash management problems for small businesses. This phase of the life cycle features building of facilities, training, growth of inventories and accounts receivable, expanding markets, and so on, all of which require cash that even the wealthy small business owner cannot provide. The road to failure is littered with the bones of those who have tried.

An annual review of the hottest movers in American business is a list of small corporations embarked on rapid growth plans. None of them making a profit. They are perpetually cash starved. They are said to be in a *cash short position*. The cash short position results from a dynamic growth plan. More facilities need to be built, requiring down payments and long-term mortgage commitments. Accounts receivable, inventories, and payroll will have to increase, generating great need for short-term cash. These short- and long-term cash demands and the absence of profit create a chronic cash short position.

From the chronic cash short position rises the true need for incorporation. Sufficient cash must be generated to provide for wages and other expenses until profit finally arrives. The incorporation process is necessary here, because a corporation can sell stock for cash for which no repayment schedule is required and no interest expense is incurred. If the entire amount is lost—which is often the case— only the speculative stockholders are out anything. The investors hope to recover their investment by virtue of an appreciation in the value of the stock they have purchased. If things work out over time, a dividend may even be declared.

51

If an entrepreneur takes up a rapid growth plan on top of learning how to deal with the conventional cash management problems listed here, the chances for success are slim.

Where Have All the Cash Cows Gone?

The term *cash cow* describes a successful business whose profits are unencumbered. That is, the company's taxes can be paid; there are no loans to repay, no inventory or accounts receivable to build, no expansion is in progress; so profits simply accumulate in the company bank accounts.

It is the cash cow that the movies have popularized as the successful business, but films have taken the cow out of context. Most businesses pass through the equity transfers—a process that usually takes years—before the companies arrive at the high green pastures of the cash cow. In the eyes of the small business owner, the question here might be most appropriately phrased, Why are there so few cash cows? The answer is that most businesses fail before they have dealt with the equity transfers.

The three equity transfers, discussed fully in this section, are actually the primary mechanisms by which you can accumulate wealth in business:

- Debt-to-equity transfer.
- Earnings-to-equity transfer.
- Labor-to-equity transfer.

The Debt-to-Equity Transfer

The *debt-to-equity transfer* is the transfer of cash from operating profits (or an owner's pocket) to a lender for the repayment of borrowed money. The amount owed is reduced. The resulting decrease in liabilities, however, is immediately offset by a decrease in the asset cash. The net result is that debt has been converted to equity, a transaction that is essentially transparent to the preparation of conventional accounting statements.

The "sinkhole" nature of the debt-to-equity transfer is difficult for the small business owner to deal with. It is only recognized as a symptom of the entrepreneurial condition. "My accountant says I'm making a good profit, I'm worth more now than before, but there never seems to be anything left over. I can't even take a vacation." The fact that the profit is being earned from a business that may owe its existence to borrowed money somehow gets lost in entrepreneurial thinking.

Paying the money back seems natural at first, but things change. Several years of Spartan living at the expense of the debt-to-equity transfer requires sacrifice. It gives the highly leveraged business startup a different hue. Before long, being in business seems like all work and no play, with apparently little to show for it. The entrepreneur must usually accept a growth in equity as his or her just reward. A simple living wage type lifestyle replaces the flashy, cash-dependent lifestyle the owner sees in the movies. The flashy, cash-dependent lifestyle usually has to wait until the entrepreneur stays in business long enough to retire most of the debt.

The transfer (debt retirement) will not show in the profit or loss figure. Interest on business debt is expensed through the profit and loss statement, but the cash required for debt retirement just disappears. The business balance sheet is a list of assets (everything owned) on the left side of a page, with liabilities (everything owed) on the right side. Equity or net worth results if the total of assets is greater than the total of liabilities. This favorable total is entered on the balance sheet at the end of the liabilities column as equity or net worth. The sheet is then "in balance." The assets total is in balance with the total of liabilities plus equity. (The No-Entry Accounting balance sheet is Figure 3.2.) The balance sheet will show no change in equity or net worth because the asset side, cash, is reduced by the same amount as the liability side, loans. For example, the following is a balance sheet before a debt-to-equity transfer:

	Assets		**Liabilities**
Equipment	$10,000	Liabilities	$ 9,000
Cash	1,000	Equity	2,000
Total	$11,000	Total	$11,000

After a $200 equipment loan principal payment, the transfer becomes:

Equipment	$10,000	Liabilities	$ 8,800
Cash	800	Equity	2,000
	$10,800		$10,800

Notice that equity began with $2,000 and remained at $2,000. Reducing the principal of a loan by making a loan payment reduces cash by the same amount as the loan balance is reduced, leaving no change in equity. What has essentially taken place is to return something that did not belong to the owners in the first place—in this case, borrowed money. Keep in mind that the cash used to repay debt is "after-tax cash." Debt repayment is not an expense so it does not reduce profit. Therefore, it does not reduce taxes either. Debt can only be repaid with the cash left over after taxes are paid.

The only place the debt-to-equity transfer becomes obvious is on the cash analysis form, which commercially available small business accounting does not usually provide. Cash analysis looks back over a month, quarter, or year for the purpose of identifying the whereabouts of every bit of cash that came out of a business. "Where did the money go?" The $200 in this example will appear as an amount that has been spent on debt retirement. Because cash analysis is not part of the typical conventional accounting package, small business is left with an information void.

Starting a business with the maximum amount of debt that can be had is committing a maximum amount of future cash to debt retirement. There is no way of being sure that cash will be available as the liability falls due. Many of the businesses that survive the first year succumb to the debt-to-equity transfer during the two-year to five-year period. The portion of cash that represents the difference between a monthly paycheck and a profitable business is consumed by the debt-to-equity transfer. Often a sizable portion of the monthly paycheck is consumed as well. The combination of borrowing too much in the beginning and the invisible nature

53

of the resulting debt-to-equity transfer often causes a cash shortfall. I call the shortfall invisible because it does not show up in conventional profit and loss statements. This shortfall is lingering, because the repayment of startup borrowed cash is usually set up for five years or more. Should the entrepreneur commit a series of errors—even small ones—the accumulating shortfall will trigger the Cycle of Demise.

The Earnings-to-Equity Transfer

The *earnings-to-equity transfer* is the building of equity through community services that are provided by taxes. This transfer moves a business's cash to community equity that is shared by the business owner. The more efficient and progressive a tax body is, the greater the increase in equity that may result. My community is an example of a favorable earnings-to-equity transfer. Good roads, excellent schools, abundant social services, effective zoning laws, and strong local leadership have combined to create a strong real estate market. The result is that my assets, both business and personal, have appreciated over 300 percent in just 14 years. It has all happened with no effort on my part, except the contribution I have made in taxes, which is small in relation to the growth in my property's value.

The transfer is not always so beneficial. Some communities suffer from decaying facilities, lack of leadership, and a declining real estate market. A business in this environment not only loses the benefit of a positive earnings-to-equity transfer but may have other gains erased by the declining value of business and personal assets.

The fiscal management challenge is to effectively manage these taxes so that each individual can receive the maximum benefit at minimum cost. There will always be heated debate over the effectiveness with which these various funds are handled and what amount is a fair share of contribution. But these topics are the subject of another book. The assumption here is that taxes are a very necessary part of earning an income and that you are best served by accepting your fair share of the load and moving along. It is important, however, to understand the law so you do not overcontribute. As a taxpayer you must also be a part of the checks and balances that keep tabs on the various tax systems to ensure reasonable efficiency.

Although the basis for tax is the level of your income, the following are several ways in which taxes are applied:

- Federal income tax is applied as a varying percent of adjusted income that increases as income rises. Adjusted income is gross income minus various deductions that are permitted. For example, $2,000 can be subtracted from gross income for each person who is dependent on the wage earner's income. The interest and property tax you pay for the purchase of a personal residence is deductible, and so forth.

- State and local income taxes may be a fixed percentage of an unadjusted gross income. In Illinois, for example, it is 3 percent of gross earnings.

- Social security is taxed on gross wages—or, in the case of the sole proprietor and partnership—on net profit. For employees, the wage earner contributes half of the total contribution and the employer contributes the other half. The sole proprietor or small corporation owner contributes the entire amount, because he or she is *both* the wage earner and the employer. For the time being, a sole proprietor is allowed a slightly smaller contribution than the corporation, but the difference is being reduced to zero. The current limit to this contribution is 15.3 percent of the first $53,400 in earnings for each employee.

- Property tax is applied based on the value of property a particular taxpayer desires to use. If the earner chooses to live and work in upscale facilities in high-demand areas, then the portion of this tax paid will be greater. All people in residences pay the tax regardless of whether they participate in ownership. Each landlord passes along all the costs associated with renting out property or the rental unit will fail as with any other entrepreneurial venture. Renters get hit twice, because they pay property tax but do not receive owner benefits by writing off those taxes against their income. The rental unit's owner receives both the rental income, which includes the property tax, and the tax writeoff.

A look at an individual earner will help bring the picture into focus. Assume the earner to be a sole proprietor with net profit of $50,000 and no other income.

Gross Income	100%
1. The entire profit amount is taxable for social security. The current rate for the sole proprietor is approximately 15.3%.	(15.3%)
2. An entrepreneur with $50,000 in profit will likely have something on the order of $10,000 worth of adjustments to income. So assume the adjusted taxable income is $40,000. The current income tax rate for adjusted taxable income of $40,000 is 18%.	(18%)
3. State and local income taxes are levied by many such governments. In Illinois, for example, the state income tax is 3%.	(3%)
4. Property taxes are of course based on property value rather than income. For this purpose, however, the assumption can be made that a sole proprietor with a $40,000 adjusted income will reside in a residence that is taxed at 3% of that adjusted income.	(3%)
Total cash available to this earner from each dollar earned.	60.7%

There are many variables among states and among families that might cause the above results to differ. But a figure between 60 percent and 70 percent should be representative of this level of income in most areas of the United States. Because the value of property or a business is part of equity, and equity depends on the political and economic climate around it, it can be said that taxes paid effectively transfer a portion of one's earnings to a community net worth or equity. For the typical sole proprietor who earns an adjusted taxable income of $40,000, the earnings-to-equity transfer equals approximately 37 percent, or $14,800 annually. Sales tax may increase this amount by another several hundred dollars.

The combination of the earnings-to-equity transfer and the debt-to-equity transfer often overwhelms the small business venture. The example just given showed that a $50,000 profit is typically reduced by $14,800 because of the earnings-to-equity transfer.

$$\begin{array}{r} \$50{,}000 \\ -\ \underline{14{,}800} \\ \$35{,}200 \end{array}$$

Debt can only be retired by the $35,200 available after the earnings-to-equity transfer has been considered. A typical progression of events is for the small business to encounter this $50,000 level of earnings somewhere between the fourth and seventh years in business. If this large piece—37 percent of net—is consumed by the earnings-to-equity transfer and a significant percentage remains from the debt-to-equity transfer, the Cycle of Demise may be triggered. This is particularly a problem for those small business owners who plan by their checkbook balances They wait until year end and take a box full of papers to the accountant to have their taxes computed. With no knowledge of their true tax obligation throughout the year, they tend to live and invest as though they had $50,000 to spend as discretionary income, rather than the $35,200 that is actually available. Satisfying the debt-to-equity transfer as well may not leave enough cash for a living wage.

The Labor-to-Equity Transfer

The *labor-to-equity transfer* involves time spent for which no immediate cash is earned. A side benefit of this transfer is that there is no contribution to the earnings-to-equity transfer (that is, no taxes due) until the labor-to-equity transfer is converted to cash by a sale.

How the Transfer Works

An example of this is a contractor who personally builds a storage shed. The materials, of course, are bought with cash, which remains a part of the contractor's equity. It is transformed, however, from cash equity to equity in the form of a building owned. This cash transfer identifies only part of the equity change. The labor expended is also transformed into equity, because part of a building's value is the labor it requires for construction. If the shed has a completed value of $20,000, half of which wás materials, the labor-to-equity transfer is $10,000.

The building of a shed will affect the contractor's equity, then, by changing $10,000 from cash to materials, and increasing that equity by $10,000 through volunteered labor. The purchase of the materials will not increase the contractor's equity, because cash was simply changed to materials of the same value. If the contractor was able to obtain the materials for 50 cents on the dollar, say at auction for $5,000, the materials purchased with cash for less than their value would also contribute to equity. This is so because the completed building should reflect its worth rather than just what it cost to build. In this case, smart shopping and the labor-to-equity transfer will have increased the contractor's equity by $15,000 ($5,000 saved on materials purchased and $10,000 saved on voluntary labor).

Preventing Opportunity Costs in the Process

Recall the old saying that, "It takes money to make money." In the absence of cash to purchase the materials, the labor-to-equity transfer opportunity would not be available. There is one problem. What does the contractor do for income while working for no cash? The business must have sufficient income so the hours required to build a shed with no wage do not detract from regular income. In other words, the owner must minimize the "opportunity cost" of building the shed personally. Also, once the shed is finished, the earnings-to-equity transfer may require some small amount of cash through a property tax.

Another example is publishing a book, which can take several work years. The big payoff that an author hopes for is writing a best-seller. Until such time as the revenue comes rolling in, the labor-to-equity transfer is at work. This type of labor-to-equity transfer is much riskier than it is for the contractor. The contractor's building will surely bring a return, but a completed book may be worthless. An advantage, however, is that no front-end cash is required.

The labor-to-equity transfer is not confined to the labor of the owner. Any labor that can be had but not paid for has the same effect. Homeowners who organize a summer work party for friends and relatives are using the labor-to-equity transfer. Whether the work party is for painting the house, planting sod, or some other chore isn't the point. What matters is that the labor will somehow increase the value of the property. The value of the labor from such a party will easily exceed the cost of a case of beer and a few hot dogs. The transfer of the net gain plus appreciation, then, falls out as cash from the increased value of the home once it is sold.

The ideal business is one that permits a comfortable living wage, and a combination debt-to-equity and labor-to-equity transfer. The transfer should be into equity, which itself will appreciate. A good example of this is a nursery at the edge of an expanding metropolitan area. As the area grows, profits should increase from expanding sales. These profits will permit the retirement of debt associated with owning the farmland on which the plants are grown. As the metropolitan area encroaches on the farmland, the property becomes more valuable as residential or commercial property than as farmland. At the same time, the amount owed is being reduced rapidly because of the extra cash available for debt retirement. The result can be the ownership of paid-up property. The value of the property often exceeds an amount that could be earned from the profitable running of the business. Occasionally the owner of such a business will sell the high-priced land and simply move the business farther out where land is cheaper.

Here is the best news in the whole book. The three types of transfers described here are the seedbed of U.S. millionaires! Periodic newspaper and magazine articles discuss the topic of being a millionaire. The most recent I have seen indicates that 80 percent of U.S. millionaires come from middle and working class families who did not inherit their wealth. They made it with 30 years of 6-day weeks, running their own businesses that cater to the ordinary needs of neighbors. Over the years, operating profits, the earnings-to-equity transfer, the debt and/or labor-to-equity transfer, and appreciation have built their equities to the $1 million level. The typical millionaire is in his early 60s, with an annual income of $121,000.

The Fourth Source of Worth

The consistent, unencumbered profits of the cash cow can be a fourth contributor to wealth—certainly, if your business becomes truly profitable itself, the profits will accumulate and increase your wealth. Another consideration, however, is the value of a business, which is discussed in detail in the case study of Chapter 11. Regular, documented, unencumbered profit is itself sellable. The highest-priced business sales are from those businesses in which profit is high and can be expected to remain high. Sale prices can exceed 10 times the annual net profit. This leverage may even exceed the accumulated equity from the three transfers. All the problems at this level are happy ones.

The Real Ratio:
A Single Calculation That Can Guide You to Profitability

The *Real Ratio* is a simple mathematical telescope that helps the user visualize the cost of entrepreneurial ignorance and everyday mistakes. Nothing has so moved No-Entry Accounting seminar attendees as the Real Ratio. Many entrepreneurs sit speechless as they ponder its piercing view into an entrepreneur's confrontation with success. Once you understand the true nature of the negative leverage the ratio reveals, you will immediately become a better manager.

Note: Proprietorships and partnerships must subtract a reasonable "wage" for the owner before a net profit percent is determined. If the proprietorship or partnership's accounting system does not result in a profit large enough to pay the owner a respectable wage, the business is actually operating at a loss. If such a loss can be traced to labor being directly transferred to equity like building a shed, that is good. If such a loss is being absorbed by the entrepreneur's willingness to work for less than could be earned elsewhere, with no such transfer, that is bad.

How the Real Ratio Identifies the Actual Cost of Waste

Let's examine the Real Ratio from the context of an actual example. My first entrepreneurial experience was to open the Old Church Inn. It was an upscale restaurant serving lunch and dinner six days a week. The days were long, so personal errands piled up for my day off. These errands never got finished, however, because restaurant demands quickly consumed much of my free time as well. The problem was solved by delegating the task of closing the restaurant several nights a week. A promising young cook was given the keys and taught how to handle the job.

Two weeks later when we performed our monthly physical inventory, a problem developed. A liquor delivery had been made just two days earlier. Part of that delivery was two cases of vodka. The inventory, however, showed only two quarts of vodka on hand. I knew at a glance that we had a problem, because it ordinarily took a month to sell that much vodka. The count was checked and it was determined that the vodka had been stolen. The promising young cook who was closing the restaurant was found to be a hard alcoholic. I

At the time, each case of vodka cost $70. The total cost of this mistake (handing the keys to the liquor cabinet to an alcoholic) was, luckily, only $140. Imagine what might have happened had there not been a monthly physical count just after the theft occurred! Anyway, it seemed like a small amount in a restaurant that had annual sales over $300,000, but look what the Real Ratio shows.

The National Restaurant Association computes average net profit percent for restaurants that have been in operation under five years to be 2.4 percent.

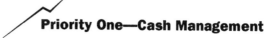

Dividing the amount of the mistake, $140, by the 2.4% or

$$140 \div 0.024$$

You move the decimal three places right to make both numbers whole,

$$140,000 \div 24 = \$5,833$$

At that time $5,833 was the approximate revenue from two good days of operating my restaurant. The $140 mistake, then, represented *two good days* of operating the restaurant for naught.

Sales from two good days:	**$5,833**
Times net profit percent of 2.4%	**x .024**
	$ 140

The Real Ratio is then calculated by dividing the cost of the mistake ($140) into the sales required to recover ($5,833). Therefore:

$$\$5,833 \div 140 = 42$$

The Real Ratio here is 42:1.

So, a typical new restaurant requires $42 in sales to recover from each $1 mistake, leaving no profit. As a series of mistakes occurs, whether the mistakes are large or small, recovery cash is essentially drawn against future profits. The same analysis applies to any amount spent beyond what is necessary. For example, spending $10 for a restaurant item when a little shopping might have found the same item or a suitable substitute for $8 is also a mistake. To let this $2 slide is to forgo $2 in profit. The only alternative way to regain this $2 with the restaurant is as profit from the next $84 in sales, a 42:1 ratio.

Now, if you consider many other mishaps that can take place from day to day (burning a few steaks, dropping a tray full of glasses, a fender bender with the company truck, and so on) it is little wonder that the failure rate for new business is so high!

This analysis is fair, in that the entire restaurant operation must be in place in order to generate the next $140 in revenue. Each new dollar in sales has a portion earmarked for cost of sales and operating expenses. We arrive at these proportions by computing the monthly profit and loss statement for each business entity. In the case of the typical new restaurant, a dollar in sales can be broken down as follows.

97.6	**cents of each dollar for expenses.**
+ 2.4	**cents are available as profit.**
100.0	**cents in sales.**

Therefore, to earn back the $140 mistake, we can only use that portion of the next dollar in sales that is represented by profit, or 2.4 cents. The other 97.6 cents are already earmarked. Recent past performance, as computed on the monthly profit and loss statement, shows that 97.6 cents of each dollar goes for expenses.

Conventional breakeven point theory may predict that the recovery cost would be only slightly greater than the cost of the mistake. In practice, however, conditions such as owner time availability, operating space, parking space, and so on, place limits on conditions necessary for this to occur.

Managing by the Real Ratio

The entrepreneur's chance for success is enhanced by learning to manage by the Real Ratio. At 42:1, the accumulation of even small errors can cause failure because they are layered on earlier business commitments for cash such as the earnings-to-equity and debt-to-equity transfers, growth of inventory, and growth of accounts receivable. Each of these cash requirements can only be met from profit. Therefore, if profit is squandered on recovering from mistakes at a ratio of 42:1, it leaves the owner continually dipping into the pocket or purse, forgoing personal income to fund the shortfall.

Few small business people ever realize what has hit them, even after every available source of cash has been tapped and exhausted. Failure comes in the form of bills due for payment for which no cash is available. All of the cash earned may have been spent on replenishing stolen inventory, or it may be tied up in accounts receivable that remain uncollected. It is for these and other, similar reasons that a significant number of failed businesses were businesses that were *profitable*. The ultimate question is not whether a business can earn a profit, but whether the profit earned *remains* in the form of cash sufficient to pay the owner's personal and business bills.

The Real Ratio, then, defines the degree of difficulty in recovering from simple ignorance and simple mistakes. It has a redeeming quality though. As profitability increases to 10 percent, for example, the negative leverage declines to 10:1. This recognition can in part account for the common belief that banks only want to lend to those who do not need to borrow. Those businesses with a low Real Ratio are better able to repay borrowed funds. They are also more readily able to recover from their mistakes.

Again, the absence of a monthly profit and loss statement, combined with a lack of personal owner involvement, leaves the entrepreneur in an uninformed position. Without knowing the actual, current, net cash profit, an owner cannot fully appreciate the impact of a given mistake. Without a full appreciation of their impact, mistakes seldom get the attention they deserve.

Summary

Whether your cash management problems stem from the expenses of starting a business, managing cash flow month by month, maintaining sufficient funds to tide your company over slow seasons, coping with success, or funding sudden growth, the effects can be devastating. The debt-to-equity transfer, earnings-to-equity transfer, and labor-to-equity transfer can combine to build the value of your business and your worth. Mastering the concept of the Real Ratio can help you understand the real cost of business losses and steer your firm around financial failure.

Chapter 5

Priority Two—Profit

Once your cash management is under control, the second priority for running a successful business is to achieve an annual net profit. This chapter explores profitability in depth. Your entrepreneurial goal must be arrival at the Node of Profitability. But before you get too excited, consider that it usually takes several years to achieve real profitability.

What is "real profitability"? The rules for sole proprietorship accounting do not provide for subtracting a wage for the owner. A profit is considered earned regardless of whether that profit is sufficient for an owner to take out a living wage. A typical sole proprietorship in the annual revenue range of $100,000 yields a 30 percent profit, or $30,000. Somewhere in this vicinity a real profit falls out. If the earnings came from a part-time venture, this level of income may represent high profitability. On the other hand, earnings of $30,000 might not provide a fair wage for all the work an owner must do as a full-time business operator to bring in $100,000 in revenue. If so, there is still no real profit. Real profit, then, comes only after the owner has taken a respectable wage from proprietorship or partnership profits.

The proprietorship profit percentages I have experienced from my varied businesses have ranged from breakeven—0 percent in a year when lending rates hit 20 percent—to a high of 62 percent. Most years' profits have fallen in the 50 percent range. The real profit has ranged from a loss (a year worked for less than a respectable wage) to a high of 22 percent. The 50 percent proprietorship profit years usually result in real profit of 8 percent or less. Here is how profitability evolves and why it takes so long to happen.

Breakeven: The Life Cycle of a Small Business

The *breakeven point* is the monetary amount at which the expenses of a business equal the revenue that the business generates. A knowledgeable estimate of the breakeven point is an absolute must for every business. There are actually three breakeven points of which the business owner should be aware: the monthly breakeven point, the cash flow breakeven point, and the inception-to-date breakeven point.

The monthly breakeven is typically reached by funding from the owner's cash. For the cash flow breakeven point, cash in equals cash out. This point must be reached for the third type, inception-to-date, to become a reality.

Earning a Living Wage

Achieving the monthly breakeven point is the first indication that a business may be viable. At this point, though, the proprietor still has no income. *Breakeven* means that expenses are equal to revenue. Profit is zero. The pay check for a proprietor is profit.

The proprietor must move beyond monthly breakeven to cash flow breakeven, which provides the owner a living wage. A living wage is just that: one that a proprietor's family can live on. At this point there is still no real profit, because all the income is consumed by the owner's need for a living wage. There is nothing left over. This is the situation I define as having "purchased a job."

Moving on to a Respectable Wage

The next step is to move from the living wage to the respectable wage category. At this point, the owners of small businesses are doing as well for themselves as they would be working for someone else at a similar level. This level is also defined as having purchased a job. The value of a business that yields this level of income, however, is still just the value of its assets, because it has not demonstrated an ability to generate a return on investment. Most small businesses fall within these categories, yielding a living or respectable wage.

Achieving Real Profit

An investment becomes a successful business only when it can move beyond the respectable wage category and contribute real profit. Real profit is cash left over after a respectable wage is provided. The ability to earn real profit is the dividing line between owning a job and owning a business.

As the years roll by, an accumulating profit brings the entrepreneur to the inception-to-date breakeven point. A respectable wage for time spent is being provided, and the business has generated sufficient profit for a long enough period to pay back the owner all the cash that was invested.

This is the point at which the job has been purchased and the purchase price refunded. At this point, all of the cash profit that is generated is discretionary cash. It is not obligated by loans or other debts. It provides the owner a respectable wage and cash left over. It may continue to do so even though the owner may have become involved only part-time or not at all.

A business at this level becomes more valuable than the value of its assets. It is generating a return on investment and positive cash flow.

Essentially, owning a successful business provides the entrepreneur with interest on all the cash invested just as though the cash were on deposit in a savings account. The purchase of a job does not. The vast majority of existing entrepreneurial ventures fall into the buying a job category. These are often the "businesses" that are for sale, so buyer beware.

A knowledge of the monthly breakeven point, the cash flow breakeven point, and inception-to-date breakeven point, relative to any business venture, serves to bring the owner's thinking into focus. The owner needs to focus on the effect that each additional expense has regarding these breakeven points. The most immediate requirement is to arrive at the monthly breakeven point, where sales equal expenses. The cash flow breakeven point is next. This is the point where all monthly cash obligations, the living wage, business loan payments, and so on, are being met on a timely basis. It must be reached before the owner's startup cash fund is exhausted. As long as the cash flow breakeven is reached and maintained, a venture can hold out indefinitely. The inception-to-date breakeven remains an achievable goal. An inability to arrive at the cash flow breakeven, however, will ultimately result in the phantomlike disappearance of the investor's cash. The business will fail before the investment can be recovered and before a respectable wage is ever earned.

You can calculate your monthly breakeven by estimating revenue and expenses. Use a blank profit and loss statement (Figure 8.4) or Schedule C as an outline and memory jogger to check that nothing is left out. To calculate the cash flow breakeven, use the cash analysis form, Figure 13.1, in the same manner. Make an effort to obtain the most accurate data available. New businesses present a special problem because they lack history on which to base accurate estimates. The following true example, however, highlights the value of calculating breakeven even in the absence of history.

A young man had started a fence building business that was doing quite well. He was working out of his home, though, so he didn't have a place to keep his equipment and the supplies he used. As he drove down the highway one day, he saw a property for sale that included a house, a large garage, and over an acre of property. The property fit his requirements exactly. He stopped and talked with the owner. The price, $125,000, seemed like an amount his business could afford. After all, he had made $65,000 and the year was only half over. A contract was signed contingent on finding financing. The young man's next step was to apply for a loan at the local savings and loan. He did so and then waited for the happy result.

Finally the result came: no loan! As it turned out, $65,000 was the young man's *gross sales*. He had just purchased a new truck and some new post-hole digging equipment. The reason the young man had so much work was that he was underbidding everyone—so much so, that rather than making a $65,000 profit, he was actually *losing* money. His expenses had exceeded the $65,000 taken in. The young man really did know how to build fences. What he didn't know was any of the simple accounting and business principles it takes to turn fence installation into a fence business.

An understanding of the breakeven point would have saved this loan applicant some embarrassment and some of the money he was losing giving fences away.

63

Even when a new business owner calculates breakeven, the tendency is to underestimate the startup expenses and overestimate starting revenues. The result (undercapitalization) may be a venture that from its inception has no chance for success. It is never able to operate above the trigger point of the Cycle of Demise.

It is wise to develop a worst-case scenario for revenue calculations in new businesses. Use the worst-case situations to think through what you might do, should some of these problems actually develop. Always leave a way out, short of forfeiting most of your equity.

The chart in Figure 5.1 gives a view of the breakeven point from my perspective.

The Stair Steps to Success

The breakeven points are always changing. Making the transition from being a sole proprietor who is the chief cook and bottle washer to being the manager of even a single employee can have a dramatic impact on company finances. The change in the breakeven points at such transitions needs to be understood before the change takes place.

Consider a person with an accounting degree who wants to develop an accounting practice. The revenue and expense breakeven point is progressively charted in Figure 5.1.

Startup Phase

The first thing the accountant will need is customers. A few clients may already be lined up as annual tax clients. These are insufficient, however, because they generate revenue only once each year. In addition, their tax work has been done on a friendly neighbor discount basis. If the clients were charged an appropriate amount for this service, they would likely go elsewhere. To make a viable business, then, the practice will need clients who require monthly accounting services. Annual tax preparation will be an additional source of revenue at year end.

The accountant will have to spend time generating the new client base. She has to prepare a marketing portfolio, set rates, and implement a marketing plan. Research and preparation of such a plan could take months, but let's assume that the accountant has the basics together in just two weeks. Keep in mind that although the accountant may not have spent a dime from the pocket, she has spent two weeks worth of labor. If the time is spent on this venture, she cannot spend it on some other means of gainful employment. Therefore, her time investment must be counted toward the breakeven point of developing her practice. The labor-to-equity transfer is at work here.

It is imperative not to confuse costs and cash. No cash has yet been spent, but two weeks in time have been. A wage of $500 per week is a minimum amount for a degreed accountant. So the inception-to-date breakeven point is already at $1,000. Let's assume that the two weeks resulted in some research, a logo design, preparation of simple brochures, printing company stationery, and the purchase of a nice leather canvassing portfolio. The cost in cash is $500. The additional cost in time is

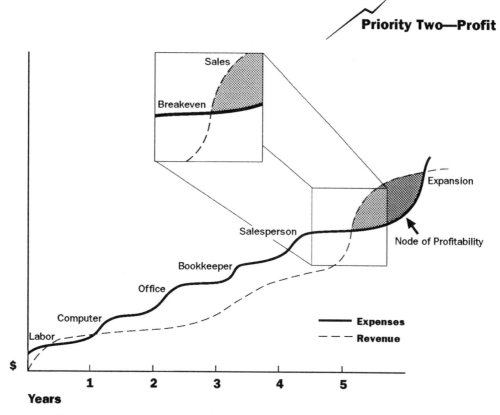

Figure 5.1. A Breakeven Analysis Showing the Node of Profitability

perhaps another day for picking up things from the print shop and for assembling a canvassing sales portfolio. Add $600 ($500 supplies, $100 for one day's labor) to the ITD breakeven point, for a total of $1,600.

The accountant is ready to begin cold canvassing (calling on prospective clients without an appointment) in the hopes of securing their accounting work. During the first week of research, she learned that 3 new clients per month is a necessary goal. Sales statistics have shown that 100 cold calls should typically result in 15 detailed presentations of her service. The 15 presentations should result in 2 new accounts. Allowing time for these presentations, travel to the various appointments, sufficient cold calls, time to set up "sold" accounts, and so on, a typical month should result in 3 new accounts.

The first month or two of intensive marketing may result in 5 or 6 new accounts, rather than the 3 from a typical month. By the end of this first month of cold calling, then, the accountant may have a client base of 5. The first week research showed that a typical monthly fee is $100, and the first month's billing should be collected in advance. Therefore, assume $500 comes in as fees from the new clients. At the same time additional costs have accrued. Four weeks of cold calling at $500 per week is a labor cost of $2,000. To date, then, the breakeven point is $3,600, and revenue is $500.

Assume that the accountant is a good marketer and she sticks with selling the service. Over the first quarter, 15 new accounts are acquired. The accountant already had $500 monthly from the first month's cold calling. The additional 10 accounts from months 2 and 3 raise monthly income by another $1,000. Total monthly income at the end of the third month, then, is $1,500.

Therefore,

Revenue:

1st month	$ 500
2nd month	1,000
3rd month	1,500
Three-month total	$ 3,000

On the cost side:

Starting research	$ 1,000
1st month calls' cost	2,000
Startup supplies	500
2nd month calls' cost	2,000
3rd month calls' cost	2,000
Three months' costs	$ 7,500

The monthly revenue at this point is just $500 below the monthly breakeven point ($1,500 monthly client revenue, compared to $2,000 monthly labor). The inception-to-date breakeven point, however, is still off in the distance (she has spent $7,500 compared to $3,000 received). The cash flow breakeven point has not yet been reached, because a living wage is not yet in hand.

At this juncture, new factors begin to make themselves felt. The successful marketing program has generated accounting work. Our accountant has discovered that it takes about a week each month to handle all the work associated with these 15 accounts. Marketing time, therefore, is reduced to just 3 weeks per month. In addition, the immediate area has been pretty well canvassed. Selling in neighboring areas requires more travel time. Another problem is that the kitchen table is no longer an adequate work place. Space for a desk, filing cabinet, typewriter, and calculator are needed. For $300, a portion of the basement must be fixed up to serve as a temporary office. Marketing and customer service phone calls have increased the family phone bill by $100 monthly as well. Postage costs have become significant at about $4 per month per account. And then there are the family interruptions just as an important call is received. It is not very professional to conduct business over the noise of a barking dog or crying children.

The net effect of these new factors is that the speed of new client acquisition begins to decline just as the cost of operating the business begins to increase. The breakeven point will become more distant before it gets any closer.

The fourth month brings only 3 new clients because of the smaller amount of time available for marketing. If the fifth month also provides 3 new clients, this new practice will have finally generated sufficient revenue to pay the owner for a 40-hour work week. Neither the monthly nor the ITD breakeven points have yet been reached, because:

Revenue:	1st three months	$ 3,000
	4th month revenue	1,800
	5th month revenue	2,100
	Five-month total	$ 6,900
Costs:	1st three months	$ 7,500
	4th month labor	2,000
	Office space	300
	Postage	72
	Telephone	100
	5th month labor	2,000
	Postage	85
	Telephone	100
		$12,157

The end of the fifth month finds the accountant with 21 clients, a monthly income of $2,100, and monthly costs of $2,185 ($2,000 in labor, $85 in postage, and $100 in telephone expense). Monthly breakeven is near, but wait! At 21 accounts, new problems surface. First, it is no longer possible to get the marketing and the accounting done in a 40-hour week. The accountant realizes that she must spend 60 hours to keep 3 new accounts coming each month and still get the work out. The temporary office will work for a couple more months, but signs of strain are beginning to show. A computer would help, but that requires an investment of several thousand dollars.

The accountant decides to stick with it and manages to obtain 3 new clients in each of months 6 and 7. The effort brings the practice to 27 accounts, yielding $2700 per month. For the first time the practice generates a 40-hour-per-week salary and pays the postage and telephone bills with cash to spare. Monthly breakeven has been reached.

But the effort has taken a toll. The startup supplies are gone. Marketing time is now down 50 percent because of the workload 27 monthly accounts generate. More than 40 hours are actually being spent working each week. If the year end should fall at this point with its associated tax work, marketing time would have to be eliminated to allow for tax preparation. The accountant wants to stop working from home, because some of the clients are uncomfortable coming to her basement. These are happy problems, though, because the first indication of business viability is in hand.

The first of the stair steps to success has been climbed. Her practice has achieved the monthly breakeven point. The accountant is now faced with a big decision. Is a monthly $2,500 pretax net profit sufficient, or must the practice be built to the next higher level? Certainly $2,500 monthly is a living wage, but it provides for few luxuries. Besides, there is no psychic income associated with working out of one's basement, so the accountant decides to take the next step.

The Expansion Phase
This step evolves around deciding which is the most efficient way to proceed. She asks herself these questions:

- Should I hire a bookkeeper to free up my time for marketing?
- Should I hire a salesperson and free up time for bookkeeping?
- Would a storefront office help by generating walk-in traffic?
- Would purchasing a personal computer free up enough time to be more cost effective than the storefront or either of the employee options?

There is one certainty at this juncture. Whichever option the accountant chooses, the result will be to increase the demand on her time. It will do so in an area in which our entrepreneur remains unskilled: training and planning the time of others. If the salesperson is hired, a significant amount of time will be required to train that person. If the bookkeeper is hired, a significant amount of time will be required to train that person. If the computer is purchased, a significant amount of time will be required to first learn it and still more time to implement the system.

The accountant makes these decisions one by one. The computer should precede the bookkeeper. A bookkeeper is less expensive than a salesperson. Having an employee at home, though, violates the zoning code, so the office would have to come before the employee. A few months later, the bookkeeper is hired. These decisions made since monthly breakeven was achieved will lock the accountant onto a course of action. A sufficient number of new clients or fee increases must now be obtained to again achieve monthly breakeven. These combined new expenses (operating costs, bookkeeper wages, the computer, and the new office) will have eaten into our accountant's $2,500 per month cash base. During this transitional period, the accountant is likely to lose a client or two, thereby pushing the next breakeven point, cash flow breakeven, farther into the future.

The decision to move ahead at this juncture is a classic example of a triggering mechanism for the Cycle of Demise. Available cash is in decline, but required cash is expanding. The situation can be complicated further by deciding to hire a salesperson in hopes of more quickly generating new business. Remember that the expense of the salesperson's wage comes before the revenue he or she might generate. The time that the accountant must spend on training will further decrease her effectiveness before the hoped-for improvement arrives. And what if the salesperson does not work out?

As a rule of thumb, the small business owner faces a minimum loss of 30 percent of the existing profit level once managerial authority is turned over to another party. This is so even if the owner is still directly involved. Not included in the 30 percent is any wage increase that the new manager's salary will add to the company's previous payroll amount. There will be a loss in efficiency due to the need to train, as discussed previously. The new person will have less specific knowledge about the business and will want to try things his or her own way. And an employee has considerably less dedication than the business's owner.

An unfortunate fact is that employees may not have much sympathy for a business owner. Employees see the cash come in but they cannot see the financial struggle going on inside the business. They see the facilities, but they do not see the

debt. They see the successful businesses around them, but they are blind to the failures. The Entrepreneurial Trojan Horse is at work in their minds.

The process of once again arriving at monthly breakeven will likely take our accountant several years. The cash shortfall during these several years must be covered in some way. One of two primary ways is a stash of startup cash that most entrepreneurs exhaust during the first year. The second is the owner's ability and willingness to work for 50, maybe 30, cents on the dollar, until the Node of Profitability is reached. The owner, essentially, will have to transfer labor to equity at the rate of 50 to 70 cents on the dollar. The equity builds in the form of monthly accounting clients that could be sold to another practicing accountant. Perhaps there is some value in paid-up fixtures and equipment as well. Unfortunately, this is not cash.

Real Profitability Phase

Somewhere around the fifth year in business, as Figure 5.1 shows, the practitioner will be at the brink of success. The arrival at the brink of success is characterized by the practice once again reaching the monthly breakeven point. This time, a complete operating business is in place and the business has arrived at the Node of Profitability. At this point cash flow goes positive. Real discretionary cash actually begins to fall out of the monthly operations.

This example reveals the rule rather than the exception, regardless of the type of business. Arrival at the Node of Profitability typically develops from a combination of factors. The important ones are these:

- The entrepreneur has learned (usually by the sink-or-swim method) how to run a business.

- Writeoffs such as depreciation, startup losses, and certain tax credits and perhaps interest expense have expired and no longer reduce profits and taxes due.

- A clientele has been developed from the previous years in business, and sales have reached a stable level sufficient to carry the business.

- The business has hired and trained enough employees to run the business efficiently.

- The owner has learned to manage cash through the startup, the rolling cash fund, and the peaks and valleys of business seasons.

The stair steps effect is created in the breakeven plot by each new decision to move the business along. The practitioner in this example arrives at the Node of Profitability in approximately five years. It is here that she encounters the final obstacles to success.

Managing a Business Through the Node of Profitability

The arrival of the Node of Profitability results in an unusual amount of cash in the bank account. The manner in which the practitioner deals with this cash is the final test that determines whether success has arrived to stay.

The accountant has worked diligently for five years with every available penny and every available moment going into the business. The family car is likely to be in a state of disrepair. The house needs fixing. There has been no time or money for a leisure weekend, much less a vacation, and so forth. On top of these considerations rests a factor that the business owner has not yet learned to deal with. No profit means no tax. Big profits mean big taxes. The first four years have resulted in little tax, because there has been little profit. The writing off of startup costs, interest on loans, tax credits, personal deductions, and so on, have moved tax liability forward just as the breakeven point has been moved forward. Once the business reaches profitability, our accountant will be required to come up with 13.2 percent of her first $53,400 for self-employment tax (social security for the self-employed). Another 20 percent to 30 percent might be due for state and federal income taxes. So $40,000 in adjusted taxable income can result in taxes from $8,000 to $15,000.

The accountant is close to the bookkeeping process and can see these things coming. For all other businesses, however, the onset of significant tax liability is not so clearly visible. Accrued taxes are due to be deposited *during* the year in which they were earned. If a business owner does not know how much profit was made and when it was made until after year end, fines and penalties will also be due. With an adjusted taxable income of $40,000, these fines and penalties can reach the four-digit level for a single year.

So, when the accounting practice arrives at the Node of Profitability, the business bank account is suddenly flush with cash. Tugging on one corner of this treasure trove is the entrepreneur, and perhaps her spouse, who have just struggled through five years of deprivation. Tugging at another corner is a large, perhaps unseen, tax liability plus penalties. If the entrepreneur makes the mistake of indulging in five years of lost pleasures before the tax bill is satisfied, the practice will again be plunged into the grip of a new cash management problem, the problem of success.

Unless an entrepreneur has learned to recognize success before it arrives, success is typically very short lived and can actually be the cause of failure. It is usually wise to ride the Node of Profitability for a year or two before withdrawing substantial amounts from the reserve funds. It helps to settle old debts, fix things up a bit, and build a cash reserve. An owner may decide to ride this Node of Profitability into the sunset. Risking it all once again in hopes of even larger gains may not be wise.

Look again at the accounting practice breakeven chart in Figure 5.1. Notice that the Node of Profitability is a very small area. It is entirely possible for an uninformed entrepreneur to ride right through the Node of Profitability without knowing it's there!

I have seen many businesses that pay for accounting statements that are three or four months delinquent. I have also seen some of these same businesses run by the erroneous assumption that if there is cash in the bank account, everything is okay. Imagine a business in which both of these conditions exist. The Node of Profitability might be arrived at, resulting in free cash. Having more cash than before might be translated as being better off than before. A spending spree could drive the breakeven point beyond the Node of Profitability. It could all happen before the delinquent statements give the entrepreneur or his or her accountant a hint about what has happened. The passing may go completely unnoticed.

An entrepreneur who is determined to build an empire overnight might succumb to the same passing. Suppose that the accountant was so excited by the arrival of the Node of Profitability that she decided to immediately copy the operation. The startup costs of a new office or two could quickly lift the total breakeven point beyond the profitability of the first office. At the same time, the practitioner's diminishing involvement in the profitable office will surely cause it to generate less profit. It may even become unprofitable. The dynamic growth plan triggers the Cycle of Demise once again. The need for cash is increasing while the availability of cash is decreasing. And so it goes.

The only way to succeed in the long run, then, is to understand accounting. An owner must see that accounting data from the business is complete and current. The owner must be able to use this data in a responsible and informed manner. There simply is no other way to survive, except by extraordinary luck.

Look once again at Figure 5.1. You may question how the accountant could afford to live from year 1 through year 4 when overall the practice was losing money. The answer lies in the labor-to-equity transfer. The accountant had to be willing and able to receive less than an appropriate wage and diminished fringe benefits to make up the cash shortfall. Once the practice becomes profitable, this shortfall is returned in the form of equity in an operating practice. If the accountant was to cash in at the Node of Profitability—that is, sell the practice—the labor-to-equity transfer will fall out as cash proceeds from the sale of a successful business. Until that time, cash is locked into the business as though it were sealed in granite.

Now that you understand the life cycle a typical small business experiences on the way to profitability, take a look at the calculations that help you determine just how profitable your business currently is.

Profit and Loss Math

The entrepreneur needs to understand the mathematical basis for computing profit and loss, because so much depends on the answer. Because of the mathematical relationships in the profit and loss formula, the results are subject to large, erroneous swings. For example, an accurate value for inventory and any calculated cost of goods sold figure computed using a certain inventory value can be the difference between success and failure. Suppose that the cost of sales figure used to compute net profit was 48 percent of total sales. Because of a combination of factors, such as spoilage, theft, poor count figure, mathematical error, and so on, the computed value should have been 52 percent of net sales.

Actual value of 52% - computed value of 48% = 4% error

The calculation of net profit in Figure 5.2 explores the relationship of the error in cost of sales (4 percent) to the resulting error in profit percent. The error is considerably magnified because of the mathematical relationship involved in computing profit and loss. Cost of sales contributes to the result as a large part of the calculation 45 percent to 55 percent is common. Profit, however, is typically a much smaller part of the whole calculation, usually less than 5 percent.

Because profit is a much smaller element in the calculation, it can be wiped out by seemingly small errors in the portion of the calculation involving larger numbers. Therefore, a 4 percent error in calculating or estimating cost of sales can lead to a 100 percent error in profit.

	Accurate Percentages	Erroneous Percentages
Sales	(100)	(100)
Cost of Sales	52	48
Operations Expense	48	48
Net Profit	0	4

Figure 5.2. Phantom Profits Lead to Phantom Taxes

The problem, as pointed out by the profit margin study, Figure 1.5, is that a typical profit margin is less than 4 percent. An error of 4 percent in cost of sales, then—52 percent as compared to 48 percent—is greater than all of a typical profit margin. In statistical terms, the entire profit margin computed with an estimate or industry standard can be within the margin for error. When a profit figure falls within the margin for error, it might actually be a loss.

A different problem develops if we reverse the error. Assume the correct cost-of-sales figure was 48 percent, but it was erroneously computed to be 52 percent. Using the same math as in Figure 5.2, the resulting profit figure would be 0 percent instead of the actual 4 percent. If the error were only discovered at year end, it would be too late to make timely income tax deposits. Penalties and interest would have accrued. An owner may also find that there is no cash to pay these surprise taxes at year end, penalties or not. And where did the money go?

Proprietorship accounting tends to mask this problem by using a profit formula that does not provide for a proprietor's wage. The proprietor's profit is the proprietor's wage and profit together. A typical proprietorship profit for businesses in the $100,000 sales range is on the order of 30 percent. All of this 30 percent typically takes the form of a wage. The error in Figure 5.2, then, would make profit swing from 34 percent to 30 percent in the first situation and from 30 percent to 34 percent in the second situation. The difference appears to be small to the unknowing entrepreneur. In fact, it can be the difference between owning a job at 30 percent and owning a business at 34 percent.

My experience has shown that the use of industry standard percentages, or an average for computing cost of sales in lieu of a physical monthly count, regularly leads to profitability errors on the magnitude of 100 percent. The practice of using one of these "estimates," together with the practice of taking a physical inventory only once a year, is ruinous. Imagine a business that used estimates and didn't even take an inventory at the end of December, as some businesses do. The owner of such

a business could end up paying income tax on a profit that could actually have been a loss. Wow! Now that's mismanaging cash.

The point is this. An owner's lack of accounting knowledge and the practice of not performing accurate and timely accounting create a snowball effect. Mistakes silently, unknowingly, consume more and more of the owner's cash, until Cycle of Demise mechanics take over the running of the business and guide it to failure.

Summary

Managing for profit is a necessary immediate and long-term goal. It is, however, secondary to cash management, because your business can subsist without profit but will quickly wither and die without cash. Profit management, however, is a higher priority than calculating and paying taxes, because no taxes are due until the business earns a profit.

Chapter 6

Priority Three—Taxes

It is important to dispel the notion that because taxes are always changing, only a professional has the time to stay current with all the changes. Although tax laws across the board may change significantly from year to year, the effect on an individual business and the way that business does its accounting seldom change. The Schedule C from the Internal Revenue Service (IRS), for example, with its many line numbers and titles, experienced only position changes on the form after the major tax overhaul of 1986. The line numbers and titles escaped virtually unchanged.

The point is, once you learn how to deal with the particular taxes involved with your business, there is little else to learn from year to year. Tax changes that do occur for a particular business can be learned from the instructions of the various tax forms that the government provides. The annual Form 1040, for example, begins with "What's new for this year?" IRS Publication 334, *Tax Guide for Small Businesses*, which is provided free by the federal government, begins with a page and a half of important changes for the year. This publication is available long before the 1040s are mailed. It even discusses pending legislation and points the reader to IRS Publication 553, which highlights changes for the coming year. The use of these two free publications provides as much advance notice as is available. Entrepreneurs can learn at a glance whether a change affects their particular type of business. The changes section is followed by two pages of important reminders. These few publications provide all the tax help a small business needs if the owner will only take the time to read them.

Research by a nationwide accounting firm assessed what small businesses fear the most. The results showed that small businesses' biggest fears were the government and taxes. Tax experts, on the other hand, indicate that taxes and the government are the last thing to fear. The fact is, those entrepreneurs who have come close to the tax system have a much greater chance to succeed than those who do not. They learn that there is nothing to fear and that mismanaged cash or insufficient profit (priorities 1 and 2 described in previous chapters) can do businesses in long before taxes are even a consideration. Almost everyone who owns a business is capable of and will benefit from doing his or her own taxes. The benefits extend well beyond the cash saved by not paying someone else to do the work. At the heart of a completed tax return is a sound understanding of information processing that occurs throughout the year behind the scenes.

So here is what I consider to be a primary goal for the small business owner. Each entrepreneur should have the ability to prepare financial statements and use that data to prepare quarterly and year-end taxes. If success should later bring in enough cash to pay someone else to do the work, so be it. But the entrepreneur who turns the financial work over before he or she has learned to do the job will have done him- or herself a great disservice. Sufficient knowledge to prepare financial statements and taxes is one of the qualities that separates the job owners from the business owners.

Why You Should Master Your Business's Tax Data

Knowledge of accounting and tax preparation serves as defense against failure. It keeps accounting and tax bills to a minimum and helps the entrepreneur fend off the Cycle of Demise. Accounting knowledge serves as a tool for generating more profit sooner and obtaining a return on investment. Entrepreneurs who achieve a working knowledge of accounting are able to think and plan their way to success. They have developed their entrepreneurial navigational skills to the point where they can make the grade with any business they choose.

The first years of operation result in losses for most businesses. Those losses can be written off against current and future profit. Taxes are, therefore, based on inception-to-date profit. The key to receiving the full benefit from a small business startup investment is to stay in business long enough to use up one's tax credits and earn the right to pay income tax. There is no way for a successful business to avoid paying income tax! Or it could be said, a business that does not pay income tax is not yet successful. My own trucking business went through four years before business and personal tax credits were exhausted. Only then was the combination of high income and low deductions sufficient to require payment of significant income tax.

One caution: Deductions that reduce income tax do not reduce self-employment tax (social security payments for self-employed people). The limit is currently 13.2 percent of the first $53,400 in profit. It is possible for a proprietor to owe the entire amount for social security and still not owe income tax.

The Form 1040 is the master tax form for our tax system. It is thought to be much more complicated than it really is. The 1040 itself is the summary sheet onto which the results of other sheets (schedules) are posted. The 1040 provides for the exemptions allowed for all a filer's dependents. Schedules B, C, D, E, and F and Forms W2 and 1099 generally contribute to the income portion of the 1040. Schedule A is the documentation of various personal deductions. The overall purpose of the 1040 is to arrive at the adjusted taxable income for each taxpayer or couple filing jointly.

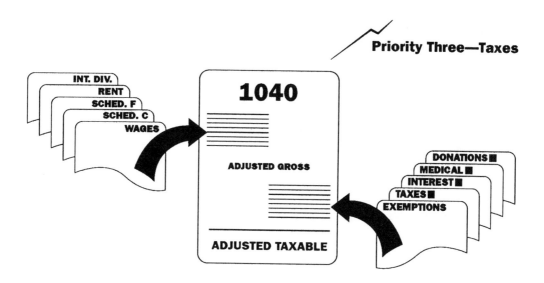

Figure 6.1. The U.S. Tax System for Small Business Returns

The science of legally reducing one's adjusted taxable income is the subject of many articles and books. Much of the manipulation possible was eliminated or curtailed by the tax revision legislation of 1986. In general, the new code is more straightforward. Most importantly, it is no longer advantageous to "lose" money in a business venture in order to turn the loss into gain with tax breaks. It would be helpful for you to read through applicable tax forms and become familiar with their intent. The 1040 booklet itself provides much of the information that most small business owners will ever require.

Forms You'll Need to Prepare a Federal Tax Return

The tax system paperwork that applies to most small business taxpayers is laid out in Figure 6.1. The forms involved in the packet may look complicated, but much of the text is simply instructions to add or subtract one number from another or move a number from one line to another. Many technical questions can be answered by obtaining a free copy of IRS Publication 334, *Tax Guide for Small Businesses*. The book can be obtained by calling the toll-free IRS phone number in your local phone book and requesting a copy. Any questions that cannot be answered by reading this booklet can be answered by calling the same number and asking for help. It is important to write down the name of the IRS person from whom you obtain information and the date you obtained it. This information is required for your protection if, during an audit, the recommended action turns out to be incorrect. Staple the person's name, phone number, and the inquiry date to the document in question.

The Form 1040 itself has three variations:

- The 1040EZ is the most basic; it only provides for wages reported through the W2 form. It provides for standard deductions only.
- Form 1040A provides for a few more deductions and options.
- Sole proprietors and anyone with a home mortgage or additional sources of income must use the full Form 1040.

SCHEDULE C (Form 1040)	**Profit or Loss From Business**	OMB No. 1545-0074
Department of the Treasury Internal Revenue Service (O)	(Sole Proprietorship) Partnerships, Joint Ventures, Etc., Must File Form 1065. ▶ Attach to Form 1040 or Form 1041. ▶ See Instructions for Schedule C (Form 1040).	**1990** Attachment Sequence No. **09**

Name of proprietor	Social security number (SSN)

A Principal business or profession, including product or service (see Instructions)

B Enter principal business code (from page 2) ▶

C Business name and address ▶ (include suite or room no.)

D Employer ID number (Not SSN)

E Accounting method: (1) ☐ Cash (2) ☐ Accrual (3) ☐ Other (specify) ▶

F Method(s) used to value closing inventory: (1) ☐ Cost (2) ☐ Lower of cost or market (3) ☐ Other (attach explanation) (4) ☐ Does not apply (if checked, go to line H)

		Yes	No
G	Was there any change in determining quantities, costs, or valuations between opening and closing inventory? (If "Yes," attach explanation.)		
H	Are you deducting expenses for business use of your home? (If "Yes," see Instructions for limitations.)		
I	Did you "materially participate" in the operation of this business during 1990? (If "No," see Instructions for limitations on losses.)		
J	If this is the first Schedule C filed for this business, check here ▶ ☐		

Part I Income

1	Gross receipts or sales. *Caution: If this income was reported to you on Form W-2 and the "Statutory employee" box on that form was checked, see the Instructions and check here* ▶ ☐	1	
2	Returns and allowances	2	
3	Subtract line 2 from line 1. Enter the result here	3	
4	Cost of goods sold (from line 38 on page 2)	4	
5	Subtract line 4 from line 3 and enter the **gross profit** here	5	
6	Other income, including Federal and state gasoline or fuel tax credit or refund (see Instructions)	6	
7	Add lines 5 and 6. This is your **gross income** ▶	7	

Part II Expenses

8	Advertising	8		21 Repairs and maintenance	21	
9	Bad debts from sales or services (see Instructions)	9		22 Supplies (not included in Part III)	22	
10	Car and truck expenses (attach Form 4562)	10		23 Taxes and licenses	23	
11	Commissions and fees	11		24 Travel, meals, and entertainment:		
12	Depletion	12		a Travel	24a	
13	Depreciation and section 179 expense deduction (not included in Part III) (see Instructions).	13		b Meals and entertainment		
14	Employee benefit programs (other than on line 19)	14		c Enter 20% of line 24b subject to limitations (see Instructions)		
15	Insurance (other than health)	15		d Subtract line 24c from line 24b	24d	
16	Interest:			25 Utilities	25	
a	Mortgage (paid to banks, etc.)	16a		26 Wages (less jobs credit)	26	
b	Other	16b		27a Other expenses (**list type and amount**):		
17	Legal and professional services	17				
18	Office expense	18				
19	Pension and profit-sharing plans	19				
20	Rent or lease (see Instructions):					
a	Vehicles, machinery, and equip.	20a				
b	Other business property	20b		27b Total other expenses	27b	

28	Add amounts in columns for lines 8 through 27b. These are your **total expenses** ▶	28	
29	**Net profit or (loss).** Subtract line 28 from line 7. If a profit, enter here and on Form 1040, line 12. Also enter the net profit on Schedule SE, line 2 (statutory employees, see Instructions). If a loss, you MUST go on to line 30 (fiduciaries, see Instructions)	29	
30	If you have a loss, you MUST check the box that describes your investment in this activity (see Instructions). ⎫ 30a ☐ All investment is at risk. ⎭ 30b ☐ Some investment is not at risk. If you checked 30a, enter the loss on Form 1040, line 12, and Schedule SE, line 2 (statutory employees, see Instructions). If you checked 30b, you MUST attach **Form 6198**.		

For Paperwork Reduction Act Notice, see Form 1040 Instructions.　　　　　Schedule C (Form 1040) 1990

Figure 6-2 Schedule C, Profit & Loss for the Sole Proprietor

Schedule A records your itemized personal deductions. The use of this form becomes advantageous when itemized deductions exceed what would be available through the standard deduction. Medical expenses, property taxes, home mortgage interest payments, and donations may be itemized on this form. The total of allowed deductions is then copied to the appropriate line on the Form 1040.

Schedule B is actually the backside of schedule A. Its purpose is to list any sources of interest or dividend income that total $400 or more.

Schedule C, shown in Figure 6.2, is the centerpiece of No-Entry Accounting. This is the form used by the largest number of American businesses. It is a simple profit and loss statement. And yet, it is so complete that millions of diverse businesses can use it to report their profit and loss on a common basis. The Schedule C embodies all the accounting principles (including all business writeoffs) you must master in order to run your own business. Therefore, to understand accounting at the practical level, what better place to begin than with a single document through which millions of businesses come together? The Schedule C is covered in depth in the sections that follow.

Note: Partnerships are required to use form 1065 and the additional forms Schedule L, a balance sheet, Schedule M and Schedule K. Corporations are required to use one of the 1120 master forms and associated schedules which are much like the partnership forms.

A subsidiary schedule to the Schedule C is the Form 4562, used to itemize depreciation expense. It provides for selecting a writeoff method for the various classes of property. Also see Chapter 6 for a complete discussion of depreciation methods. Publication 334, *Tax Guide for Small Businesses*, covers depreciation and the Form 4562 in detail.

Schedule D is the form used to report gains and losses from the sale of stocks and bonds or other securities.

Schedule E is another profit and loss form. It is designed to report profit or loss from rental properties and to report royalty income. It also provides for income from part ownership of partnerships or S corporations.

Schedule F is the profit and loss form for a farming operation. It is different from the Schedule C in that certain farm reporting requirements break revenue into such categories as cattle, eggs, vegetables, fruit and nuts, and so on, instead of the single line Schedule C provides for revenue.

Form 1099 may be a part of an individual tax return. The 1099 is used to report interest and dividend income. It is also used to report income received by freelance entrepreneurs when no tax was withheld by a client. The 1099 must be prepared when the fees or commissions paid to any outside contractor exceed $600 in a year, just as that contractor must report the fees as income. The proprietor who fails to report such earnings paid to contractors on a 1099 is liable for the taxes and penalties the freelancer should have paid but probably did not.

The W2 is also used with the 1040 to report the wages of a business owner or spouse. A sole proprietor will not have a W2 from his or her own business but may have one or more from having worked for someone else during a tax year. The owner may have a series of 1099s as well. The biggest part of the job involved with using these various forms is collecting and tallying the data that they require. Once the forms have been completed for one year, succeeding years are much easier. An entrepreneur who has used No-Entry Accounting through the year will find that much of the tax work is nothing more than a copy job.

A typical small business owner's filing, therefore, will require the 1040, Schedule A, and Schedule C. If the owner learns No-Entry Accounting and keeps records accordingly, he or she should require no more than two hours to complete preparation of a personal tax return at year end.

Schedule C in Detail

Schedule C essentially outlines the accounting concepts a small business operator must understand. Figure 6.2 illustrates a recent Schedule C so you can follow along.

Line A: Principal Business or Profession
The purpose of this line is to specifically identify the business for statistical purposes in conjunction with the code in line B.

Line B: Principal Business Code
This code helps the IRS to classify information by line of business. This data, available through such publications as the *United States Statistical Abstract* and computerized mailing lists, helps business owners, accountants, bankers, the government, and other groups develop programs and plan for the future. You take the code from Part IV of Schedule C, Principal Business or Professional Activity Codes.

Line C: Business Name and Address
This line is simply the business name and address.

Line D: Employer ID Number
Line D is a unique computer identification number that is assigned by the federal government to each business when it begins using employees. The number must be applied for by using a form you can obtain from the IRS. This employer ID number is used for the deposit of withheld employee income taxes and for reporting corporate income tax.

Line E: Method(s) Used to Value Closing Inventory
On this line you indicate which method you use for placing a value on inventory. The requirement for declaring a particular method stems from the need to compute cost of goods sold. The proper valuing of inventory on a regular and timely basis is critical to the success of any enterprise involving inventory. Inventory typically represents a substantial portion of a business's need for cash. Inventory must be available in the right quantities, sizes, prices, and so on. It is easy for a business to find itself with too much of a slow-moving product and too little of a fast mover. The slow movers tie up cash that might otherwise be used to purchase more fast movers.

The Cycle of Demise can be triggered by this lock on cash. A wide variety of other inventory problems, such as waste, theft, or spoilage, can trigger the cycle as

well. It is, therefore, important to manage inventory with great care so that it doesn't become the anchor that sinks the ship.

Tax law mandates that a physical inventory be taken at least once a year as part of computing the annual tax bill. Once a year might be good enough for the tax collector, but it is not good enough for the entrepreneur. Every effort should be made to perform a physical inventory every month. The wrong accounting method used to compute the value of physical inventory can make the process more time consuming and difficult.

One of the methods will be more appropriate for your particular business than the others. For a business heavily involved with inventory, such as a restaurant, I would recommend the "Cost of the Last Item Purchased" method. Each method discussed in detail later in this chapter.

Taking Inventory

An inventory of several thousand items can be taken quickly if it is organized well. Three-by-five cards can contain the basic inventory data for each item. For example:

Date	Item	On Hand	PriceLast Paid	Total $ Amount
03/03	Any description	15	$1.00	$15.00

The cards can be kept in some logical sequence, such as by all items in the cooler, or all items in some section of the storeroom. I was able to take a complete inventory (2,300 items) every month in my restaurant, including forks, spoons, meat produce, and supplies, in approximately three hours. The cards were divided among employees who each counted a particular section. The office manager was able to extend and price everything in another two to three hours with a calculator and the cards. A computer would be helpful with this pricing and extension if the owner knows how to run one. With this data in hand, the entrepreneur becomes master of the enterprise. Cost of sales can then be computed with accuracy. Any resulting profit can be relied on to be real.

A common practice among small businesses is to use an estimate of cost of sales rather than computing cost of sales from a physical inventory. Even if such a practice resulted in a year-end figure of reasonable accuracy, a business could fail from cash flow problems during the year. The erroneous swings in estimated profit through the year could lead to spending decisions that cause the business to fail. Waiting for results of an annual inventory might be too late. Estimates and industry standards are too much like weather reports for the entrepreneur who really wants to succeed. They just are not reliable enough.

Look what else happens with a monthly physical inventory.

- The specific knowledge of how much cash is tied up in inventory is as valuable to the entrepreneur as is an accurate cost of sales figure. Inventory value and cost of sales are the two largest pieces of the successful business puzzle, and the two most difficult to obtain. Therefore, accurate data from these two pieces means that the largest part of the cash management problem is in control.

- If the business has a theft problem, it does not continue more than 30 days without being identified. Hopefully, this is before the problem becomes fatal to your business.

- Employees are involved in the process, so they learn how easy it is to get caught stealing. They are, therefore, less likely to try theft in the first place.

- The monthly review keeps the owner completely informed regarding the movement of specific items. More informed buying decisions can then be made and more timely and appropriate sales can be run.

- The annual tax position can be more accurately forecast because the monthly accounting is more accurate. Year-end tax surprises, penalties, and interest are thus eliminated.

- The computed value of inventory also keeps the entrepreneur up to date with regard to the balance sheet. The value adds to one's assets, which are used to compute net worth. Collateral value is then current.

The likelihood for success is considerably enhanced in such an operation, because the entrepreneur "knows" where the business is going. The business is being guided by the owner rather than the owner following the business. Sufficient information is available to adjust and correct and keep a business on the road to profitability.

Methods Used to Value Inventory

The method chosen to value inventory can have a significant impact. Figure 6.3 is sample data used to discuss how the various inventory valuation methods are computed. Each line on the inventory records represents a different purchase of the same part on a different day and so sometimes at a different price. The examples show that a change in the method used can cause significant change in the value of every single item. The changes range from $21 to $25 in the inventory value of an item, and from $44 to $50 in the same item's cost of sales value, simply by using a different computation method. There can also be a significant change in the clerical work required to support the chosen method.

Widgets

Date	Purchases	Unit Cost	Total
1/1	3	$4.00	$12.00
3/30	3	4.50	13.50
6/30	3	4.50	13.50
9/30	3	5.00	15.00
12/30	3	5.00	15.00
Available	15	Spent	$69.00
Year End Inv.	5 remaining		
Sold	10		

Figure 6.3. Sample Inventory Record

Cost of the Last Purchase Method

This method is calculated by multiplying the price paid for the last purchase of an item by all like items in inventory. From a cash management perspective, this method provides the most relevant result for the typical small business involved

with inventory. It reflects the current operating condition of a business in terms of replacement cost. This method is the easiest to compute, because there is only one cost figure involved in the calculation. Therefore, the widgets record using this method would show:

5 items on hand, times the last purchase price of $5 =
Inventory value = $25
10 items sold, times the last purchase price of $5 =
Cost of sales = $50

This method yields a reasonable current value of inventory that may be used for loan collateral. It involves none of the accounting rehash necessary under other methods. It also yields the highest cost of goods sold figure in an increasing market, which leads to a lower profit figure, which means less cash available. Whichever direction the market is moving, this method provides the most direct and most efficient method for staying on top of your cash position.

Average Cost Method

An inventory system that uses this method must provide for storing all the purchase prices and quantities of each item purchased throughout the year as in Figure 6.3. Some computer programs do not permit storage of enough individual purchases to use this method. This cost figure is computed by dividing the total cost of the units available throughout the year by the number of units available for the year. The value needs to be recomputed monthly and can become a clerical load. Using Figure 6.3 again:

$$\frac{\text{Total Value} \quad \$69}{\text{Units Available} \quad 15} = \$4.60 \text{ Average Cost}$$

Therefore,

$4.60 times 5 units on hand = Inventory value of $23.00
$4.60 times 10 units sold = Cost of sales of $46.00

The average cost figures fall somewhere in the midrange of the other methods and add a certain practicality to the chore of cash management. There can be more math required, however, in computing the average. If prices have changed little since a prior valuation, this is no great problem. But in a changing marketplace, this method may add significantly to the clerical time required to do an inventory. The small business owner may decide to forgo a regular inventory, because some or all of this clerical time may be his or her own. Remember that the need is for greater owner involvement, rather than less.

FIFO, the First-In, First-Out Method

The FIFO method of valuing inventory relies on the principle that when an item is sold, the particular item that is delivered to the customer is the particular item that was first received into inventory. An example is the milkman at the grocery store. He puts his latest delivery at the back of the cooler. Then, when a customer removes a gallon through the front door, it is the milk that has been in the store the longest (first delivered) that the customer removes. This method will result in a cost of goods sold figure that could lag considerably behind a current replacement price, especially with slow-moving items. Because FIFO inventory is relieved on a first-in, first-out basis, if five remaining units consist of the last ones to be received into inventory, two of those may remain from those purchased in September, and all three from the purchase in December. See Figure 6.3. So:

12/30	3 units	x	$5.00	$15.00
9/30	2 units	x	5.00	10.00
		inventory value of =		$25.00

The 10 that were sold consist of all those purchased in January, March, and June, plus 1 from the September purchase. They had a value of:

1/1	3 units	x	$4.00	$12.00
3/30	3 units	x	4.50	13.50
6/30	3 units	x	4.50	13.50
9/30	1 unit	x	5.00	5.00
		Cost of Goods Sold =		$44.00

LIFO, the Last-In, First-Out Method

The LIFO method of valuing inventory relies on the principle that when an item is sold, it is the last such item received into inventory that is actually delivered to the customer. If the milkman stocked his cooler using this method he would stock it through the front door. Customers would then be removing the latest delivery first, rather than the oldest delivery first. LIFO inventory is relieved on a last-in, first-out basis.

Therefore, the five remaining in inventory consist of the first ones received into inventory. See Figure 6.3.

1/1	3 units	$4.00	$12.00
3/30	2 units	4.50	9.00
	Inventory value =		$21.00

The ten that were sold had a value of:

12/30	3 units	$5.00	$15.00
9/30	3 units	5.00	15.00
6/30	3 units	4.50	13.50
3/30	1 unit	4.50	4.50
	Cost of Goods Sold =		$48.00

Actual Cost Method

This method should be used where there are a small number of high-priced items in inventory, each of which has a different price. A used car dealership is a good example. The price that was paid for each car is recorded on an individual card. Any repairs or added costs are added to the purchase price, showing the total cost. Once an item is sold, the card is removed from inventory. The value of inventory is simply the sum of the unsold cost cards. Cost of sales is the sum of the costs of those cars that were sold. Figure 6.3 is, therefore, not an appropriate record for this type of inventory.

Lower of Cost or Market Method

This method of valuing an inventory provides for choosing which of two values of an inventory item is most appropriate. The business owner must choose between the actual cost that was paid and the current market value, whichever is less. The very obvious shortcoming of this method is the time and logistics involved in arriving at the current market value. This method is appropriate for valuing a portfolio of stocks for which current market value is readily available and conservatism is important. The data in Figure 6.3 is insufficient to value inventory and cost of sales by this method, because the card does not include current market value.

Back to line E. The method used to value inventory in an existing business has almost always been selected by an accountant. It would have been selected at the time the first tax return was filed by marking one of the choices on line E. Once selected, written permission from the IRS must be obtained in order to change that selection. This restriction is necessary, as the taxable income figure would be subject to manipulation if the method used could be changed regularly. The extra work a chosen method may require may be reduced each month by using a simpler method.

One word of caution: The two methods may yield a slightly different result for taxes due. One who follows this recommendation, then, should take time in advance of year end to roughly calculate any projected year-end difference.

Line F: Accounting Method

The accounting method choice that must be made on Line F deals with the two basic approaches to accounting statements: cash method and accrual method. Just as the methods for valuing inventory cause different results, so do these two different methods. The basic difference lies in when, and under what conditions, the transactions a business generates are to be counted.

No-Entry Accounting is a cash basis system that is faster than a computerized financial statements system. At year end it becomes a modified cash system because of IRS reporting rules for cost of sales and depreciation. Each of these modifications is dealt with in detail later.

The Cash Method

Transactions under the cash method are counted when the actual cash changes hands. For example, the owner of a shoe store sells a pair of shoes to a friend but gives the friend 30 days to pay for the purchase. The sale would not be reflected in the shoe store accounting until the cash is actually received 30 days later. In the case of something like insurance, which is typically prepaid, the complete year's expense is counted when it is paid even though it may cover an entire year.

The particular value of this method is that it lends itself directly to the management of cash without some intervening accounting work. As items like the annual insurance premium pass through the system, periodic cash losses occur. These losses directly flag cash management problems, because they show the owner that there is likely no cash available for immediate use.

Figure 6.4 compares the numbers for a typical month in which insurance is not due and one in which insurance must be paid.

Month When No Insurance Is Due

Sales	$10,000
Cost of Sales	(4,500)
Normal Operations	(4,500)
Profit	$1,000

Month When Insurance Is Due

Sales	$10,000
Cost of Sales	(4,500)
Normal Operations	(4,500)
Annual Insurance	(1,200)
Loss	$ (200)

Figure 6.4. Cash Versus Accrual: Two Different Profit Pictures

My conclusion is that the sight of a $1,000 profit one month and a $200 loss in a similar month is the shock treatment most small business owners need to properly manage cash. The fact that insurance is used equally throughout the year does not matter. What matters is whether there is enough cash to carry the company over the crunch. Any process that can speed up and simplify the gathering of cash management data, such as the cash method of accounting, is a process that needs to be used by the small business owner.

Cash accounting also reduces the level of knowledge required to prepare regular statements as compared to the accrual method. It requires no monthly adjusting entries from reserves such as prepaid insurance or depreciation. If it is faster and simpler and can be learned in a much shorter time, the chances that a harried business owner will use it are greater, thus the greater opportunity for the company's financial success.

The Accrual Method

The accrual method counts a transaction when it is effective. The passing of cash from one hand to another is not a consideration. Recall the sale of a pair of shoes discussed previously. The owner let a friend take the shoes and pay later. Once the shoes were taken out of the store, accrual accounting considers the sale to have been made. Company revenue would have increased by the amount of the sale price of the shoes. Whether the cash will actually ever be received is a matter for another day. If the cash is received, it will simply be treated as cash received against accounts receivable. If it is not collected, it will at some point have to be written off as a bad debt. The effect of writing off a bad debt is to decrease the sales of the period in which it is written off.

A plumbing contractor who attended a No-Entry Accounting Seminar is an example of how accrual accounting can work to one's disadvantage. His business was doing large government plumbing projects. These projects would be done in three phases and would often take as long as two years. The work would have to be completed through a particular phase before the contractor could receive a payout. Several months, worth of labor and material could be involved in a single billing. Once a bill was submitted, it took another 30 to 60 days to receive payment. At year end there were always several projects partially complete for which cash had been expended but for which no cash had been received. Accrual accounting dictates that the portion of work completed—and

86

therefore, the portion that has been effectively earned—must be counted as that year's income, whether it has been paid for or not.

This plumbing business naturally developed cash management complications. Income tax had to be paid on income that had not yet been received and often was not received for another quarter. The result was a business that had to plan to have sufficient cash to meet payroll and buy materials for perhaps three or four months, not to mention payment of income tax on profits that had been earned but not yet received.

In this plumber's case, the cash float required would occasionally approach $100,000. If a snag developed on a job, the receipt of cash could be delayed even longer. The whole time, the plumbing contractor was seeing monthly statements that showed a profit. The profit was not cash, however, because the sale was counted before any cash was received. Other contractors who work in the industrial and residential segment experience similar conditions. Their business is also likely, however, to experience the additional burden of an occasional bad debt.

Compare the example used in Figure 6.4 for cash accounting with the same data as seen through accrual accounting, shown in Figure 6.5.

Month When No Insurance Payment Is Due

Sales	$10,000
Cost of Sales	(4,500)
Operations Expense	(4,500)
Insurance Expense	(100)
Profit	$ 900

Month When Insurance Payment Is Due

Sales	$10,000
Cost of Sales	(4,500)
Operations Expense	(4,500)
Insurance Expense	(100)
Profit	$900

Figure 6.5. The Accrual System's Cover-up

Right! The records show no difference, but nonetheless the cash flow is affected.

The untrained business owner typically becomes comfortable and confident that things are fine when monthly statements show consistent profit. The problem, of course, is not profit but cash. Figure 6.4 accurately reflects the cash management problem the small business owner must deal with when the accounting papers don't provide the actual cash flow data. The swing from $1,000 in profit from a cash accounting month with no insurance to a $200 loss in a cash accounting month with insurance is real. Seeing it in the cash method's monthly profit and loss statement is the shock small entrepreneurs need to stop and evaluate their position. Smoothing this type of large swing over with accrual accounting in Figure 6.5 only increases the number of failed small businesses.

Commercially available accounting reports rarely alert the business owner to the impending cash crisis outlined in this example. The difference as I see it is enhanced pictorially in Figures 6.6 and 6.7.

Figure 6.6. A Business Venture as Seen Through Accrual Accounting

Figure 6.7. The Same Venture as Seen Through Cash Accounting

A contractor I know was told by his accountant in January that he had made a $45,000 profit in the preceding year. The contractor promptly scheduled a vacation trip to Las Vegas. Upon his return, the quarterly tax deposit from employee withholding was due. Also due was his personal income tax and self-employment tax. The total came to something on the order of $15,000.

The $45,000 profit had been computed using the accrual method, which as Figures 6.4 and 6.5 show causes cash management data to fall through the cracks. The combination of the contractor's ignorance regarding what a $45,000 profit really meant and the complete lack of any cash management information caused the contractor to trigger the Cycle of Demise. Three months later he filed for bankruptcy; another profitable business had failed.

Line G: Changes Between Opening and Closing Inventories

This bit of information is necessary to prevent unscrupulous business owners from changing their inventory methods to manipulate their tax position. Changes to your inventory method can be made, but only after a written and acceptable explanation. It must be clear to the IRS that no attempt is being made to avoid taxes. The plumbing contractor discussed in the accrual accounting example may have a basis for requesting a change to cash accounting. It would not eliminate his tax obligation, but it would bring it more in line with his ability to pay on time and without incurring penalties and interest. Also eliminated would be much of the interest expense caused by borrowing operating cash to meet accrual accounting imposed deadlines.

Line H: Home Office Expenses

The office in the home deduction reflects costs of using one's home for running a business. The deduction has been abused in the past, though, so the IRS rules regarding the applicability of this deduction are very specific. A special calculation sheet has been included as Figure 13.6 for use by businesses that qualify. It is also discussed in Chapter 13's discussion of cash analysis. In general, a home office can only be deducted if a special room or space is set aside for the sole use of the business and that business is regularly conducted there. If an owner operates out of an office, storefront, shop, or other location, the home office is not deductible.

Lines I and J: Material Participation in Business and Tax Shelters

These two lines are directed at discovering whether the filer had any material risk in a business operation. Prior to the rewriting of the tax code in 1986, certain tax shelters were available that would permit an individual to increase after-tax income by generating paper losses. The investors were essentially involved in a no-lose situation. This type of investment is no longer allowed except to the extent one participates in the risk. Most of those for whom this book has been prepared will have no need to explore these two lines in detail.

Schedule C, Part I—Income.

Lines 1: Gross Receipts or Sales

On this line you record the total sales from the last year. Line 1b is for recording any returns. Returns are those sales that for some reason were returned or canceled. They will be subtracted from sales on Line 3 so that the sales figure will not be overstated.

Line 4: Cost of Goods Sold and/or Operations

Transfer the cost of sales computed on the back of Schedule C, Line 38 to Line 4. This amount will be subtracted from the adjusted sales figure in Line 3, to arrive at the gross profit figure on Part I, Line 7. Gross profit means sales, minus the actual cost of the items that were purchased for resale. In a shoe store, for example, gross profit would be sales minus the cost of the actual shoes that were sold.

Line 6: Other Income

On Line 6 you record any other income the business had as well. List the rent from the upstairs rooms over the shoe store, for example.

Schedule C, Part II—Expenses

In Part II you record those operating expenses that were generated by the business throughout the year. Operating expenses are all expenses incurred *except* those for the purchase of something to be resold. Typical operating expenses are rent, utilities, and wages. The No-Entry Accounting system, described fully in Part II of this book, tracks all of the expenses you list on this part of the schedule.

One of the operating expense categories that needs some extra explanation is depreciation, discussed in full momentarily. Its impact on cash flow and the bookkeeping mechanics involved with depreciation is discussed in Part II of this book. A depreciation spreadsheet is included later in the chapter. A glance at this form will answer many questions you may have. Depreciation is discussed in even greater detail in IRS Publication 334, *Tax Guide for Small Businesses*.

Schedule C, Part III—Cost of Goods Sold and/or Operations

Part III describes the cost of sales for your business. Cost of sale items are only ones you have purchased specifically for resale. One example is the shoes sold in a shoe store. Another example is the subcontractors a general contractor pays to get a house built. The subcontractor's bill will include labor and material but to the contractor the entire amount is meant for resale to the homeowner. Therefore, the entire bill is treated as cost of sales.

Many service businesses have no cost of sales at all. Some businesses have cost of sales but no inventory, because they buy cost-of-sales items only for specific jobs. The local truck mechanic is a case in point. The mechanic buys only those parts needed to fix a particular truck. The mechanic may keep some items, such as fan belts, filters, or lubricants, as spare parts inventory. These items would fit the requirements for calculating cost of goods sold.

This section of the schedule is for the calculation of the cost of goods sold where inventory is involved. The math instructions written into this section result in using the accrual method of computing cost of goods sold. Regardless of whether an entrepreneur elects cash basis or accrual basis accounting, the method used to compute cost of sales for tax purposes is always the accrual basis. Here is why.

Suppose a company had elected the cash basis method of accounting and was permitted to exercise full cash basis theory in its accounting for taxes. If the company found itself in a strong cash position at year end, it could purchase and pay for a large quantity of goods for resale. Because the cash had changed hands, theory would dictate that the cost of goods sold figure would rise accordingly. It could conceivably rise enough that a loss would be generated.

	Before	*After*
Sales	$1,000	$1,000
Cost of Sales	500	600
Operations Exp.	400	400
Profit	$100	$0

90

Notice that the additional $100 spent as cost of goods sold took net profit down to 0. Because taxes are based on profit, no tax would be due. Profit generated before the extra $100 in goods for resale was spent is wiped out. Under this theory, a business could roll its tax liability into the future by simply stocking up on inventory at the end of each year. The mandatory use of accrual accounting dictates that only those cost of sale items that have been sold and delivered can be expensed. Inventory could still be built up at year end but with no tax advantage, because the new purchases would not be sold and delivered. Accrual accounting closes a tax loophole for the cost of sales.

No-Entry Accounting uses the cash basis theory because it relates directly to the cash position of the business. Cost of sale checks and other cost of sale documents are subtracted under pure cash theory. The result may lead to a tax due figure at year end that varies from this method of computation.

To handle this variation, the reverse side of the monthly No-Entry Accounting profit and loss statement (Figure 8.4) provides a quick method for recomputing taxable profit. It uses the cost of sales data that is generated from the monthly physical inventory. The math used is from the accrual method on Schedule C. This procedure permits the cash management advantage of expensing cost of sale purchases outright. At the same time, the process provides the cash management advantage of looking ahead to the year end's real tax position. Both procedures help you keep cash management problems under control.

The actual application of these separate principles is covered in more detail in Chapter 10's case problem for Joe's Cafe.

Depreciation

Depreciation is an accounting technique used to spread the cost of large purchases over their useful life. The modified accelerated cost-recovery system (MACRS) is the method now permitted on the depreciation tax form. Note: Every public library carries a complete set of tax forms and instructions. These forms are in a binder that is kept with the reference librarian. You can copy the forms for personal use. The depreciation report, Form 4562, is one of these. The accompanying instructions explain how to compute MACRS. Except for some small percentage difference, MACRS works the same as straight line depreciation. MACRS permits businesses to more rapidly write off depreciable assets than under other previously used methods, hence, the use of *accelerated*.

The straight line method applies an equal amount of an asset's depreciation expense over the useful life of the asset. A new $10,000 truck, for example, would be expensed at the rate of $2,000 per year for 5 years. If a business expects a sizable profit, it may choose to purchase some depreciable item at year end. The business can claim an entire year's depreciation expense for that item even though it may have been purchased on December 30. This technique, via Section 179 discussed in a moment, is a tax device used to induce profitable businesses to buy more assets sooner, in hopes of stimulating the economy. The straight line method may be elected in preference to MACRS to push depreciation expense into the future. If profits, and therefore taxes, are small at present, moving depreciation to the future will decrease future taxes. Following are key points with respect to depreciation:

- What is the useful life of your business assets? Form 4562 expresses useful life in terms of 3-year property, 5-year property, 7-year property, and so on.

- The rules for 3-year property are quite limiting. This property essentially includes over-the-road semitractors and some animals.

- Rules for 5-year assets allow new cars, trucks, light equipment, computers, trailers, busses, planes, test equipment, and animals such as cows and sheep in this category.

- Rules for 7-year property provide for essentially furniture, fixtures, and heavy machinery and equipment.

- Types of items counted as 10-year property include most boats or barges.

- Included as 20-year property are most farm buildings.

- Rules for 27.5- and 31.5-year property stipulate residential rental property and all other rental property, respectively.

Contact your area IRS office for free help on any questions that may arise about depreciation. The IRS does have an 800 number.

The monthly depreciation expense can be computed by using the depreciation form in Figure 6.8. Enter the date an asset was purchased, the name of the asset, and its purchase price. Then divide the purchase price by the number of years it is expected to be in service. A new truck would be five years. If the purchase price was $10,000, then:

$$\frac{\$10,000}{5 \text{ years}} = \$2,000 \text{ per year}$$

Begin in the column representing the year the asset was put into service. Enter $2,000 on the truck line in the year it was put into service, and the four succeeding years. If the purchase date was December 14, 1989, then 89, 90, 91, 92, and 93 would have $2,000 entries.

Perform the same operation with each asset. Once all the assets are listed down the left side of the form and all the annual depreciation expense amounts are spread in the manner shown above, total each yearly column. Divide these annual totals by 12 months to arrive at the monthly depreciation expense. (Use a pencil so that the numbers can be changed as necessary.) In this truck example, the monthly expense would be:

$$\frac{\$2,000}{12 \text{ months}} = \$166.66 \text{ per month}$$

The monthly total amount will fluctuate as some items are completely ex-pensed and others are added. Unless the change is significant, the schedule need not be changed except annually. The annual depreciation expense needs to be accurate for the purpose of filing income tax, but accuracy on a monthly basis is not necessary. Depreciation expense can be copied from one month to the next until some major change takes place.

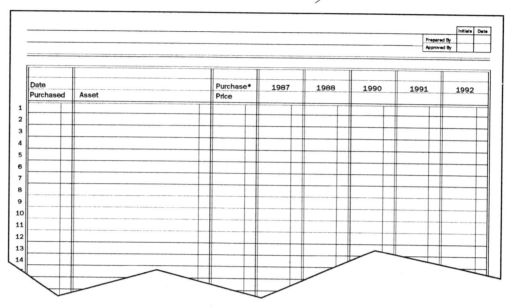

Figure 6.8 A Sample Depreciation Spreadsheet

Any profit made by selling a depreciated asset must be declared as income. Suppose the $10,000 truck was used for four years and then sold for $3,500. Because we have depreciated the truck at the rate of $2,000 per year for four years, its book value is said to be $2,000, that is, the undepreciated year that remains on the schedule. The book value becomes the cost of the item sold.

In this example, the used truck was sold for $3,500. Its book value, or cost, is $2,000. The profit on the sale of the truck, therefore, is $1,500. This $1,500 must be treated the same as $1,500 in profit generated from operations. Had the truck been sold for less than book value, a loss would have been generated. The loss may be written off as with any other business expense.

Section 179

Section 179 essentially replaces and simplifies the investment tax credit. Its purpose is to stimulate investment in new equipment by allowing immediate writeoff of certain equipment purchases. Check with your local IRS office to see what types of equipment are included or review IRS Publication 334, *Tax Guide for Small Businesses*.

This section of the tax code permits the entrepreneur to expense completely the amount of equipment purchases in any business year without regard for depreciation rules. This treatment is limited to $10,000 annually and is only permitted in the year of purchase. The owner has the option to invoke Section 179 if the year has been good. The immediate writeoff of up to $10,000 in new purchases will reduce the tax burden for the year. In a poor income year, the election would probably be to use the straight line or MACRS method. To do so would move depreciation expense into years in which a greater profit is expected. The resulting depreciation expense will then serve to reduce taxes in future years.

93

An example: Jason buys a used truck for his trucking business. The purchase price is $14,000. Jason has had a good year, so he elects Section 179, which allows immediate writeoff of the first $10,000 of his purchase. This procedure will immediately reduce the current year's tax obligation. The remaining $4,000 will be placed on Jason's depreciation schedule using the straight line method. The used equipment balance of $4,000 will then be expensed over the next five years at $800 per year ($1,000 ÷ 5 = $800.)

The depreciation amount for year 1, $800, would be recorded in the column of the first year after the year of purchase. This is because the first year was taken by the Section 179 $10,000 deduction. The second-year deduction of $800 would be entered in the next year column, and the third-year deduction, and so on, would follow . These depreciation entries will be added to all the others involved with the same year. The sum of the depreciation entries for a year is then divided by 12 to arrive at the monthly depreciation expense.

Summary

Taxes are an important element in the mix of required knowledge for small business owners. Despite this importance, however, cash and profit management come first. An understanding of tax law and a practical knowledge of preparing your tax forms serve to complete the entrepreneurial financial package much like frosting completes the cake.

Part II

Getting a Handle on Your Money— No-Entry Accounting Manual

No-Entry Accounting is the ultimate condensation of accounting, recordkeeping, and learning tools through which the small business owner can learn to survive and prosper. For small businesses, nothing is easier, nothing is faster, and nothing is more thorough.

To quote a retired IRS district director of the Criminal Investigative Division, "No-Entry Accounting is an exquisitely uncomplicated accounting system and a practical course of instruction in how to succeed in business." A CPA, MBA from the University of Iowa says, "In my 15 years of teaching accounting at Iowa State University I have never seen anything so informative and so vital in such a condensed form." These quotes are reprinted here in the hopes that you will be impressed enough to read this section thoroughly and complete the case problems.

Biting the Bullet

Any form of accounting is dry for people who hate working with numbers. This and all other math required for business is drudgery for those who hate recordkeeping. This is as easy and as fast as business records get.

No-Entry Accounting works equally well whether your business exists or you have not yet begun. If you are thinking of starting a business and find that you cannot bring yourself to read and do this section entirely, don't try to start a business. If you are already in business and cannot get through this section, there is a very high likelihood that your business is already in the grips of the Cycle of Demise.

Learning enough to complete the case problems and understand the answers will put you in direct touch with the heartbeat of a successful business venture. This process is the litmus test of entrepreneurial capability. I don't say you have to love it, or even like it. You don't have to answer the questions 100 percent correctly (no one ever has). You don't even have to use all this work in your own business (even though it is certainly recommended). However, if you cannot get yourself through this section and learn to use these basic concepts, your chances for success are slim indeed.

A couple of quick analogies might help prove how necessary No-Entry Accounting is to your business. Imagine the young hotshot who wants to be a jet fighter pilot but cannot deal with motion sickness. Or think of someone who wants to be a nuclear submarine captain who cannot stand confinement. This section will let you know if you suffer from entrepreneurial motion sickness or entrepreneurial claustrophobia—before you lose your life savings finding out.

Starting Up or Changing Over

You can adopt the No-Entry Accounting system easily whether your business is new or existing. Essentially, you simply learn to sort original transaction documents— deposit tickets, canceled checks, and paid cash receipts—so they become the detailed accounting record. For an existing business, the No-Entry Accounting system-generated totals are simply combined with the year-to-date totals from any other system to make the changeover. Chapter 12 discusses some conversion considerations that have to do with cash and accrual accounting and cutoff dates that may affect conversion from an existing accounting system. None of these considerations, however, alters the way you perform No-Entry Accounting.

To convert from a manual system or a computer system to No-Entry Accounting, you can order the materials for sorting, filing, and reporting. (The order form appears in the back of the text.) You can also master the system using the forms in Chapter 10's case study. Either way you learn, Part II of this book is your instruction manual. A sort sheet that replaces the need for these materials in a learning environment has been included in the text.

Part II begins with a system comparison. No-Entry Accounting is compared in detail with conventional accounting for both manual and computerized systems. This chapter is followed by one that teaches you how to perform No-Entry Accounting.

Part II concludes with two case problems. Joe's Cafe is designed to be a universal flight test for the entrepreneur. The concept and techniques it teaches are universal. It includes a wide variety of transaction types, system considerations, and tax considerations that are relevant to all businesses. The fact that you may own a business that has no inventory, or some other type of inventory, should not deter you from doing the problem. The payoff comes in the answers review section when you learn that there are three separate sets of correct answers for the problem, as there are three sets of answers for every real life business.

The entrepreneur needs to know how to generate and use all three sets if he or she hopes to succeed. Why? Commercially available accounting provides only two of the sets. Because it is not available commercially, the missing set can only come from your own effort.

The Ace Trucking case problem deals with buying and selling a small business. Many businesses fail from the moment a purchase contract is signed, because the owners pay too high a price or start with severely constricted cash flow. So it is certainly worthwhile for both prospective buyers and prospective sellers to understand the valuation process.

Chapter 7

Why No-Entry Accounting?

Traditional but complex accounting systems are designed to accomplish the same results as the No-Entry Accounting system. Throughout the long history of business enterprises, accounting systems have adapted to innovative data processing, computers, and the needs of financial analysis and reporting. However, as they underwent changes, the traditional accounting systems kept the historical trappings of the "system." This has caused traditional accounting methods to become needlessly time consuming, costly, and complex for most small business enterprises.

The historical baggage accumulated by traditional accounting systems is often justified by the assumption that these systems provide accurate net figures and that this accuracy can be certified. A careful and informed observer, however, recognizes that the net figure is really an estimate. The results are never more accurate than the least accurate amount that is included in the computation. Inventory valuation and depreciation, for example, are recognized as estimates even though they may be computed by formula and without fraudulent intent. Therefore, the net profit (or loss) derived from figures that include estimates is an estimate itself.

The successful owner or manager of a typical business is likely to have learned to make commonsense adjustments and decisions to meet current conditions. This manual is intended to provide a commonsense alternative to traditional, complicated accounting. Small business owners have the right to question any accounting system that requires trained specialists to operate and interpret it.

Switching to No-Entry Accounting is as easy as getting a checking account; it doesn't even have to be a business account. A CPA firm that tested this system states that "all a beginning student needs to understand cash basis accounting are a bank statement and deposits and canceled checks." These and many other types of documents are included in the case problems so that the owner of almost any business can see how the system applies to him or her.

The beauty and simplicity of No-Entry Accounting is that it is designed around the Schedule C business income tax reporting form through which 10 million nonfarm businesses report their profits and losses. Just as all 10 million businesses are able to report their profitability and, therefore, their tax status with a single 8-1/2-by-11-inch form, now they can manage their record keeping just as easily. Schedule C provides a reporting structure that works for many, many types of businesses. The type you want to start or already own is almost certainly one of them.

The focus here is cash management, then profit, and then taxes—the top three priorities discussed in Part I. These are *universal* problems. Not having enough money to pay the rent is the same for a beauty salon or a restaurant; lacking funds to buy a new set of tools is the same as not enough money to pay the book binder.

Remember: The world's most used profit and loss statement is the Schedule C. It doesn't matter whether your income is rent, fees, royalties, commission, or sales—these are all "sales" on the Schedule C.

Schedule C, the "final report" for business taxation, consists of some 30 lines. That's all! I would dare to say that none of the 10 million businesses using it use all 30 some lines; most use fewer than 20. The comparable forms for partnerships and corporations use different line numbers, but the profit and loss considerations are identical. The No-Entry Accounting forms from this book can be used by corporations and partnerships through the year just as for proprietorships. At year end the numbers are simply transferred to the appropriate tax forms.

To start using No-Entry Accounting, just begin saving business checks and receipts and filing them using the instructions in this part of the book. If you follow the step-by-step guide to accounting and report generation in Chapter 18, you will be up and running.

Rethinking the General Ledger

General ledger is a term taken from conventional accounting. It is the name for that portion of accounting that results in the preparation of the profit and loss statement, or income statement, and the balance sheet. It is the portion of accounting work that forms the basis for an accountant's monthly service. Computer salespeople often use maintenance of the general ledger as a justification for the purchase of a computer and accounting software. Little mention is ever made that use of a computerized general ledger system is complicated and considerably more time consuming than most manual methods. During my years of computer experience, the general ledger system was always the last application to be installed—sometimes delayed years after the initial system installation.

There is another problem with other general ledger systems. General ledger programs require their operator to have a solid grasp of double-entry accounting mechanics. I have never seen such an operator with less than an accounting degree. The monthly and year-end closing procedures have high potential for errors.

In fact, this potential for error is the basis for double-entry bookkeeping. The object of the double-entry accounting is to arrive at a balancing figure from two different directions to ensure that all data has been posted and/or entered into a computer correctly. When an out-of-balance condition develops, an error has been generated that must be tracked down before processing can proceed. Several types of errors can still pass through the system undetected and cause considerable delay before they are corrected. Some programs demand that the ledgers be "in balance" in order to create checks.

I have seen an example where the general ledger was so out of balance that days of effort could not balance the books. Use of the program had to be discontinued and the work done by hand. Pay checks had to be done on a typewriter and later reentered in the computer. Because this situation is not infrequent, a standard feature in many commercial general ledger computer packages is the provision to plug in a bogus balancing number. Once the computer thinks the system is in balance, transaction lists and a bogus statement can be printed to help find the error or errors.

Each step eliminated in the accounting process can reduce the time spent generating cash management information. If a necessary process can be made faster and easier, the business owner is more likely to do what is necessary and, therefore, is more likely to succeed. Herein lies the impetus for the development of No-Entry Accounting.

No-Entry Accounting is more than a general ledger package. It is a small business information system designed to help you get the job done in an absolute minimum amount of time. The case problems and instructions are also designed to alleviate the fear of taxes that small business owners often experience. The Joe's Cafe problem shows that accounting is simple and that taxes are mostly a copy job.

Thus, No-Entry Accounting, which is organized around the Schedule C, simplifies small business accounting to the point where you can keep track of your business yourself.

One Shortcut

Here's a tip you might find helpful if you already run a small business and use a personal computer. A simple spreadsheet program can be used with No-Entry Accounting to carry forward account balances (such as adding February's figures to January's to generate new year-to-date totals). A spreadsheet program will also help you print out a set of statements in case you or another user of your records would not be satisfied with "fill-in-the-blank," handwritten statements.

No-Entry Accounting Versus Conventional Accounting

The following is a list of documents and procedures you eliminate when you implement No-Entry Accounting as opposed to conventional accounting:

- The need to take courses to learn debits and credits (double-entry mechanics)
- The need for and use of journals, ledgers, trial balances, and check register in manual accounting

- The need for a daily/monthly transaction journal and year-to-date transaction journal in computerized accounting
- All the time-consuming "posting" of each transaction that is associated with either manual or computerized systems
- The monthly and annual closing entries worksheet and closing entries
- In a sole proprietorship, the need for a separate checking account(s)
- The need for a petty cash fund and its associated accounting
- Learning and continual use of transaction reference numbers

Figure 7.1 compares No-Entry Accounting procedures with those of conventional manual accounting. Figure 7.2 compares No-Entry Accounting procedures with those of a conventional computerized accounting package.

The Reference Number Dilemma

What transaction reference number for a computerized accounting system would be assigned to a transaction that involves a cash receipt such as one from the local gas station? What number would be assigned to an adjustment or correction for which there is no supporting document? Because the computer will not permit duplicate reference numbers, how do you keep track of numbers already assigned?

One way accountants deal with this reference number problem is to establish a petty cash fund. It can be funded and replenished by a check that has a reference number. The numerous small cash transactions that can occur monthly with no reference number are then handled outside the computer system with a submanual system. The various amounts must be summarized manually and posted en masse to the appropriate expense ledgers periodically.

Any number that goes into the computer must be checked for accuracy. This accuracy check consists of making two adding machine tapes of both the reference numbers and the amounts of transactions to be entered. Once two tapes each have been obtained with the same total—one set for reference numbers and one set for amounts—these totals are checked against a third total. The third total (called a *hash total*) is generated as a by-product of handling all the numbers once again by entering them into the computer system. If the third total does not agree with the others, the error must be found and corrected before processing can begin. Some simplified general ledger programs—those that prepare financial statements—do not provide for generating this third total as a by-product of entering the data. The use of this type of program could result in paying taxes on profit that was not earned, a giant cash management no-no.

Here is how.

Say that $500 was to be added to account number 304 but was entered as 403, instead. Or suppose that the account number is correct but the amount went in as $5,000 instead of $500. What if $109 went in as $901? Without the accuracy check, the data may end up in a location that has an effect exactly opposite of the effect intended. The amount may easily be overstated by a factor of 10, as in the $5,000 to $500 example. It is foolish to spend hours each month generating accurate data for the preparation of financial statements only to lose it all by reentering that data in a computer without checking the

Traditional Accounting System

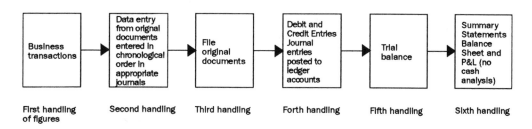

First handling of figures   Second handling   Third handling   Forth handling   Fifth handling   Sixth handling

No-Entry Accounting System

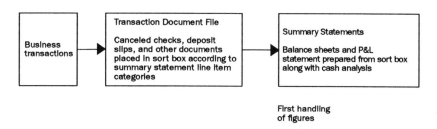

First handling of figures

An Example: Steps taken to record and transfer transaction information of cash sales for the day amounting to $562.

Traditional Accounting

1. A deposit is made at the bank for $562.
2. $562 is recorded in cash receipts journal.
3. $562 is recorded in the sales journal.
4. The cash receipts total for month (including $562) transferred to the cash account in the ledger.
5. The sale total for month (including $562) is transferred to the sales account in ledger.
6. A worksheet is completed as a first step in preparing summary statements.
7. Information is transferred to the balance sheet and profit and loss statement. This includes the $562 sales transaction as a part of the subtotals and totals.

No-Entry Accounting System

1. A deposit is made at the bank for $562.
2. The bank deposit ticket is filed in the Sales compartment of the No-Entry Accounting system sort box.
3. All deposit tickets for Sales are added. The total becomes the amount shown as Sales in the profit and loss statement for the month.
4. The $562 deposited is included in the bank statement from which the amount of cash as an asset in the balance sheet is determined.

Figure 7.1. Manual System Data Handling Compared to No-Entry Handling

Computerized Accounting System

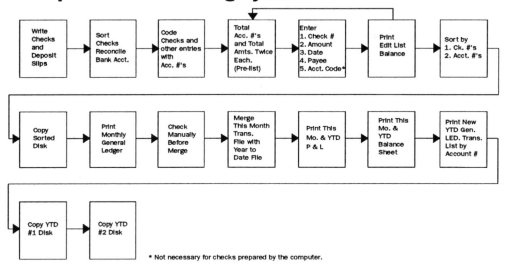

* Not necessary for checks prepared by the computer.

No-Entry System

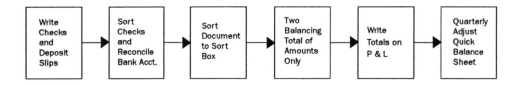

Figure 7.2. Computer Data Handling Compared to No-Entry Handling

accuracy of the transfer. Figure 7.2 deals with the extra work associated with a chart of accounts program for computerized financial statements.

It is important to note that this discussion is concerned with the more complicated computerized accounting packages, some of which even require a professional to set up. In recent years, however, a number of simpler computerized systems have been developed. These systems, in fact, resemble an electronic checkbook and can be used in conjunction with the No-Entry Accounting system to replace the manual sorting of checks and deposit slips. Small business owners may find this sort of system a useful compromise: a speedy method of restructuring information as it is needed, but simple enough to do yourself on a consistent basis.

Chapter 17 discusses conditions under which you may want to use the computer for accounts receivable, check writing for accounts payable, and inventory management.

Features Unique to No-Entry Accounting

The advantages of using No-Entry Accounting increase when you consider the information that No-Entry Accounting provides that is lacking in other systems:

- The cash analysis statement is integral to No-Entry Accounting. As you saw in Part I, such statements are the heart of what small business owners need to stay afloat financially. The system directly complements the monthly preparation and use of this extremely important statement.

- Business records are kept in perpetual audit-ready condition. No intervening or additional steps are required to put the records in shape for an audit. No other system, manual or computerized, compares with the audit-ready feature of No-Entry Accounting records. The retired IRS district director quoted earlier states that "The system when used as directed will meet the requirements of the most demanding IRS auditor."

- The sort box used in No-Entry Accounting is an important learning tool for distinguishing between transactions that affect the income statement and those that affect the balance sheet, an area of common confusion for learners. Documents ordinarily sorted to a compartment without a Schedule C line number are balance sheet transactions. Documents sorted into numbered compartments are income statement items.

- For sole proprietorships, the sort box points directly to the line number of the Schedule C on which a particular transaction will ultimately reside. This feature significantly enhances your chances of preparing your own tax return.

- The accounting and tax cycle discussion in Chapter 18 guides you in completing the accounting, filing, and tax work for each month, the quarter, and the year end.

- The balance sheet has been modified to meet the needs of the entrepreneur, rather than the needs of double-entry accounting. It is directly applicable in preparation of a loan application and as a monitor of the labor-to-equity, debt-to-equity, and earnings-to-equity transfers, the most important uses of the balance sheet.

- No-Entry Accounting provides for the actual types of documents a small business requires for its daily functions. Cash receipts, personal checks, and charge card receipts used to pay business expenses do not fall through the cracks.

- The system provides directly for "office in the home" accounting. The complete auditable record is generated as an automatic by-product of routine monthly accounting. A year-end cost computation form is included and becomes part of the tax record and audit trail.

- The system provides for handling receipts necessary for warranties and refunds. The expense is taken and the documents necessary to obtain warranty adjustments and refunds are retained. (Have you ever received a refund on a garbage can that was guaranteed for five years and only lasted four? I have, because my No-Entry Accounting system made it easy to put my hands on the receipt/warranty!)

Tracking Receipts

Many No-Entry Accounting seminar attendees admit that most paid cash receipts for their business simply fall through the cracks, even if they have an accountant.

No-Entry Accounting provides the simplest way possible to ensure that these cash transactions are not omitted and that there is no duplicity or subsystems to deal with.

Another way that accountants handle the problem of cash receipts is by insisting that there be no cash transactions. "Pay everything with a check," they say. Such rigid demands serve only the computer and the accountant. I have seen companies writing 150 to 175 checks per month when 50 or 60 would have gotten the job done nicely. The extra 100 checks create substantial extra bookwork, which translates to extra cost and opportunity for error. Only when a business grows large enough for employees to be involved in an unsupervised way with cash disbursements does such confinement become necessary.

Summary

No-Entry Accounting strives to cut the fat and complications from your recordkeeping chores. The system was designed by a small business owner for small businesses like yours. Many users have already proven that it works. The remainder of Part II describes in detail how to implement and use No-Entry Accounting easily.

Chapter 8

Basic Principles, Procedures, and Results

This chapter explains the nitty-gritty steps in learning and using the No-Entry Accounting system. You will see how typical business transaction papers that an enterprise receives or originates are sorted in order to prepare financial statements. This transaction reporting system provides a direct method of sorting transaction documents in a sort box from which profit or loss and balance sheet summaries may be prepared quickly. One important benefit of No-Entry Accounting is that it eliminates double entries and duplication of effort.

There are several additional advantages to be gained from this system that the figures in Chapter 7 did not show. One is the ease with which you can learn No-Entry Accounting compared with traditional accounting and computer accounting packages. Many entrepreneurs have learned to do their own accounting in a single day through our seminar series. This book now provides you with the opportunity to learn at your own pace in your own home or office. It may take more than a day, but there is no faster way to learn at home.

The figures also do not show how much time you can save through No-Entry Accounting. Experience has shown that a typical small business owner can finish financial statements and taxes in the same amount of or less time than it takes to prepare and forward the raw data to an accountant. The 14- to 30-day turnaround time the accountant requires is eliminated as well.

A certified public accountant found the No-Entry Accounting system to be 75 percent faster than the manual system and 15 percent faster than a computer-based system. The system was tested on clients with annual revenue ranging from $55,000 to $678,000 and a monthly checking count ranging from 15 to 130 checks. A review of Figures 1.3 and 1.4 show that well over 90 percent of all American businesses fall under the $678,000 level.

Since that accountant's test, No-Entry Accounting has been installed in businesses where the monthly check count approaches 200 and where annual revenue is into the millions.

No-Entry Accounting is based on Schedule C and the use of a sort box into which a businessperson places receipts for a specified time period.

Each sole proprietorship must prepare a yearly summary report using Schedule C as a minimum legal requirement. The schedule essentially creates a profit or loss statement that you can also use for management analysis and guidance for the business. Partnerships and corporations use forms whose line numbers are different. The Schedule C is used in this book, however, because sole proprietorships compose the largest group.

The Sort Box

The No-Entry Accounting system sort box is essential to the system. It permits you to sort tight all your business documents into the same order you would get from a computerized accounting system, but without the need for ledgers, journals, or repetitive data entry. In practice, you hang the sort box on a wall or place it on a desk so you can insert documents directly into the sort box through the course of the month.

In this way, paid cash receipts, charge card receipts, and all the other papers do not get lost by statement preparation time. You will get all the deductions you have coming.

The sort box has five functions:

- It is an excellent lab tool for learning accounting. It speeds the learning process considerably and facilitates monthly processing.
- It quickly sorts checks numerically, as described in Sorting Checks in this chapter. This sort results in preparing the permanent record in order by check number and date and account, just as though it had been entered into a computerized system.
- It helps separate balance sheet items and income statement items as documents are sorted into their appropriate category.
- It helps to remove nonpertinent (duplicate records such as the canceled check to the charge company and the charge receipts) and personal documents, such as the mortgage payment and school tuition, from your business papers.
- It helps to eliminate your fear of taxes by pointing directly to the line number on the Schedule C tax form where the data will ultimately reside. Once you understand that taxes are mostly a copy job, your fear dissipates. The pigeonholes and physical nature of sorting your paperwork make the learning process involved in accounting more concrete. You should be able to easily absorb the conceptual basis for accounting entries and easily separate balance sheet and income items using the sort box.

Understand that each numbered compartment is, therefore, found only in the profit and loss statement. The unnumbered compartments are Assets, Liabilities, Draw, Capital, and Outsort. Assets, Liabilities, and Capital are net compartments.

They receive both transaction documents (for additions and subtractions) and information documents (such as loan papers and titles). Any documents sorted into these compartments are automatically excluded from the profit and loss statement preparation. The rules or conditions by which a document would find its way into these compartments is discussed in detail in Chapter 9's explanation of the transaction index.

Sorting Checks

If your bank does not return canceled checks each period, skip this discussion and compare your carbon copies of checks against checks listed in the monthly bank statement. Remove the checks listed on the bank statement for sorting and storage in the permanent storage box.

If your bank returns canceled checks, you should sort them before you compare them with the monthly statement. As a first use of the checks, once your checks are in numerical order you can compare them more quickly against the check stubs to verify the amounts. Check, too, that the bank encoded the same amount at the bottom of the check that you wrote on the top. This process reduces the time you spend reconciling the account. To help you sort the checks into numeric order before you reconcile your bank statement and checkbook register, the No-Entry Accounting sort box includes a sorting mechanism. The sort numbers appear as large gold numbers over the sort box compartments. Follow these steps:

1. If the check numbers span more than 1000, first create stacks separated by the thousands' digits (such as 1990 through 1999 in one stack, 2000 through 2112 in the second).

2. If you have written more than 100 checks, you next sort each stack of the checks by their 100's digits. (For example, your 2000 through 2112 stack would become 2000 through 2099 and 2100 through 2112.)

3. Now sort checks by their 10's digits, using the sort box labels 0 through 9 to represent the 10's columns of the check numbers. (For example, checks 1990 through 1999 are sorted in the 9 compartment, whereas 2000-2009 are sorted in the 0 compartment.)

4. Now remove the checks from the compartments, starting with the lowest-numbered checks (that is, the 1990s before the 2000s, and so on). Sort each compartment's checks in order, 0 through 9, on the 1's column.

Now stack the numerically sorted checks into a single pile, in ascending order. They are ready to use in checking your bank's statement.

A second use of these canceled checks is for your permanent record. After you use them to reconcile the statement, re-sort the checks into their account categories in the sort box, keeping the groups of checks in numeric order within the compartment. For example, you sort check 244 with which you bought stamps into the Office Supplies/Postage compartment, then check 256 with which you paid for typewriter ribbons behind check 244.

Now your checks are in the same compartments as the paid cash receipts for transactions. Remove the receipts and checks category by category to prepare your financial statements, as described in this chapter under Monthly Statement Preparation Procedure.

Then the sorted documents are moved by category to the permanent storage box, where they are combined with previously stored checks and receipts for the same categories. In the end, your permanent record is in sequence just as if you printed a general ledger spreadsheet with computer accounting software.

Separating Personal and Business Transactions

One of the most common problems in small business record keeping is intermingling personal and business funds. Business transactions are represented by cash receipts, personal checks, business checks, charge card receipts (both business and personal) and sometimes by barter. Personal transactions that become mixed in with business transactions are easily removed from the business accounting by sorting them into either the Draw compartment or the Outsort compartment. Handwritten memos or other documents can be used to keep track of barter transactions and the signed and dated memos can be sorted directly into the permanent record.

The Draw compartment provides one of the more important ways you can look at what is happening to business cash because it reveals how much cash you are taking out of the business each month. It can be eye opening to receive 35 or 40 canceled checks with the monthly bank statement and find 30 of them sorted into the Draw compartment.

The Outsort compartment provides for duplicate transaction documents and documents that are worth keeping but are not involved directly as part of the accounting record.

The Permanent Storage Box

You use the permanent storage box for documents that have been placed in the proper category in the sort box during preparation of the monthly profit and loss statement. The permanent storage box includes a set of tab dividers with the same titles as the sort box compartments.

At the end of each month the documents in each compartment in the sort box are transferred to the permanent storage box for future reference. Some of the data will be used later to prepare quarterly, year-to-date, and annual reports.

The permanent storage box provides for the storage of *all* business documents. A loan packet filed in Liabilities, for example, will include an amortization schedule, the original and renewal loan papers, the original deposit receipt showing the proceeds going into the company account, and the canceled checks that represent principal reductions. Once a loan—a car loan, for example—is paid in full, the title will be included and the entire packet will be moved to the Assets compartment for permanent storage. The balance sheet can be quickly prepared by reviewing the documents filed behind the Assets and Liabilities tabs.

No-Entry Accounting is therefore a filing system as well as an accounting system. It leaves the complete set of business documents in a perpetual audit-ready state with virtually no duplication of effort. And it's all in one place for easy access.

Figures 8.1 and 8.2 graphically illustrate the connection between the U.S. tax system and the sort box of No-Entry Accounting. The line number titles on IRS Schedule C (discussed in Chapter 6 and shown as Figure 8.1) are duplicated as compartment names on the sort box (Figure 8.2), and vice versa. If the sort box compartment used to appropriately sort a document has a line number (the small numbers printed in some sort box compartments), any activity associated with that compartment is automatically associated with the profit and loss statement process. A check made payable for a newspaper ad, for example, would be sorted into the advertising compartment, which is identified with the Schedule C line number 8. The profit and loss process involves documents that involve income and expenses.

If a document is sorted into a box compartment that has no small number (a receipt for depositing loan proceeds into the company account is sorted into Liabilities, for example), then that document is automatically associated with the balance sheet process. The Liabilities compartment has no small number. The balance sheet process involves documents that define what is owed and what is owned.

Figure 8.3 is Part III of Schedule C. Your business may use it to compute cost of sales by the mandatory accrual method. The considerations involved with using this portion of the Schedule C are discussed in Chapter 6 under Lines E and F and Part III.

Key Uses of the No-Entry Accounting System

Income Tax Preparation

In practice, the dollar values used for preparing Schedule C can be obtained from business transaction documents placed in the No-Entry Accounting sort box, Figure 8.2. A sort box look-alike answer sheet has been included in Chapter 10 so you can learn the No-Entry Accounting process without the sort box for purposes of completing that chapter's case study. The actual preparation of monthly statements and providing for an audit trail, however, are considerably simplified and take much less time if the sort box and the rest of the No-Entry Accounting system is used. Most small businesses will be able to complete their monthly statements (cash forecast, profit and loss statement, and balance sheet) in less than one hour per month. (For your convenience, an order form for No-Entry Accounting materials is included in the back of the book.)

The sorting procedure is orderly and direct. No additional entries are made to journal or ledger accounts, reducing the chance for errors and minimizing recordkeeping time. Should an audit be required, the original business transaction documents stored in the permanent storage box provide certification. Incidentally, none of the journals or ledgers or posting in conventional accounting is sufficient as audit proof. These items only provide the *means* to track and locate the proof. Only paid cash receipts and canceled checks will suffice. For several audits by the state tax collector and by insurance companies, my preparation took only minutes, because the required data was already in audit-ready condition after each month's accounting work. More common from the IRS are queries regarding a tax deposit. These can be handled in minutes, because the documents supporting each deposit are filed as a complete packet as the documents pass through the system.

SCHEDULE C
(Form 1040)

Department of the Treasury
Internal Revenue Service (0)

Profit or Loss From Business
(Sole Proprietorship)
Partnerships, Joint Ventures, Etc., Must File Form 1065.
▶ **Attach to Form 1040 or Form 1041.**   ▶ **See Instructions for Schedule C (Form 1040).**

OMB No. 1545-0074

1990

Attachment
Sequence No. **09**

Name of proprietor

Social security number (SSN)

A Principal business or profession, including product or service (see Instructions)

B Enter principal business code
(from page 2) ▶

C Business name and address ▶
(include suite or room no.)

D Employer ID number (Not SSN)

E Accounting method: **(1)** ☐ Cash   **(2)** ☐ Accrual   **(3)** ☐ Other (specify) ▶

F Method(s) used to
value closing inventory: **(1)** ☐ Cost   **(2)** ☐ Lower of cost or market   **(3)** ☐ Other (attach explanation)   **(4)** ☐ Does not apply (if checked, go to line H)

	Yes	No

G Was there any change in determining quantities, costs, or valuations between opening and closing inventory? (If "Yes," attach explanation.)

H Are you deducting expenses for business use of your home? (If "Yes," see Instructions for limitations.) . . . .

I Did you "materially participate" in the operation of this business during 1990? (If "No," see Instructions for limitations on losses.) . . . .

J If this is the first Schedule C filed for this business, check here . . . . ▶ ☐

Part I   Income

1	Gross receipts or sales. *Caution: If this income was reported to you on Form W-2 and the "Statutory employee" box on that form was checked, see the Instructions and check here* . . . . ▶ ☐	**1**	Ⓐ
2	Returns and allowances	**2**	
3	Subtract line 2 from line 1. Enter the result here	**3**	
4	Cost of goods sold (from line 38 on page 2)	**4**	Ⓑ
5	Subtract line 4 from line 3 and enter the **gross profit** here	**5**	
6	Other income, including Federal and state gasoline or fuel tax credit or refund (see Instructions)	**6**	
7	Add lines 5 and 6. This is your **gross income** . . . . ▶	**7**	

Part II   Expenses

8	Advertising . . .	**8**		**21**	Repairs and maintenance . . .	**21**
9	Bad debts from sales or services (see Instructions)	**9**	Ⓒ	**22**	Supplies (not included in Part III) .	**22**
				23	Taxes and licenses	**23**
10	Car and truck expenses (attach **Form 4562**) .	**10**		**24**	Travel, meals, and entertainment:	
11	Commissions and fees . . .	**11**		**a**	Travel	**24a**
12	Depletion	**12**		**b**	Meals and entertainment .	
13	Depreciation and section 179 expense deduction (not included in Part III) (see Instructions). . .	**13**		**c**	Enter 20% of line 24b subject to limitations (see Instructions) .	
14	Employee benefit programs (other than on line 19)	**14**		**d**	Subtract line 24c from line 24b .	**24d**
15	Insurance (other than health) .	**15**		**25**	Utilities	**25**
16	Interest:			**26**	Wages (less jobs credit) . . .	**26**
a	Mortgage (paid to banks, etc.).	**16a**		**27a**	Other expenses (**list type and amount**):	
b	Other	**16b**				
17	Legal and professional services .	**17**				Ⓔ
18	Office expense.	**18**				
19	Pension and profit sharing plans .	**19**	Ⓓ			
20	Rent or lease (see Instructions):					
a	Vehicles, machinery, and equip. .	**20a**				
b	Other business property. . .	**20b**		**27b**	Total other expenses . . .	**27b**

28 Add amounts in columns for lines 8 through 27b. These are your **total expenses** . . . . ▶ | **28**

29 **Net profit or (loss).** Subtract line 28 from line 7. If a profit, enter here and on Form 1040, line 12. Also enter the net profit on Schedule SE, line 2 (statutory employees, see Instructions). If a loss, you MUST go on to line 30 (fiduciaries, see Instructions) . . . . | **29**

30 If you have a loss, you MUST check the box that describes your investment in this activity (see Instructions). . .
If you checked 30a, enter the loss on Form 1040, line 12, and Schedule SE, line 2 (statutory employees, see Instructions). If you checked 30b, you MUST attach **Form 6198.**

30a ☐ All investment is at risk.
30b ☐ Some investment is not at risk.

For Paperwork Reduction Act Notice, see Form 1040 Instructions.

Schedule C (Form 1040) 1990

Figure 8.1. IRS Schedule C

Assets	Sales Line 1 **A**	(Returns & Allowances) Line 2	Cost of Sales Line 4 **B**
Liabilities	Draw 0	Capital 1	Outsort 2
Ads & Promotion Line 8	Car & Truck Line 10 **C** 3	Commissions Line 11 4	Wages Line 26 5
Insurance Line 15	Business Interest Line 16 6	Legal Professional Line 17 7	Office and Postage Line 18 8
Rent Line 20 **D**	Repairs Line 21 9	Supplies Not Inventoried Line 22	Taxes Line 23
Travel Entertainment Line 24	Utilities Telephone Line 25	Bank Charges Line 27a	Donations Line 27a
Laundry Cleaning Line 27a	Misc. Line 27a **E**		
	Medical	Office in the Home	Warrenties/ Receipts

Figure 8.2. No-Entry Accounting Sort Box

Schedule C (Form 1040) 1990

Part III Cost of Goods Sold (See Instructions.)

31 Inventory at beginning of year. (If different from last year's closing inventory, attach explanation.)	31	
32 Purchases less cost of items withdrawn for personal use	32	
33 Cost of labor. (Do not include salary paid to yourself.)	33	
34 Materials and supplies	34	
35 Other costs	35	
36 Add lines 31 through 35	36	
37 Inventory at end of year	37	
38 **Cost of goods sold.** Subtract line 37 from line 36. Enter the result here and on page 1, line 4	38	

Part IV Principal Business or Professional Activity Codes

Locate the major category that best describes your activity. Within the major category, select the activity code that most closely identifies the business or profession that is the principal source of your sales or receipts. **Enter this 4-digit code on page 1, line B.** *For example, a grocery store is under the major category of "Retail Trade," and the code is "3210."* (**Note:** *If your principal source of income is from farming activities, you should file* **Schedule F** (Form 1040), Farm Income and Expenses.)

Construction	2675 Agent or broker for other firms— more than 50% of gross sales on commission	**Finance, Insurance, Real Estate, and Related Services**	7856 Mailing, reproduction, commercial art and photography, and stenographic services
Code		5520 Real estate agents or brokers	7872 Computer programming, processing, data preparation, and related services
0018 Operative builders (for own account)	**Retail Trade—Selling Goods to Individuals and Households**	5579 Real estate property managers	
General contractors		5710 Subdividers and developers, except cemeteries	7922 Computer repair, maintenance, and leasing
0034 Residential building	3012 Selling door-to-door, by telephone or party plan, or from mobile unit	5538 Operators and lessors of buildings, including residential	7773 Equipment rental and leasing (except computer or automotive)
0059 Nonresidential building	3038 Catalog or mail order	5553 Operators and lessors of other real property	7914 Investigative and protective services
0075 Highway and street construction	3053 Vending machine selling		
3889 Other heavy construction (pipe laying, bridge construction, etc.)	**Selling From Showroom, Store, or Other Fixed Location**	5702 Insurance agents or brokers	7880 Other business services
		5744 Other insurance services	
Building trade contractors, including repairs		6064 Security brokers and dealers	**Personal services**
0232 Plumbing, heating, air conditioning	**Food, beverages, and drugs**	6080 Commodity contracts brokers and dealers, and security and commodity exchanges	8110 Beauty shops (or beauticians)
0257 Painting and paper hanging	3079 Eating places (meals or snacks)		8318 Barber shop (or barber)
0273 Electrical work	3086 Catering services	6130 Investment advisors and services	8334 Photographic portrait studios
0299 Masonry, dry wall, stone, tile	3095 Drinking places (alcoholic beverages)	6148 Credit institutions and mortgage bankers	8532 Funeral services and crematories
0414 Carpentering and flooring	3210 Grocery stores (general line)		8714 Child day care
0430 Roofing, siding, and sheet metal	0612 Bakeries selling at retail	6155 Title abstract offices	8730 Teaching or tutoring
0455 Concrete work	3236 Other food stores (meat, produce, candy, etc.)	5777 Other finance and real estate	8755 Counseling (except health practitioners)
0885 Other building trade contractors (excavation, glazing, etc.)			

Figure 8.3. Part III of Schedule C

In one case a deposit was made at a local bank for the quarterly payroll taxes. The bank did not pass the deposit along. The mistake was documented in a moment because the canceled check, the bank's deposit receipt, and the appropriate tax form were all filed together in the appropriate permanent storage box compartment.

In another case the IRS tried to penalize me for $1,200 because I had not made four even quarterly deposits of estimated taxes. I knew that there would be a penalty because I didn't have the cash at the time the deposits were due. What I did have, though, were monthly profit and loss statements showing that I had not earned the money evenly; most of it came in the third and fourth quarters. I was able to use my records to quickly prepare Form 2210 showing that the fine and penalties were grossly overstated because the taxes were not due until late in the year. You can imagine the relief I felt when the fines and penalties turned out to be only $570. I know for sure that had I not done the monthly accounting so that the job was easy (it required knowing my profit at the end of the third, fifth, eighth, and twelfth months) or if I had had to go to an accountant to see whether the IRS figure was correct, I would not have gone to the trouble. Essentially, I earned $630 in the hour it took me to complete the form. Assuming a 5 percent net profit and using the Real Ratio computation in Chapter 4, that one hour of tax work put the same $630 in my pocket as would $12,600 in additional sales. Wow! And the accountant's fee would have been an additional expense!

Reports to Associates

Good communication within a business enterprise is required for long-term success. Producing accurate and timely financial reports that are likely to be read and understood by owners and managers is one of the objectives of the No-Entry Accounting system. Should there be questions about the components of any of the totals or subtotals in the profit and loss or the balance sheet report, the sources of these data are immediately available in an organized form in the permanent storage box.

Bank Loan Requirements

Although individual banks vary in their financial report requirements for a loan application, your bank most likely will not require more financial information than the system provides. A current profit and loss statement in the form of Schedule C (Figure 8.1) or the year-to-date income statement (Figure 8.4) would be included for several years, if available. A listing of assets and liabilities—both business and personal—using the No-Entry Accounting balance sheet, Figure 8.5, should be included. And finally, the completion of the cash analysis form (Figure 13.1, to be discussed in full in Chapter 13) reflects how cash was used through the last year.

A second copy that forecasts cash requirements and indicates how loan proceeds would be used in the next year would also be included in loan application paperwork. The No-Entry Accounting system is a proven means of providing the financial information required for bank loans.

Operational Analysis

A final key use of this accounting system is to help the owner or manager determine how his or her company is operating and why it is operating that way. For example, managers may want to compare the dollar and percentage expense figures across time, or they may want to compare their company's figures with industry-wide figures. Having values available from the basic summary reports provides the base for answering the elusive but necessary questions:

- Where has all the money gone?
- How and why has our business reached its current position?
- What is the basis for making decisions about the future?

This accounting system provides the information for operational analysis in direct, organized, and available form with no duplication of effort.

Transactions Involved in No-Entry Accounting Procedures

Some banks no longer return canceled checks. Rather, the banks often issue carbon-set checks so the carbon copy of each check remains in the checkbook. The statements these banks provide include the appropriate check number and amount for checks that have cleared the bank. If your bank does not return canceled checks, remove your carbon copies of the checks from your checkbook for checks listed in the bank statement. Use those for sorting instead. If you use the cash basis for accounting on Schedule C the checks are sorted once they appear on the bank statement. For accrual accounting, the process is more complex. See Chapter 12 for specific details involving cutoff dates and accrual versus cash accounting as you convert to the No-Entry Accounting system.

Sales

A bank deposit slip, for many businesses, identifies the sales income for a day. You can use deposit slips as the business documents for the Sales compartment in the sort box. Some businesses find that the sales record made at the time or point of sale—

Income Statement

Date _____

	This Month	%	Year To Date	%
Sales				
Category A	_____	___	_____	___
Category B	_____	___	_____	___
Returns	(_____)	___	(_____)	___
Total Sales	_____	___	_____	___
Cost of Sales				
Category A	_____	___	_____	___
Category B	_____	___	_____	___
Total Cost of Sales	(_____)	___	(_____)	___
Gross Profit	_____	___	_____	___
Operating Expenses				
Advertising	_____	___	_____	___
Car and Truck	_____	___	_____	___
Commissions	_____	___	_____	___
Depreciation & Section 179	_____	___	_____	___
Wages	_____	___	_____	___
Insurance	_____	___	_____	___
Interest on Business Debt	_____	___	_____	___
Legal, Professional	_____	___	_____	___
Office Supplies, Postage	_____	___	_____	___
Rent & Leases	_____	___	_____	___
Repairs & Maintenance	_____	___	_____	___
Supplies Not For Resale	_____	___	_____	___
Taxes & Licenses	_____	___	_____	___
Travel, Meals, Entertainment	_____	___	_____	___
Utilities, Telephone	_____	___	_____	___
Bank Charges	_____	___	_____	___
Donations	_____	___	_____	___
Office Expense	_____	___	_____	___
Laundry, Cleaning	_____	___	_____	___
_____	_____	___	_____	___
_____	_____	___	_____	___
_____	_____	___	_____	___
Miscellaneous	_____	___	_____	___
Total Operating Expenses	(_____)	___	(_____)	___
Net Profit or (Loss)	_____	___	_____	___

Figure 8.4. Income Statement for No-Entry Accounting

Date:_____

Balance Sheet

Assets	Liabilities

Assets

Cash on Hand and in Banks

_____ _____

_____ _____

_____ _____

U.S. Government & Marketable Securities

_____ _____

_____ _____

Nonmarketable Securities

_____ _____

_____ _____

Securities Held by Broker in Margin Accounts

_____ _____

_____ _____

Restricted or Control Stocks

_____ _____

Partial Interest Real Estate Equities

_____ _____

_____ _____

Real Estate Owned

_____ _____

_____ _____

_____ _____

Loans Receivable

_____ _____

_____ _____

_____ _____

Automobile and Other Personal Property

_____ _____

_____ _____

_____ _____

Cash Value—Life Ins.

_____ _____

Business, Other Assets

_____ _____

_____ _____

_____ _____

Total Assets (A)   _____

Liabilities

Notes Payable to Banks (Secured)

_____ _____

_____ _____

_____ _____

Notes Payable to Banks (Unsecured)

_____ _____

_____ _____

Due to Brokers

_____ _____

_____ _____

Amounts Payable Others (Secured)

_____ _____

_____ _____

_____ _____

Amounts Payable Others (Unsecured)

_____ _____

_____ _____

_____ _____

Accounts and Bills Due

_____ _____

_____ _____

_____ _____

Unpaid Income Tax

_____ _____

_____ _____

_____ _____

Other Unpaid Taxes and Interest

_____ _____

Real Estate Mortgages Payable

_____ _____

_____ _____

Other Debts—Itemized

_____ _____

_____ _____

_____ _____

Total Liabilities (B)   _____

Net Worth (A) – (B)   _____

Total Liabilities and Net Worth _____

Figure 8.5. No-Entry Accounting Balance Sheet

117

the sales invoice, sales ticket, or cash register tape—will serve best as the business document that reflects the business transaction. In any event, there is no need to transfer the sales amount to a journal or ledger account.

If your business requires a sales journal listing the various checks deposited, the back of the deposit slip provides ample space to record these multiple receipts. It serves quite well as a permanent detailed record if you include each customer's name, check number, and amount.

Purchases
Purchases are usually paid for by check, so your canceled checks may be used as the business documents that record your purchases. The purposes of various purchases are reflected in summary statement categories. In each case the checks are distributed to an appropriate category in the sort box, as explained later in the chapter.

Wages and Salaries
Wages and salaries are paid by check, so again your checks serve as the business documents representing payroll transactions. These business costs and expenses may fall under different sections in the financial summary statements, so the checks will be placed in appropriate compartments in the sort box as explained later in the chapter.

Expenses
Expenses such as rent, utilities, and interest are paid by check, so again the check becomes the business document that may be used to identify the transaction. Checks representing the same expense category are assembled in the sort box category and totaled for the appropriate line item value as you prepare summary statements.

Adjustments
Adjustments are infrequently made outside the regular flow of business transactions. If you need such adjustments and they do not involve making a deposit or writing a check, a transaction memorandum (supplied as part of the No-Entry Accounting materials) explaining the adjustment serves as the business document.

Procedures for Statement Preparation with No-Entry Accounting

Documents You Need
Canceled Checks
Your checks returned each month by the bank (or carbon sets, if no checks are returned) are the primary documents used to support business transactions. It will be helpful to make descriptive notations on each check when you write it to ensure that it finds its way to the correct sort box compartment.

Deposit Slips
Bank deposit slips are important in recording business transactions. Deposit slips may record one of several different transactions involving the income statement and the balance sheet. For example, you insert sales deposits in the Sales compartment, the deposit ticket for loan proceeds in Liabilities, the return of an overpayment (an insurance overpayment, for example) in the Insurance compartment and add instead of subtract it, and so on.

Paid Cash Receipts

Receipts for items you purchase with cash play a major role in recording transactions in some business types. Receipts are often overlooked in computerized accounting systems because they have no usable reference number, which is required to track an item through a computerized system. Accountants, therefore, discourage use of cash receipts for reasons other than audit viability.

The No-Entry Accounting method provides a direct, simple way to handle these documents: sorting them directly into the sort box throughout the month, where they remain until you prepare the next statement. Once the expenses that the documents represent are added to the checks, they should be filed with the canceled checks as part of the permanent record detail.

Charge Card Receipts

Slips you receive when you use credit cards are often the documents that prove business transactions. Take care to distinguish business from personal charges. Only the charge ticket copies are sorted into the sort box. The canceled check for payment to the charge card company is out sorted because it does not provide sufficient detail and would result in a double deduction.

Notes or Loan Papers

Paperwork from a lender provides verification of funds you have borrowed and also shows the interest you pay so you can charge it as an expense. These papers are filed in an individual loan packet with all other documents pertaining to that specific loan.

Bills of Sale

Bills of sale show the purchase price of the various assets of a business that have been paid for. These documents provide proof of expenditures, particularly when cash only is used. These are sorted into assets as they represent paid-in-full purchases.

Transaction Memos

Transaction memos provide for any necessary adjustments such as returned sales or separating multiple items paid for with a single check (such as interest and principal). In general, a transaction memo is used in the absence of any other document that would sufficiently support a business transaction. Take care to provide sufficient information on the memo to support the transaction.

Government Reporting Forms

Government forms such as payroll and sales tax deposit receipts or Form 941 (both state and federal) are to be stapled to the canceled check that pays the amount due. In this way the audit trail is complete. Should there ever be an audit, the form you filed and the canceled check that paid the required amount are immediately at hand. The Transaction Index provides more detail on the use of these forms.

After You Write Checks

Writing a check is a very common way to complete a business transaction. The canceled check is then used as the business document to represent a specific transaction. You place it, with other similar checks, under the appropriate category in the sort box. The total of this category is then recorded in the profit and loss statement or the balance sheet. Deciding when to sort a particular document (as the check is written or when it returns as a canceled check) is discussed in Chapter 12. The following section demonstrates how canceled checks are sorted in the sort box so you can prepare a profit and loss statement and a balance sheet that reflect the changes brought about by the writing of these checks.

Schedule C: Profit and Loss Statement

Checks written to pay for the following deductions are placed in the corresponding compartments in the sort box as identified and numbered using the line numbers listed in Table 8.1.

Table 8.1. Schedule C Line Numbers and Their Categories

Schedule C Line No.	Category
8	Advertising
9	Bad debts from sales or services
10	Car and truck expenses
11	Commissions
15	Insurance
16	Interest on business indebtedness
17	Legal and professional services
18	Office expense (See Figure 8.6)
20	Rent or lease
21	Repairs
22	Supplies not for resale
23	Taxes
24	Travel and entertainment
25	Utilities and telephone
26	Wages
27	a. Bank service charges (checks are not written for this charge; in place of a check, a memorandum may be used).
	b. Other expenses

Depletion (12), Employee benefit programs (14), and Pension (19) are not used often enough to warrant a separate category in the sort box. Use a blank compartment if you need one of these items.

Depreciation (13) is discussed in Procedures Initiated by Adjustments and Nonroutine Transactions.

Part III: Cost of Goods Sold and/or Operations

Line 32, Purchases of items for resale; 33, Cost of labor; 34, Materials and supplies added to items for resale; and 35, Other costs, are included. Lines 33 and 34 deal with adding labor and/or materials before a product is resold. Typically, most retail, wholesale, and service companies do not perform these functions, so they skip these lines.

Balance Sheet

The Assets compartment should contain only documents representing "paid in full" transactions. Documents for loans used to purchase assets should be handled

To meet the requirements of an office in the home, the office must be:

1. Exclusively used as your business office. It can be a whole room or part of a room, but it must be used exclusively for business.

2. Furnished with a business telephone, desk, chair, filing space, etc.

3. Used as such regularly. Note: The use of the home for other business purposes applies as well. The same form may be used with a note explaining the business use.

Calculation of Office in The Home Expense

Residence mortgage interest expense _____

Residence property taxes _____

Business telephone (if not already
deducted on P & L) _____

Residence gas usage or other heating fuel _____

Residence electricity usage _____

Garbage collection, water & sewage charges _____

Residence repairs (only those which affect the
residence as a whole, such as roofing or exterior
painting job, plumbing, etc.) _____

Casualty losses such as storm damage _____

Residence insurance _____

Total cost of residence operations _____

Repairs or other expenses solely for business use* _____

Use this method to calculate your office expense.

> Calculate the percent of square footage your office occupies, as compared to the whole residence. Multiply this percentage times the total cost of residence operations to arrive at your office expense.

You may choose the method which generates the greatest benefit. The portion of interest and taxes not taken here may be taken on the 1040 form Schedule A, so that the entire interest and tax deduction may be taken.

* These repairs may be expensed in their entirety and should be excluded from the above calculation. Add in total to the calculated office expense (line 18, schedule C).

Figure 8.6. Office in the Home Expense Computation Sheet

through Liabilities and compartment 16, Interest on Business Debt, until the loans are paid in full. The Assets tab and associated documents should be moved annually to the current year's permanent storage box. Any item that appears on the depreciation schedule and is fully paid should have supporting documents stored here. The balance of Asset items not yet fully paid will be found in a loan packet under Liabilities.

The value of an asset such as inventory should be entered directly to the balance sheet as Inventory from the worksheets periodically used to compute this value. No inventory documents should be sorted in the Assets compartment. Passbooks and checkbooks for company savings and money market accounts would also be stored here.

Procedures Initiated After Bank Deposits Have Been Made

Bank deposit tickets typically represent money that can be used by the business. In most cases, the bank deposit has been generated through sales, but it may also represent proceeds from a loan or from startup cash.

This discussion explains how to handle deposit tickets for the sort box and how the transaction is treated in the profit and loss statement and the balance sheet.

Schedule C: Profit and Loss Statement

In Part I, Income, bank deposit tickets represent income from various sources. Deposit tickets representing income from sales are placed in the 1 Sales compartment of the sort box. If an item is returned or if an adjustment is made on a previous sale, a transaction memo is written describing this transaction. This memo is then placed in the 2 Returns & Allowances compartment.

Balance Sheet

In the Assets compartment, store only complete sets of documents supporting paid-in-full, depreciable items. The initial cash deposit for a corporation goes into the Capital compartment. Deposit tickets from loan proceeds should remain in a loan papers packet stored in the Liabilities compartment until the loan is fully paid.

An envelope packet should be established for each loan. It should include any finance papers or note, a deposit slip showing borrowed funds going into the company account, an interest amortization schedule, a bill of sale, and other legal papers. Any document that can support the business use of borrowed money or purchase contracts should be kept in the appropriate packet. Insert the forms into an envelope and title it with the loan number or bank name. As canceled checks for principal reduction come in, store them as well in the appropriate envelope. If a check was in payment of principal and interest, note on the front of the check what portion was for interest and what portion was for principal. Use the front of the envelope to record principal reductions and a running balance. If personal funds are used to pay business debts, make a personal loans packet to keep these items separate.

Some new No-Entry Accounting users have been shocked to find out how much money they put into the business without knowing it. Interest may be charged on these personal loans, but it must then be reported as interest income on the Schedule B, Interest and Dividend Income, with the year-end tax filing. If the interest exceeds $600 the business must provide the lender with a Form 1099 at year end. The 1099 reports income to the government from which taxes were not withheld.

Procedures Initiated by Adjustments and Nonroutine Transactions

Assets are depreciated by an amount that is commonly determined by IRS rules. Because no checks are written for depreciation, the amount that can be applied each month is entered in the monthly profit and loss statement directly. At year end the total amount is moved to Line 13, Depreciation, on the Schedule C. Chapter 6 covers this topic in detail. Form 4562 is used to report depreciation. More detailed information is available in IRS Publication 334, *Tax Guide for Small Businesses*. Form 4562 is included in the tax and accounting cycle flow chart, in Chapter 18.

Expenses may be paid by cash rather than by check. Cash receipts are sorted into the appropriate expense compartment in the same manner that checks would be sorted.

Monthly Statement Preparation Procedure

The profit and loss statement or income statement is a list of all income from which all expenses are subtracted. The monthly preparation of the profit and loss statement begins once the checks have been received from the bank, have been numerically sorted, and the bank account has been reconciled. (See Chapter 12 for details about cutoff dates.) Prepare a memorandum for any transaction whose only documentation is on the bank statement. Such transactions might include bank service charges, the purchase of checks, or any bank drafts that might be processed for which no document is received.

When you begin the sort box should be empty, except for any paid cash receipts that may have been sorted into the box during the month for safekeeping. *All* other business documents that have been generated during the month should be sorted into the sort box at this time, regardless of whether they are balance sheet items, profit and loss items, or neither. Be careful to separate personal items from business items by using the Draw and Outsort compartments. Sort each document into the sort box compartment that most closely deals with the nature of the transaction.

Here are several examples:

- A check in payment of an advertising bill would be sorted into compartment 8, Advertising.
- A deposit slip representing the proceeds of a loan would be sorted into the Liabilities compartment, along with the loan papers and an interest amortization schedule. A loan packet envelope would be set up to store the document set in the permanent storage box.
- A personal check paying a company phone bill would be sorted into the Liabilities compartment, because it represents a loan to the business. A memo for the amount of the check must then be sorted into compartment 25, Utilities, Telephone. The memo should include the check number and an indication that

a loan was made. If the loan is repaid, the canceled check will be removed from Liabilities and sorted into Utilities, Telephone. Be sure to remove the memo then, to avoid a double count.

* A company check used to make a home mortgage payment would be sorted into the Draw compartment, because it represents taking money out of the business. Corporations cannot use draw!

The transaction index, described in Chapter 9, explains how to handle a wide variety of routine transactions in detail.

Once the sorting process is complete, the profit and loss statement can be prepared. The first time you prepare a statement, you may want to use Schedule C. It provides helpful math instructions and are identified with the same line numbers found on the sort box.

Remember, only compartments with the small number in their title are involved with the profit and loss statement. The number identifies the compartment's line number on Schedule C. Once you understand the math and the process, it is better to use a copy of the blank profit and loss statement (Figure 8.4) that permits current month and year-to-date computations. In practice, the December year-to-date figures will be transferred to Schedule C for tax reporting. Some adjustments to these year-end figures may be required, as discussed in Chapter 12. The Joe's Cafe case problem provides examples and explanations of these possible adjustments.

Income Statement Preparation
Follow these steps to prepare your income statement:

1. Begin by getting a copy of the income statement (Figure 8.4), then removing the documents from the sort box, one numbered compartment at a time.

2. Write the total value of a compartment's documents on the appropriate line of Schedule C or monthly profit and loss statement.

3. Reinsert the documents into their compartment and proceed to the next numbered compartment containing documents.

4. Repeat this process until all the document totals have been recorded on the income statement.

Note: The Cost of Sales compartment and the Wages compartment are out of numeric sequence. The vast majority of transactions in a typical business involve these two items. Therefore, placing them together in the center conserves your time and motion.

P&L Statement Preparation
The monthly profit or loss can now be computed:

1. Be sure to make *two* adding machine tapes of each compartment total before you transfer the total to the income statement. The two tapes should, of course, agree.

2. Combine the current month's figures with the year-to-date figures to arrive at a new year-to-date total. Again, be sure to make two adding machine tapes of this new total to ensure its accuracy.

3. You can prepare this report on Schedule C, but that form has no month or year-to-date columns. In practice, the Schedule C is only used for reporting the year-end totals.

4. Move all documents to the appropriate permanent storage space.

Balance Sheet Preparation

The balance sheet (Figure 8.5) is a list of everything you own and everything you owe. A No-Entry Accounting balance sheet differs significantly from a conventional balance sheet in that it combines business and personal items and it is not involved with double entry mechanics. It is simply a list into which known values are plugged! Directions for completing the balance sheet are within its text.

The purpose of the balance sheet is to compute your net worth or equity. Net worth or equity is computed by subtracting the list of what you owe from the list of what you own. These two values are in a constant state of flux but not to the same degree as the items in the income statement. Most small businesses, therefore, find little value in recomputing their net worth on a monthly basis. An annual recalculation is a must and a quarterly recalculation is recommended.

The primary use for the balance sheet is as a written statement of financial condition required by lending institutions. Most lenders require a biannual update. The primary use to the small business owner is as a yardstick of economic progress. A transformation takes place in small businesses that to most entrepreneurs is invisible, almost mystical. (There is profit but no cash.) This invisible transformation is the transfer of cash to equity. The cash equity transfer may take place in your personal affairs, business affairs, or both. The result of the equity transfers, debt, labor, and earnings will fall out on the balance sheet as increased net worth. The only way to get a look at what has transpired is to periodically review your net worth or equity.

In general, net worth should show a steady increase year after year. The increase may result from less debt, more inventory, more accounts receivable, a more valuable home, and so on.

A corporation or a partnership must file a corporate balance sheet annually with its tax return. This balance sheet is incorporated into the same form as the profit and loss statement for the corporation or partnership, and it must reflect only business items.

Business items such as inventory value, equipment and fixtures, salable contracts, and accounts receivable can be entered under "other" on the balance sheet. If you need more space, rename some of the unused items listed on the balance sheet.

Cash Analysis Preparation

The cash analysis is probably the most important accounting function you can perform for your business in order to ensure its permanence. The high failure rate of new businesses is well documented. A study of these failures indicates that poor cash management is at the root of the vast majority of cases. One report calls the problem undercapitalization; another blames too low a sales figure; another blames the irresistible temptation of new owners to begin with large cash outlays for new equipment and remodeled buildings. The irony of the problem is that good cash management information is relatively easy to obtain.

The cash analysis form (Figure 13.1) lists all the sources and uses of cash a small business is likely to encounter. The review of cash used and the forecast of cash required can both be accomplished by filling in the blanks on the form. One of the major input items is a cash profit or loss, so the ideal time to prepare an analysis or forecast is the moment you complete the income statement.

You may want a look at your company's cash position monthly with a cash forecast period of 30, 60, or 90 days. A review of all sources of cash and uses of cash year-to-date can be the answer to one of the business world's most troubling questions, "Where did all the money go?" With the answer in hand, you are in a position to guide a business around the Cycle of Demise rather than follow the business into the Cycle of Demise. Chapters 13 and 14 deal with each source of cash and each use of cash in detail.

Summary

At this point in the No-Entry cycle, the profit and loss statement, balance sheet, and cash analysis are in hand, and you've balanced your checking account to boot. All these financial records were prepared by handling your business's figures just twice—once to create the original document as transactions occurred and once to enter them as totals on the statements. Accounting can't get any easier or faster.

Chapter 9

The No-Entry Alphabetical Transaction Index

To conveniently check whether you're using the proper procedure for sorting transaction documents into the sort box, refer to this chapter's transaction index. Some of these transactions have been explained previously, but this transaction index is organized by alphabetic headings. Reading through each of these transactions will prepare you for the Joe's Cafe case problem in Chapter 10 as well as for the use of No-Entry Accounting in your own business.

Whether or not you ever intend to implement No-Entry Accounting, read this chapter in order to learn the important concepts embodied in the Joe's Cafe case study. In practice, small businesses may handle several of these transactions infrequently. This index is intended to be a simple and fast way to review an infrequently used transaction as time passes.

Adjustments: Any necessary adjustment can be accomplished by preparing a transaction memorandum and inserting the memo into the appropriate sort box compartment. Be sure to include sufficient information on the memorandum to support an audit, such as a date, check reference number, and an explanation of the adjustment.

Assets: Documents sorted into this category have to do with increasing the amount you own. Documents sorted here reflect paid-in-full, depreciable assets. (In general, items such as your car or building are depreciable. An asset such as an extended contract or inventory is not.) Documents dealing with company savings or money market accounts would also be sorted here. Staple bills of sale and other receipts to the checks associated with the purchase. Documents for assets purchased through any financing method are not placed here until the financing is fully paid. Once paid, the entire supporting packet from Liabilities is moved here. A complete asset picture is arrived at by filling in the balance sheet (Figure 8.5) with the appropriate values. The documents stored behind the Assets tab are moved each year to the current year permanent storage box.

Bank Service Charge: This charge is levied by banks as a charge for using a checking account. It is one of the few business transactions that does not generate a document that can readily be sorted in the sort box. The charge is usually included in the bank statement. Therefore, you should prepare a transaction memo noting the date and amount of the charge from the bank statement, together with the notation, "bank service charge." This document should be sorted into the Miscellaneous or other Line 27 category. This compartment is also used in businesses that are involved with credit cards. The charges associated with the use of a credit card service and bank service charges for the card are also sorted here. Overdraft notices and new checks charged to a business account would also be sorted here.

Cash Receipts for Business Expenses: Sort cash receipts into the appropriate category, as with canceled checks. If the business purpose is not readily apparent from the receipt itself, write a description on it.

Cost of Sales: Checks written in payment of items for resale are sorted to the Cost of Sales compartment of the sort box. By sorting cost of sales documents here as you complete the payment or in accordance with the cutoff date considerations discussed in Chapter 12, you work with the cash basis accounting method. Recall that the cash basis counts a business transaction only when the cash involved actually changes hands. (See Schedule C, Part III and cash accrual line E 1 and 2.) The line-by-line instructions on the Schedule C for computing Cost of Sales result in the accrual method.

Understanding the difference between cost of sales under each accounting method is important to any business owner. The process of sorting cost of sales documents directly into the Cost of Sales compartment and subtracting them directly from sales does not necessarily mean they have been delivered to the customer. The resulting profit figure, however, will directly yield the cash management figure that is so important to the business owner. Conceivably, the difference between "paid-for items" and "actually delivered items" could cause a year-end profit figure that is different for tax purposes than it is for cash management purposes. By year end, most small businesses experience little difference in the results computed from both methods. Each business, however, should periodically make the accrual calculation to be sure that there will be no year-end surprises. The front of the No-Entry Accounting income statement (Figure 8.4) uses the cash method.

Depreciation: Assets are depreciated by an amount that is commonly determined by IRS rules. The concept of depreciation is discussed in Chapter 6. A detailed explanation of IRS rules and regulations and depreciation theory can be found in IRS Publication 334. Because no check is ever written for depreciation, there is no sort compartment for it. The correct amount chargeable for a given month is entered directly to the monthly profit or loss statement from the No-Entry Accounting depreciation spreadsheet in Figure 6.8. The total of these monthly entries may need adjustment when taxes are filed. For most small businesses, the large purchases that typically find their way to the depreciation schedule happen infrequently. Most of the time the monthly amount will remain unchanged.

Draw: The Draw category reflects the removal of cash, inventory, or services from a business by the proprietor. Draw checks include cash taken as the owner's income, checks written for personal expenses, and memorandum tickets indicating some dollar amount of business inventory or services used for personal purposes. Without all these documents at hand, you cannot reasonably reconcile annual cash flow through a business. An annual review of where cash came from and where cash has been spent is a mandatory requirement for small business owners who hope to succeed. These items remain in the permanent storage box of the year in which they were incurred.

Corporations are not permitted draws for their officers. A tax court has held that use of a corporate checking account for personal expenses can result in loss of corporate status.

Expense Check: Checks for expenses are sorted into the category that most closely represents the expense that the check pays. For example, a check written to pay for a newspaper ad is sorted into the advertising category. These items remain in the permanent storage box for the year in which they were incurred.

Gain From Sale of Assets: See Sales, example 2.

Liabilities: Documents to be inserted in the Liabilities compartment have to do with increasing or decreasing the amount you owe. Any deposit that represents loan proceeds going into the company account is sorted here. Such a deposit reflects an increase in liabilities. Any check that in whole or in part represents the reduction of what you owe is also sorted here. "In part" refers to the common practice of making a loan payment with a single check, part of which is interest expense and does not reduce the liability. Both the interest amount and the principal amount should be noted on the check that you sort here. Prepare a memo ticket for the interest amount and sort it into "Interest on Business Debt." In this way the loan payment is completely processed. The sum of all deposited loan proceeds minus the amount paid back with monthly or other payments equals the liability amount that appears on the balance sheet. A different liability amount should be shown for each separate loan.

In general, a deposit slip represents loan proceeds, and a check represents a reduction of loans. When you obtain a loan always request an *amortization schedule* (computer printout indicating how much of each payment is interest and how much is principal). This information is essential to an accurate cash forecast.

It is advisable to clip the deposit slip to the loan papers, including subsequent renewals and the amortization schedule. Insert them into the loan packet that is supplied with No-Entry Accounting materials. Insert the canceled checks that retire loans into the appropriate loan packet. This procedure will provide a complete loan audit trail from which the outstanding amount can easily be determined. The complete liabilities section of the permanent storage box is moved annually to the current year permanent storage box.

Loan from the Bank: (See also Liabilities.) The proceeds from a loan should be deposited into your business checking account. The resulting deposit slip should be sorted into the Liabilities compartment. Make note on the deposit ticket that the money was received as a loan and not from sales. This ensures that the amount is sorted out of the profit and loss process and into the balance sheet process.

Loan from the Owner: (See also Liabilities.) This type of loan is the same as one from the bank. Be sure to include any personal check or cash payment for business expenses as a loan from the owner. One separate loan packet for all personal loans should be established.

Loan Payment: (See also Liabilities.) Loan payments usually consist of two elements: interest and principal. The interest part is an expense item that enters into the profit and loss statement. The principal payment portion of the check affects the liabilities section of the balance sheet. Note the principal portion on the check and sort the check to the appropriate loan packet in Liabilities. A memorandum is written for the interest portion which is sorted into the Interest on Business Debt (16) compartment. A check written for only interest or principal would be sorted accordingly.

The interest memorandum should include the following information: (1) The date and check number of the payment check, (2) the amount of interest, and (3) the word "Interest." If more than one loan exists with a single bank or more than one bank is involved, be sure the document is sorted into the appropriate loan packet.

Money Market Deposit: See Assets and Draw.

Mortgage, Business: See Loan Payment.

Mortgage, Personal: Sort personal mortgage payments to the owner's Draw compartment for a proprietorship; such payments are not permitted in a corporation. Do not pay personal bills with a corporate checking account!

NSF Check: A check returned for lack of funds was most likely received in a sales transaction. If after two attempts to clear the check it remains NSF, sort it into the Returns compartment. See also Sales Returns.

Office in the Home: Your office is computed per the form of the same name (Figure 8.6). Sort all documents that relate to the home office into its compartment in the sort box. Personal or business checks and paid cash receipts in payment of all home utilities (garbage collection, home mortgage interest, insurance, property taxes) and general repairs (roofing or an exterior paint job) are all sorted here. If you use a personal checking account to occasionally pay any of these expenses, sort the canceled checks directly to the sort box when the bank statement is received. This procedure will save time at year end and will keep important documents from being misplaced.

The same is true of the property tax bill and the annual 1099 form received from your mortgage company for residence mortgage interest. At year end, the computation is made per the form Office in the Home (Figure 8.6). The computed amount is added to items already sorted to office expense category, line 18. Items sorted directly to the office expense category are those items whose only purpose or use is in, or for, the office, such as an office paint job, office repairs, stationery, and supplies.

To simplify generating the monthly expense, divide the prior year's Office in the Home expense by 12 and use that number monthly until the actual figure can be computed at year end. If you purchase an item of equipment such as a calculator or typewriter, see Assets and Depreciation. If your place of business is other than your home, the office in your home cannot be deducted.

Outsort: The Outsort compartments in the sort box and in the permanent storage box provide for double documents and storage for documents no longer of use to the permanent record. For example:

- You use a charge card for three purchases, resulting in a $300 bill from the charge card company. At the time you incurred the charges, you obtained a detailed receipt for each purchase, establishing proof of business use. You pay the charge card bill with a single check for the entire balance. The check duplicates the more detailed, more audit-acceptable charge card ticket copies. The check is also a single document, whereas each of the three purchases might be expensed in different categories or draw if the use was personal. The individual receipts can be sorted individually as needed. You may need the canceled check, though, because the credit card company could lose the payment and later ask for proof that you paid the amount. The Outsort compartment keeps the monthly bill from being double counted in the system but preserves it for another possible use. The canceled check and credit card statement should be kept together in Outsort. If the account is personal, the company check depositing the amount is a draw document.

- The monthly bank statement is also sorted into Outsort.

- Another example deals with documents other than checks. Suppose a company had a money market or savings account into which it made periodic deposits of excess cash. The resulting documents would certainly pertain to the business but not in the conventional way. You could write a company check for the deposit and a deposit ticket would be generated from depositing the money into the company money market account. The deposit ticket and any supporting documents—such as a pass book or check book—should go into Assets but the check, because it is a duplicate record, should be sorted into Outsort.

Payroll: Payroll costs consists of:

- The net paycheck.

- The federal withholding and FICA tax withheld (FICA tax = 7.56 percent from the employee plus 7.65 percent from the company) from employee checks.

- Any state income or other tax.

- Workmen's compensation insurance premiums.

- Unemployment insurance premiums. It has two forms, SUTA for the state portion and FUTA for the federal portion. The premiums are based upon an employer's experience with unemployment claims. SUTA is filed monthly. FUTA is filed annually at 0.008 percent of gross wages up to $7,000 for each employee.

Documents sorted into the Wages compartment include the canceled net pay checks and the memos that are described in the payroll section of Chapter 17. The memo is for the amount of the federal withholding and FICA tax that was withheld from the employee paycheck. (Do not include the company's 7.56 percent, because this portion is sorted into taxes.) The net paycheck, this memo amount, plus any other deductions, such as state tax, should equal the gross wages amount.

If state tax is withheld from the employees' paychecks, a memo reflecting this amount is sorted into Wages as well. The canceled check that is in payment of these tax deposits is stored in the Federal, State, or Personal tax packets, whichever is appropriate. These packets are provided with the No-Entry Accounting materials and are filed behind the Taxes tab in the permanent storage box. This procedure helps to deal with tax inquiries and keeps the tax records in a perpetual state of audit readiness should a question arise.

Workmen's compensation and unemployment canceled checks are sorted into the Insurance compartment. Keep in mind that these costs are directly related to the cost of wages. When you decide to hire another employee, bear in mind that these two items can cost an additional 12 percent of the gross wage.

Additional payroll information is provided in Chapter 13. Figures 13.4 and 13.5 deal with employee withholding deposit requirements and the impact of employee taxes on payroll expense, and Chapter 18 describes the timing of deposits.

Petty Cash: For a proprietorship, a petty cash check is sorted into the Draw compartment, indicating that money was taken out of the business. If the money is used for business purposes, the resulting paid cash receipts are sorted into the appropriate expense categories of the sort box, and the check is removed from Draw and put in Outsort.

For a corporation, the Draw compartment can be renamed Petty Cash. Each month the cash receipts are reconciled against the remaining cash in the fund to ensure that the money was spent for business purposes. The receipts are then sorted into the appropriate compartment of the sort box for the monthly preparation of the No-Entry Accounting profit and loss statement. The receipts would then be moved to the appropriate permanent storage compartment.

Sales: Receipts from daily sales are deposited into the bank account. Be sure to note "sales" on the deposit slip to ensure that you sort it properly.

Any gain from the sale of a company property should be handled as a memorandum if no deposit slip results from the transaction. Such "Gain" is discussed in Chapter 6, which covers Depreciation. Basically, gain is generated if an asset was purchased for, say, $1,000, then fully depreciated to zero, and then later sold. If it was sold for $500, a gain of $500 has been accomplished. Any time that company property is sold for more than it cost, depreciated or not. A memo describing the gain transaction must be sorted into the sales compartment where the gain will be counted as ordinary income.

Sales Returns: If an item is returned or a portion of a previous sale amount is forgiven, such as the writing off of a bad debt, a transaction memo must be prepared.

Record the date, amount, any identifying document or number such as a sales ticket number, and a brief reason for the return. Sort this memo into Returns in the sort box and it will be subtracted from sales on the next profit and loss statement.

Savings or Money Market Deposits: See Outsort, example 3.

Taxes: The No-Entry Accounting System considers taxes to fall into two categories: employer taxes and all others.

Employer taxes consist only of federal social security matching contributions. (FICA is 7.56 percent of the first $53,400 in annual wages at present.) Federal withholding is an employee tax that the employer is directed to collect and pass along. Proprietor withholding and self-employment tax (social security for self-employed people) are not business expenses but personal expenses of the self-employed. They are, therefore, not deductible as a business expense. The No-Entry Accounting method provides for these personal taxes by maintaining the deposit record in the Personal Tax packet that is filed behind the Taxes tab in permanent storage.

A considerable amount of time may pass between the actual writing of a net payroll check and the time when the associated taxes are due to be deposited. Neither the net payroll check nor the tax deposit checks are actual expenses to the business until the checks actually clear the bank.

The fact that these items can remain in float for some time contributes to your cash management problem. To keep the true wage figure, the employee's portion of any taxes deposited should be recorded on a memo that is sorted into the Wages compartment. The sum of the memos and the net paychecks then equals the gross payroll amount. The canceled check and a memo for the company's portion of any deposit become part of the tax record by being stored in the Federal, State, or Personal tax packets.

Note: The tax deposit receipt from the bank should be sorted to the appropriate tax packet. Once the canceled check for the deposit is returned, the receipt and check should be stapled together with the appropriate report document for storage in the appropriate tax packet. This procedure helps to facilitate any audit or necessary future correspondence.

All Other Taxes: Business property taxes and sales taxes should be sorted into Taxes (23). Staple a copy of the completed reporting forms or tax bill to the canceled check for storage in the permanent storage box. Sales tax documents are generally stored in the State tax packet. The property tax documents will be sorted into the permanent storage tax compartment. No packet is provided. Personal property documents should be sorted to office in the home as appropriate.

Unemployment Compensation, Federal and State: Unemployment compensation is an insurance program designed to help workers who have lost their jobs through no fault of their own. Premiums are paid to the state as the primary provider of benefits, but a portion must be paid to the federal government as well. The federal portion serves as a backup for hard-hit areas or states that exhaust their state funds.

The federal portion is paid annually. These checks should be sorted into Insurance (15) even though they are directly related to wages. The premium for these two insurance programs is calculated as a percent (from 1 percent to 7 percent) on the first $7,000 of each individual's gross wages. The percentage varies with the experience an employer has had with claims. The federal portion is 0.008, or 8/10 of 1 percent of gross wages.

Wages: See Payroll.

Warranties/Receipts: Occasionally, an item such as a car battery may be purchased with cash. The receipt is also the warranty. Such warranties should be kept in the Warranty packet and filed behind the Warranty/Receipts tab. Therefore, the receipt document itself is not available for use as the sorted transaction document. In this case, prepare a transaction memo with all the pertinent information and sort it into the appropriate expense category. The Warranty/Receipts packet should be moved annually and stored behind the current year's Warranty/Receipts tab.

Workmen's Compensation: Workmen's compensation is an insurance program intended to protect employees from loss of wages if the employees are injured and to reimburse expenses involved in job-related injuries. Checks for this expense may be sorted into the Insurance (15) compartment. The expense is in fact an insurance premium, the rate of which is based on the gross payroll amount.

Chapter 10

Using No-Entry Accounting— Joe's Cafe Case Study

This chapter gives you the opportunity to use the No-Entry Accounting principles you have been reading about by working through one month's worth of bookkeeping for Joe's Cafe. I strongly advise you to complete the exercise. Accounting, like any other skill, requires you to pull out a pencil, roll up your sleeves, and try it for yourself. It is not inherently difficult but, like riding a bicycle, you must practice, not just read about it. When you finish this chapter, you should be able to do all necessary monthly accounting and all of your tax calculations. Once you learn to do No-Entry Accounting, you will find that going through your records every month is not so much a chore as a way to understand the financial fundamentals of your enterprise.

Many entrepreneurs believe that their businesses are unique and require highly specialized accounting practices. There are, of course, special requirements in different industries. Meat packers, for example, protect themselves from fluctuations in commodity prices by closing their books every week, so that every year they have 52 profit and loss statements and balance sheets. "Monthly" accounts are usually arranged as 13 four-week months (13 x 4 = 52), rather than the 12 calendar months of about four-and-a-half weeks each. However, at some level all businesses must describe their operations—for the perusal of owners and the IRS among others—using generally accepted accounting practices. Every business must use cash analysis forms, profit and loss statements, balance sheets, and tax forms. Although the chances are that your business (or contemplated business) will not be much like Joe's Cafe, you will discover that the basic financial accounting tools you learn to use will be as applicable to your business as they are to Joe's. If you learn financial skills—like how to deal with employee payroll or depreciate an asset—that you don't need today, you may well need them next quarter or next year.

Preparing to Work the Case Study

Ideally, I would give you an envelope with Joe's bank statement, cancelled checks and deposit tickets, Joe's credit card bills, and miscellaneous cash receipts. You would have a sort box, a permanent storage box, and blank or partially completed copies of all the necessary forms. As an approximation, this chapter includes printed facsimiles of checks and receipts and copies of the various forms. The chapter also has a "virtual sort box," Figure 10.1, which is just a printed form in which you can write values of transactions. To minimize the arithmetic drudgery, most transactions are in whole dollars. Because an exercise of this sort is pointless unless you can tell whether you have the correct answer (or, as is common in accounting, one of the correct answers), the text includes detailed descriptions of what you should have done and why. Of course, rather than just reading the answer, you will learn more if, when you are uncertain what to do, you go back and reread pertinent chapters.

After looking over Joe's checks and receipts, follow these steps to complete the case study:

1. Put everything into the appropriate sort box pigeon holes. If you are using the virtual sort box, just copy the value of each transaction into the appropriate compartment.

2. After tallying the value in each sort box compartment, you should copy the totals to the blank Schedule C in Figure 10.2. The instructions for Line 4 of Schedule C say to use the instructions on the reverse to compute Cost of Sales. I return to this topic later, but for now use the Cost of Sales figures from the sort sheet instead.

3. After you have finished with Schedule C, complete the This Month column in the No-Entry Accounting monthly income statement shown in Figure 10.3. Be sure you read all the instructions on the forms and reread earlier sections of the book as necessary.

4. Then complete the Cash In and Cash Out sheet in Figure 10.4 to summarize how cash came into Joe's business and how it went out and whether Joe's Cafe made an actual profit.

Remember that although all of this seems tedious, it really is the only way to become comfortable with doing your own accounting.

Case Study Solution and Discussion

In Figure 10.5 are the completed sort box entries. You should check your values against these and, at a minimum, read any of the following sections where your figures and mine disagree (they are in the same order as the entries in the sort box). It is probably worthwhile to at least scan everything and, at the risk of sounding like your third-grade teacher, it is very good idea to try it for yourself before reading the answers.

Assets	Sales Line 1	(Returns & Allowances) Line 2	Cost of Sales Line 4
Liabilities	Draw 0	Capital 1	Outsort 2
Ads & Promotion Line 8	Car & Truck Line 10 3	Commissions Line 11 4	Wages Line 26 5
Insurance Line 15	Business Interest Line 16 6	Legal Professional Line 17 7	Office and Postage Line 18 8
Rent Line 20	Repairs Line 21 9	Supplies Not Inventoried Line 22	Taxes Line 23
Travel Entertainment Line 24	Utilities Telephone Line 25	Bank Charges Line 27a	Donations Line 27a
Laundry Cleaning Line 27a	Misc. Line 27a		
	Medical	Office in the Home	Warrenties/ Receipts

Figure 10.1. Blank Sort Sheet

JOE'S CAFE
HOMETOWN, U.S.A.

No. 1001

_____ 19 ___   70-2406
719

PAY
TO THE
ORDER OF Major Insurance Company $ 75.00

Seventy five dollars & 00/100   DOLLARS

AMERICAN NATIONAL BANK
HOMETOWN, U.S.A.

FOR liability   Joe Smith

JOE'S CAFE
HOMETOWN, U.S.A.

No. 1002

_____ 19 ___   70-2406
719

PAY
TO THE
ORDER OF ASF Provisions $ 600.00

Six hundred dollars & 00/100   DOLLARS

AMERICAN NATIONAL BANK
HOMETOWN, U.S.A.

FOR canned foods, frozen foods   Joe Smith

JOE'S CAFE
HOMETOWN, U.S.A.

No. 1003

_____ 19 ___   70-2406
719

PAY
TO THE
ORDER OF T. Grove $ 1,000.00

One thousand dollars & 00/100   DOLLARS

AMERICAN NATIONAL BANK
HOMETOWN, U.S.A.

FOR Rent   Joe Smith

JOE'S CAFE
HOMETOWN, U.S.A.

No. 1004

_____ 19 ___   70-2406
719

PAY
TO THE
ORDER OF Milwaukee Cheese $ 300.00

Three hundred dollars & 00/100   DOLLARS

AMERICAN NATIONAL BANK
HOMETOWN, U.S.A.

FOR _____   Joe Smith

138

JOE'S CAFE
HOMETOWN, U.S.A.

No. 1005

19 _____ 70-2406 / 719

PAY TO THE ORDER OF _Elgin Beverage Company_ $ 400.00

Four hundred dollars & 00/100 _____ DOLLARS

AMERICAN NATIONAL BANK
HOMETOWN, U.S.A.

FOR _____ Joe Smith

JOE'S CAFE
HOMETOWN, U.S.A.

No. 1006

19 _____ 70-2406 / 719

PAY TO THE ORDER OF _Fairfax Business Machines_ $ 500.00

Five hundred dollars & 00/100 _____ DOLLARS

AMERICAN NATIONAL BANK
HOMETOWN, U.S.A.

FOR _Cash register—Paid in full_ Joe Smith

JOE'S CAFE
HOMETOWN, U.S.A.

No. 1008

19 _____ 70-2406 / 719

PAY TO THE ORDER OF _Secretary of State_ $ 300.00

Three hundred dollars & 00/100 _____ DOLLARS

AMERICAN NATIONAL BANK
HOMETOWN, U.S.A.

FOR _sales tax_ Joe Smith

JOE'S CAFE
HOMETOWN, U.S.A.

No. 1009

19 _____ 70-2406 / 719

PAY TO THE ORDER OF _Secretary of State_ $ 50.00

Fifty dollars & 00/100 _____ DOLLARS

AMERICAN NATIONAL BANK
HOMETOWN, U.S.A.

FOR _Unemployment insurance_ Joe Smith

JOE'S CAFE		No. 1011
HOMETOWN, U.S.A.		

19 _____ 70-2406 / 719

PAY TO THE ORDER OF __Commonwealth Edison_____ $ | 150.00 |

One hundred fifty dollars & 00/100 _____ DOLLARS

AMERICAN NEIONAL BANK
HOMETOWN, U.S.A.

Joe Smith

FOR _____

JOE'S CAFE		No. 1012
HOMETOWN, U.S.A.		

19 _____ 70-2406 / 719

PAY TO THE ORDER OF __Big Bread Company_____ $ | 250.00 |

Two hundred fifty dollars & 00/100 _____ DOLLARS

AMERICAN NEIONAL BANK
HOMETOWN, U.S.A.

Joe Smith

FOR _____

JOE'S CAFE		No. 1013
HOMETOWN, U.S.A.		

19 _____ 70-2406 / 719

PAY TO THE ORDER OF __Internal Revenue Service_____ $ | 193.00 |

One hundred ninety-three dollars & 00/100 _____ DOLLARS

AMERICAN NATIONAL BANK
HOMETOWN, U.S.A.

FOR __payroll tax deposit_____ Joe Smith

JOE'S CAFE		No. 1014
HOMETOWN, U.S.A.		

19 _____ 70-2406 / 719

PAY TO THE ORDER OF __E. Jaffke_____ $ | 200.00 |

Two hundred dollars & 00/100 _____ DOLLARS

AMERICAN NEIONAL BANK
HOMETOWN, U.S.A.

FOR __250 gross, 25 FICA, 2 St., 23 W/H__ Joe Smith

JOE'S CAFE
HOMETOWN, U.S.A.

No. 1015

19 _____   70-2406
719

PAY TO THE ORDER OF ___Sislers Dairy___ $ 300.00

Three hundred dollars & 00/100 _____ DOLLARS

AMERICAN NATIONAL BANK
HOMETOWN, U.S.A.

Joe Smith

FOR _____

JOE'S CAFE
HOMETOWN, U.S.A.

No. 1016

19 _____   70-2406
719

PAY TO THE ORDER OF ___Cash___ $ 400.00

Four hundred dollars & 00/100 _____ DOLLARS

AMERICAN NATIONAL BANK
HOMETOWN, U.S.A.

Joe Smith

FOR _____

JOE'S CAFE
HOMETOWN, U.S.A.

No. 1017

19 _____   70-2406
719

PAY TO THE ORDER OF ___Bank of New York, Agent___ $ 500.00

Five hundred dollars & 00/100 _____ DOLLARS

AMERICAN NATIONAL BANK
HOMETOWN, U.S.A.

FOR ___money market (wife's) acct.___

Joe Smith

JOE'S CAFE
HOMETOWN, U.S.A.

No. 1018

19 _____   70-2406
719

PAY TO THE ORDER OF ___VISA___ $ 300.00

Three hundred dollars & 00/100 _____ DOLLARS

AMERICAN NATIONAL BANK
HOMETOWN, U.S.A.

FOR ___current payment___

Joe Smith

JOE'S CAFE
HOMETOWN, U.S.A.

No. 1019

_____ 19____ 70-2406 / 719

PAY TO THE ORDER OF The Daily News _____ $ 100.00

One hundred dollars & 00/100 _____ DOLLARS

AMERICAN NATIONAL BANK
HOMETOWN, U.S.A.

FOR Ads _____   Joe Smith

JOE'S CAFE
HOMETOWN, U.S.A.

No. 1020

_____ 19____ 70-2406 / 719

PAY TO THE ORDER OF Economic Labs _____ $ 50.00

Fifty dollars & 00/100 _____ DOLLARS

AMERICAN NATIONAL BANK
HOMETOWN, U.S.A.

FOR Dishwasher chemicals   Joe Smith

JOE'S CAFE
HOMETOWN, U.S.A.

No. 1021

_____ 19____ 70-2406 / 719

PAY TO THE ORDER OF Ottawa Meat Company _____ $ 600.00

Six hundred dollars & 00/100 _____ DOLLARS

AMERICAN NATIONAL BANK
HOMETOWN, U.S.A.

FOR _____   Joe Smith

JOE'S CAFE
HOMETOWN, U.S.A.

No. 1023

_____ 19____ 70-2406 / 719

PAY TO THE ORDER OF Ajax Office Supply _____ $ 50.00

Fifty dollars & 00/100 _____ DOLLARS

AMERICAN NATIONAL BANK
HOMETOWN, U.S.A.

FOR pens, ribbons, etc.   Joe Smith

JOE'S CAFE	No. 1024
HOMETOWN, U.S.A.	

19_____ 70-2406 / 719

PAY TO THE ORDER OF __Ed's Knife Sharpening_____ $ | 25.00 |

Twenty five & 00/100 _____ DOLLARS

AMERICAN NATIONAL BANK
HOMETOWN, U.S.A.

FOR _____   Joe Smith

JOE'S CAFE	No. 1026
HOMETOWN, U.S.A.	

19_____ 70-2406 / 719

PAY TO THE ORDER OF __Local Savings & Loan_____ $ | 650.00 |

Six hundred fifty dollars & 00/100 _____ DOLLARS

AMERICAN NATIONAL BANK
HOMETOWN, U.S.A.

FOR __Home mortgage_____   Joe Smith

JOE'S CAFE	No. 1027
HOMETOWN, U.S.A.	

19_____ 70-2406 / 719

PAY TO THE ORDER OF __Schweepes_____ $ | 50.00 |

Fifty dollars & 00/100 _____ DOLLARS

AMERICAN NAIONAL BANK
HOMETOWN, U.S.A.

FOR pans _____   Joe Smith

JOE'S CAFE	No. 1029
HOMETOWN, U.S.A.	

19_____ 70-2406 / 719

PAY TO THE ORDER OF __S. Delvecio_____ $ | 500.00 |

Five hundred dollars & 00/100 _____ DOLLARS

AMERICAN NAIONAL BANK
HOMETOWN, U.S.A.

FOR 575 gross, 50 FICA, 20 W/H, 5 St.   Joe Smith

JOE'S CAFE
HOMETOWN, U.S.A.

No. 1031

19 ___   70-2406
719

PAY TO THE ORDER OF High Flying Poultry $ 300.00

Three hundred dollars & 00/100

DOLLARS

AMERICAN NATIONAL BANK
HOMETOWN, U.S.A.

FOR _____   Joe Smith

JOE'S CAFE
HOMETOWN, U.S.A.

No. 1032

19 ___   70-2406
719

PAY TO THE ORDER OF City Government $ 50.00

Fifty dollars & 00/100

DOLLARS

AMERICAN NATIONAL BANK
HOMETOWN, U.S.A.

FOR Permit   Joe Smith

JOE'S CAFE
HOMETOWN, U.S.A.

No. 1033

19 ___   70-2406
719

PAY TO THE ORDER OF Home Town Bank $ 700.00

Seven hundred dollars & 00/100

DOLLARS

AMERICAN NATIONAL BANK
HOMETOWN, U.S.A.

FOR $550 Interest, 150 principal   Joe Smith

JOE'S CAFE
HOMETOWN, U.S.A.

No. 1035

19 ___   70-2406
719

PAY TO THE ORDER OF M. Jones $ 100.00

One hundred dollars & 00/100

DOLLARS

AMERICAN NATIONAL BANK
HOMETOWN, U.S.A.

FOR Wages (contract-labor)   Joe Smith

144

JOE'S CAFE
HOMETOWN, U.S.A.

No. 1037

_____ 19 ___ 70-2406
                          719

PAY
TO THE
ORDER OF _Ace Hardware_____ $ | 15.00 |

_Fifteen & 00/100_____ DOLLARS

AMERICAN NATIONAL BANK
HOMETOWN, U.S.A.

FOR _tools_____   _Joe Smith_____

JOE'S CAFE
HOMETOWN, U.S.A.

No. 1039

_____ 19 ___ 70-2406
                          719

PAY
TO THE
ORDER OF _Hames Refrigeration_____ $ | 300.00 |

_Three hundred dollars & 00/100_____ DOLLARS

AMERICAN NATIONAL BANK
HOMETOWN, U.S.A.

FOR _Repair walk-in cooler_____   _Joe Smith_____

JOE'S CAFE
HOMETOWN, U.S.A.

No. 1041

_____ 19 ___ 70-2406
                          719

PAY
TO THE
ORDER OF _Little League Baseball_____ $ | 25.00 |

_Twenty five dollars & 00/100_____ DOLLARS

AMERICAN NATIONAL BANK
HOMETOWN, U.S.A.

FOR _sign up son_____   _Joe Smith_____

JOE'S CAFE
HOMETOWN, U.S.A.

No. 1042

_____ 19 ___ 70-2406
                          719

PAY
TO THE
ORDER OF _Northern Illinois University_____ $ | 1,200.00 |

_One thousand two hundred dollars & 00/100_____ DOLLARS

AMERICAN NATIONAL BANK
HOMETOWN, U.S.A.

FOR _Rita's tuition_____   _Joe Smith_____

JOE'S CAFE
HOMETOWN, U.S.A.

No. 1043

_____ 19____ $\frac{70\text{-}2406}{719}$

PAY
TO THE
ORDER OF _Hometown Bank_____ $ | 350.00

_Three hundred fifty dollars & 00/100_____
DOLLARS

AMERICAN NEIONAL BANK
HOMETOWN, U.S.A.

FOR _$3oo principal $50 interest_____ Joe Smith

JOE'S CAFE
HOMETOWN, U.S.A.

No. 1045

_____ 19____ $\frac{70\text{-}2406}{719}$

PAY
TO THE
ORDER OF _Village Decorator_____ $ | 10.00

_Ten dollars & 00/100_____
DOLLARS

AMERICAN NEIONAL BANK
HOMETOWN, U.S.A.

FOR _wall paper—rest. foyer_____ Joe Smith

JOE SMITH
HOMETOWN, U.S.A.

176

_____ 19____ $\frac{70\text{-}2406}{719}$

PAY
TO THE
ORDER OF _Northern Gas Company_____ $ | 100.00

_One hundred & 00/100_____
DOLLARS

Savings & LoaAssociation
HOMETOWN, U.S.A.

MEMO _(restaurant)_____ Joe Smith

JOE'S CAFE
HOMETOWN, U.S.A.

④

CURRENCY	2,100	00
COINS		
TOTAL CHECKS		
TOTAL	2,100	00

$\frac{70\text{-}2406}{719}$

Checks and other items are
received for deposit subject
to the provisions of the
Uniform Commercial Code
or any applicable collection
agreement.

DEPOSIT TICKET DATE _____ 19____
DEPOSITS MAY NOT BE MADE FOR IMMEDIATE WITHDRAWAL

AMERICAN NEIONAL BANK
HOMETOWN, U.S.A.

Sales

JOE'S CAFE

HOMETOWN, U.S.A.

(8)

CURRENCY	1,800	00
COINS	50	00
TOTAL CHECKS	200	00
TOTAL	2,050	00

70-2406
719
Checks and other items are
received for deposit subject
to the provisions of the
Uniform Commercial Code
or any applicable collection
agreement.

DEPOSIT TICKET DATE _____ 19 ___

DEPOSITS MAY NOT BE MADE FOR IMMEDIATE WITHDRAWAL

AMERICAN NATIONAL BANK
HOMETOWN, U.S.A.

Sales

JOE'S CAFE

HOMETOWN, U.S.A.

(9)

CURRENCY	2,000	00
COINS		
TOTAL CHECKS		
TOTAL	2,000	00

70-2406
719
Checks and other items are
received for deposit subject
to the provisions of the
Uniform Commercial Code
or any applicable collection
agreement.

DEPOSIT TICKET DATE _____ 19 ___

DEPOSITS MAY NOT BE MADE FOR IMMEDIATE WITHDRAWAL

AMERICAN NATIONAL BANK
HOMETOWN, U.S.A.

Loan proceeds

JOE'S CAFE

HOMETOWN, U.S.A.

(13)

CURRENCY	2,200	00
COINS		
TOTAL CHECKS		
TOTAL	2,200	00

70-2406
719
Checks and other items are
received for deposit subject
to the provisions of the
Uniform Commercial Code
or any applicable collection
agreement.

DEPOSIT TICKET DATE _____ 19 ___

DEPOSITS MAY NOT BE MADE FOR IMMEDIATE WITHDRAWAL

AMERICAN NATIONAL BANK
HOMETOWN, U.S.A.

Sales

JOE'S CAFE

HOMETOWN, U.S.A.

(18)

CURRENCY	2,150	00
COINS		
TOTAL CHECKS		
TOTAL	2,150	00

70-2406
719
Checks and other items are
received for deposit subject
to the provisions of the
Uniform Commercial Code
or any applicable collection
agreement.

DEPOSIT TICKET DATE _____ 19 ___

DEPOSITS MAY NOT BE MADE FOR IMMEDIATE WITHDRAWAL

AMERICAN NATIONAL BANK
HOMETOWN, U.S.A.

Sales

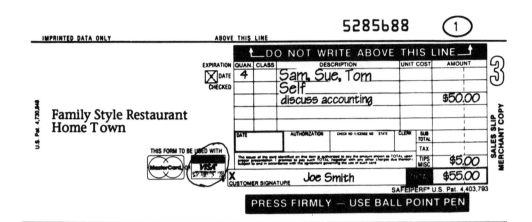

5285688 ①

IMPRINTED DATA ONLY   ABOVE THIS LINE

Family Style Restaurant
Home Town

QUAN.	CLASS	DESCRIPTION	UNIT COST	AMOUNT
4		Sam, Sue, Tom Self		
		discuss accounting		$50.00

SUB TOTAL
TAX
TIPS MISC. $5.00
Joe Smith $55.00

PRESS FIRMLY — USE BALL POINT PEN

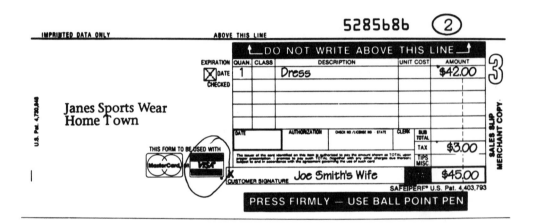

5285686 ②

IMPRINTED DATA ONLY   ABOVE THIS LINE

Janes Sports Wear
Home Town

QUAN.	CLASS	DESCRIPTION	UNIT COST	AMOUNT
1		Dress		$42.00

SUB TOTAL
TAX $3.00
TIPS MISC.
Joe Smith's Wife $45.00

PRESS FIRMLY — USE BALL POINT PEN

5285687 ③

IMPRINTED DATA ONLY   ABOVE THIS LINE

Little Bitty Motel
Duckbill, Miss.

Restaurant convention

QUAN.	CLASS	DESCRIPTION	UNIT COST	AMOUNT
		Lodging 2 nights		$190.00

SUB TOTAL
TAX 10.00
TIPS MISC.
Joe Smith $200.00

PRESS FIRMLY — USE BALL POINT PEN

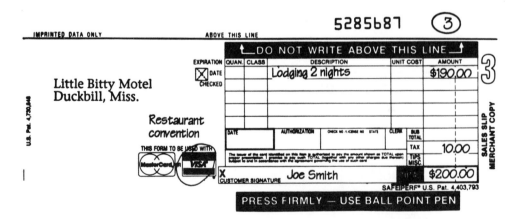

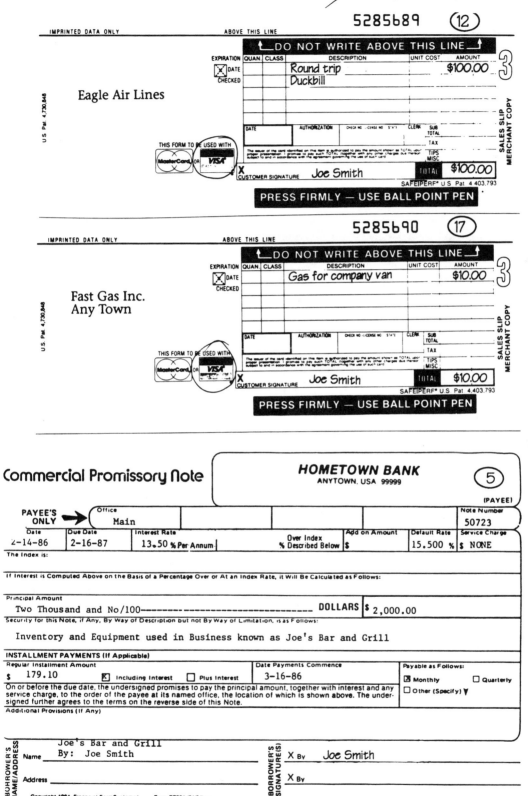

5285689 (12)

IMPRINTED DATA ONLY   ABOVE THIS LINE

↓ DO NOT WRITE ABOVE THIS LINE ↓

EXPIRATION	QUAN.	CLASS	DESCRIPTION	UNIT COST	AMOUNT
☒ DATE CHECKED			Round trip Duckbill		$100.00

Eagle Air Lines

THIS FORM TO BE USED WITH
MasterCard OR VISA

DATE	AUTHORIZATION	CHECK NO. LICENSE NO. STATE	CLEAR	SUB TOTAL	
				TAX	
				TIPS MISC	
X CUSTOMER SIGNATURE   Joe Smith | | | | TOTAL | $100.00 |

SAFE/PERF® U.S. Pat. 4.403,793

SALES SLIP MERCHANT COPY

PRESS FIRMLY — USE BALL POINT PEN

5285690 (17)

IMPRINTED DATA ONLY   ABOVE THIS LINE

↓ DO NOT WRITE ABOVE THIS LINE ↓

EXPIRATION	QUAN.	CLASS	DESCRIPTION	UNIT COST	AMOUNT
☒ DATE CHECKED			Gas for company van		$10.00

Fast Gas Inc.
Any Town

THIS FORM TO BE USED WITH
MasterCard OR VISA

DATE	AUTHORIZATION	CHECK NO. LICENSE NO. STATE	CLEAR	SUB TOTAL	
				TAX	
				TIPS MISC	
X CUSTOMER SIGNATURE   Joe Smith | | | | TOTAL | $10.00 |

SAFE/PERF® U.S. Pat. 4.403,793

SALES SLIP MERCHANT COPY

PRESS FIRMLY — USE BALL POINT PEN

Commercial Promissory Note

HOMETOWN BANK
ANYTOWN, USA 99999   (5)

(PAYEE)

PAYEE'S ONLY → Office: Main

Note Number: 50723

Date	Due Date	Interest Rate	Over Index % Described Below	Add on Amount	Default Rate	Service Charge
2-14-86	2-16-87	13.50 % Per Annum	$	$	15.500 %	$ NONE

The Index is:

If Interest is Computed Above on the Basis of a Percentage Over or At an Index Rate, it Will Be Calculated as Follows:

Principal Amount
Two Thousand and No/100———————————————————— DOLLARS $ 2,000.00

Security for this Note, if Any, By Way of Description but not By Way of Limitation, is as Follows:

Inventory and Equipment used in Business known as Joe's Bar and Grill

INSTALLMENT PAYMENTS (If Applicable)

Regular Installment Amount	Date Payments Commence	Payable as Follows:
$ 179.10 ☒ Including Interest ☐ Plus Interest	3-16-86	☒ Monthly ☐ Quarterly ☐ Other (Specify) ▼

On or before the due date, the undersigned promises to pay the principal amount, together with interest and any service charge, to the order of the payee at its named office, the location of which is shown above. The undersigned further agrees to the terms on the reverse side of this Note.

Additional Provisions (If Any)

BORROWER'S NAME/ADDRESS
Name: Joe's Bar and Grill
By: Joe Smith
Address _____

BORROWER'S SIGNATURE(S)
X By Joe Smith
X By _____

Copyright 1984, Financial FormSystems™   Form FF301 (01/84)

ORIGINAL

GO GAS
SERVICE STATION

⑥

REGULAR
NO LEAD
PREMIUM
DIESEL

DATE_____
GALLONS___8.7___
$___10.00___

Thank You

---

⑭   1/1/

House call to
start car.
Rec. cash
$30.00

Brett Fleury

Qwick Copies
fast service! good quality!

Date:_____ ⑦

# of copies	unit price	total price
59	.08	4.72
		tax .28
		$5.00

---

⑯

*cleaning
supplies*

THANK YOU
CALL AGAIN

$10.00
3.96
2.00
8.41
11.63
$25.00 TOTAL

---

⑮

AIRPORT
PARKING

$10.00

CASH RECEIPT
GAS & GO MART

⑩

DATE _____

DOLLARS ___$10.00___

GALLONS ___8.9___

INITIALS ___MRP___

Cash Receipt   Postage

six dollars & 54/100   ⑪

Amount
_____

Purpose
_____

$ 6.54

Initials SBB
_____

SCHEDULE C **(Form 1040)** Department of the Treasury Internal Revenue Service (O)	**Profit or Loss From Business** (Sole Proprietorship) **Partnerships, Joint Ventures, Etc., Must File Form 1065.** ▶ **Attach to Form 1040 or Form 1041.** ▶ **See Instructions for Schedule C (Form 1040).**	OMB No. 1545-0074 **19⎯90** Attachment Sequence No. **09**

Name of proprietor	Social security number (SSN)

A Principal business or profession, including product or service (see Instructions)   **B** Enter principal business code (from page 2) ▶

C Business name and address ▶ ....
(include suite or room no.)   **D** Employer ID number (Not SSN)

E Accounting method: **(1)** ☐ Cash   **(2)** ☐ Accrual   **(3)** ☐ Other (specify)▶.........................

F Method(s) used to
value closing inventory: **(1)** ☐ Cost   **(2)** ☐ Lower of cost or market   **(3)** ☐ Other (attach explanation)   **(4)** ☐ Does not apply (if checked, go to line H) | Yes | No |

G Was there any change in determining quantities, costs, or valuations between opening and closing inventory? (If "Yes," attach explanation.)

H Are you deducting expenses for business use of your home? (If "Yes," see Instructions for limitations.) . . . . . .

I Did you "materially participate" in the operation of this business during 1990? (If "No," see Instructions for limitations on losses.) . . .

J If this is the first Schedule C filed for this business, check here . . . . ▶ ☐

Part I Income

1	Gross receipts or sales. *Caution: If this income was reported to you on Form W-2 and the "Statutory employee" box on that form was checked, see the Instructions and check here* . . . . ▶ ☐	**1**
2	Returns and allowances	**2**
3	Subtract line 2 from line 1. Enter the result here	**3**
4	Cost of goods sold (from line 38 on page 2)	**4**
5	Subtract line 4 from line 3 and enter the **gross profit** here	**5**
6	Other income, including Federal and state gasoline or fuel tax credit or refund (see Instructions)	**6**
7	Add lines 5 and 6. This is your **gross income** . . . . ▶	**7**

Part II Expenses

8	Advertising	**8**	**21** Repairs and maintenance . . .	**21**	
9	Bad debts from sales or services (see Instructions)	**9**	**22** Supplies (not included in Part III) .	**22**	
			23 Taxes and licenses	**23**	
10	Car and truck expenses (attach **Form 4562**) .	**10**	**24** Travel, meals, and entertainment:		
11	Commissions and fees	**11**	**a** Travel	**24a**	
12	Depletion	**12**	**b** Meals and entertainment .		
13	Depreciation and section 179 expense deduction (not included in Part III) (see Instructions).	**13**	**c** Enter 20% of line 24b subject to limitations (see Instructions) .		
14	Employee benefit programs (other than on line 19)	**14**	**d** Subtract line 24c from line 24b	**24d**	
15	Insurance (other than health) . .	**15**	**25** Utilities	**25**	
16	Interest:		**26** Wages (less jobs credit) . . .	**26**	
a	Mortgage (paid to banks, etc.) .	**16a**	**27a** Other expenses (**list type and amount**):		
b	Other	**16b**	....		
17	Legal and professional services	**17**	....		
18	Office expense.	**18**	....		
19	Pension and profit-sharing plans .	**19**	....		
20	Rent or lease (see Instructions):		....		
a	Vehicles, machinery, and equip. .	**20a**			
b	Other business property. . .	**20b**	**27b** Total other expenses	**27b**	

28 Add amounts in columns for lines 8 through 27b. These are your **total expenses** . . . . ▶   **28**

29 **Net profit or (loss).** Subtract line 28 from line 7. If a profit, enter here and on Form 1040, line 12. Also enter the net profit on Schedule SE, line 2 (statutory employees, see Instructions). If a loss, you MUST go on to line 30 (fiduciaries, see Instructions) **29**

30 If you have a loss, you MUST check the box that describes your investment in this activity (see Instructions). . .   **30a** ☐ All investment is at risk.
If you checked 30a, enter the loss on Form 1040, line 12, and Schedule SE, line 2 (statutory employees, see Instructions). If you checked 30b, you MUST attach **Form 6198.**   **30b** ☐ Some investment is not at risk.

For Paperwork Reduction Act Notice, see Form 1040 Instructions.   Schedule C (Form 1040) 1990

Figure 10.2. Blank Schedule C for Sort Sheet Totals

Income Statement

Date _____

	This Month	%	Year To Date	%
Sales				
Category A	_____	___	_____	___
Category B	_____	___	_____	___
Returns	(_____)	___	(_____)	___
Total Sales	_____	___	_____	___
Cost of Sales				
Category A	_____	___	_____	___
Category B	_____	___	_____	___
Total Cost of Sales	(_____)	___	(_____)	___
Gross Profit	_____	___	_____	___
Operating Expenses				
Advertising	_____	___	_____	___
Car and Truck	_____	___	_____	___
Commissions	_____	___	_____	___
Depreciation & Section 179	_____	___	_____	___
Wages	_____	___	_____	___
Insurance	_____	___	_____	___
Interest on Business Debt	_____	___	_____	___
Legal, Professional	_____	___	_____	___
Office Supplies, Postage	_____	___	_____	___
Rent & Leases	_____	___	_____	___
Repairs & Maintenance	_____	___	_____	___
Supplies Not For Resale	_____	___	_____	___
Taxes & Licenses	_____	___	_____	___
Travel, Meals, Entertainment	_____	___	_____	___
Utilities, Telephone	_____	___	_____	___
Bank Charges	_____	___	_____	___
Donations	_____	___	_____	___
Office Expense	_____	___	_____	___
Laundry, Cleaning	_____	___	_____	___
_____	_____	___	_____	___
_____	_____	___	_____	___
_____	_____	___	_____	___
Miscellaneous	_____	___	_____	___
Total Operating Expenses	(_____)	___	(_____)	___
Net Profit or (Loss)	_____	___	_____	___

Figure 10.3. Blank Monthly Income Statement

Cash In from	Amount	Cash Out to	Amount
_____	_____	_____	_____
_____	_____	_____	_____
_____	_____	_____	_____
_____	_____	_____	_____
_____	_____	_____	_____
_____	_____	_____	_____
_____	_____	_____	_____
_____	_____	_____	_____
Total:	$	Total	$
Cash surplus	$		
Cash shortfall	($	)	

Figure 10.4. Blank Cash In and Cash Out Sheet

Sort Box Entries

Assets Compartment

Handling assets is probably the most difficult step in No-Entry Accounting, mostly because the "generally accepted accounting practices" and IRS regulations are complicated. (Because there are firms with billion-dollar assets, it is understandable that accountants and the government look closely at how these assets are carried on a business's books.) Fortunately, most small business have relatively few asset transactions.

The Assets compartment should contain a single document, canceled check 1006 for full payment for a cash register (warranties, and any paid receipts would also be in permanent storage). To be a depreciable asset, an item must have several years of useful life and cost at least $500, so the cash register is the only purchase this month that would qualify. The depreciation for the cash register would be computed using the spreadsheet in Chapter 6. You may also wish to review IRS Publication 334, *Tax Guide for Small Businesses*. The three possible answers that might appear on Line 12 of Schedule C (Depreciation) would be:

- $8: The new equipment straight-line depreciation method calls for dividing the original purchase price ($500) by 5 years (estimated useful life) for an annual depreciation of $100. Dividing $100 by 12 gives $8 (approximately) as this month's share of the depreciation.

- $17: The Modified Accelerated Cost Recovery System (MARCS) yields a different result. MARCS depreciates the undepreciated balance remaining by 40 percent each year ($500 times 0.4 = $200 ÷ 12 MONTHS = $17). The following year, 40 percent of the $300 balance is taken, and so on, through the fifth year, at which point all remaining depreciation is taken.

Assets	Sales Line 1	(Returns & Allowances) Line 2	Cost of Sales Line 4
1006 500.–	4 2,100.– 8 2,050.– 13 2,200.– 18 2,150.– $8,500.–		1015 300.– 1004 300.– 1012 250.– 1031 300.– 1021 600.– 1005 400.– 1002 600.– $2,750.–
Liabilities	Draw	Capital	Outsort
1033 150.– 5 0.– 9 2,000.– 1043 300.– 176 100.– $1,650.–	2 45.– 1042 1200.– 1026 650.– 1017 500.– 1041 25.– 1016 400.– $2,820.– 0	1	1018 0.– 2
Ads & Promotion Line 8	Car & Truck Line 10	Commissions & Fees Line 11	Wages Line 26
1019 100.–	6 10.– 10 10.– 17 10.– $30.– 3	4	1014 200.– 1035 100.– 1029 500.– $800.– 5
Insurance Line 15	Business Interest Line 16	Legal Professional Line 17	Office and Postage Line 18
1001 75.– 1009 50.– $125.–	1033M 550.– 1043M 50.– $600.– 6	7	7 5.– 1023 50.– 11 6.54 $62. 8
Rent Line 20	Repairs Line 21	Supplies Not Inventoried Line 22	Taxes Line 23
1003 1,000.–	1039 300.– 14 30.– $330.– 9	1020 50.– 1027 50.– 16 25.– $125.–	1008 300.– 1013 193.– 1032 50.– $543.–
Travel Entertainment Line 24	Utilities Telephone Line 25	Bank Charges Line 27a	Donations Line 27a
1 55.– 3 200.– 12 100.– 15 10.– $365.–	1011 150.– 176M 100.– $250.–		
Laundry Cleaning Line 27a	Misc. Line 27a		
	1037 15.– 1024 25.– 1045 10.– $50.–		
	Medical	Office in the Home	Warrenties/ Receipts

Figure 10.5. Completed Sort Sheet for Joe's Cafe

- $500: The entire purchase price could be expensed in the year of purchase if Section 179 were elected.

Sales Compartment

The sales compartment should contain four checking account deposit receipts (numbered 4, 8, 13, and 18), each with the handwritten notation "Sales." The deposit receipt for loan proceeds ($2,000, Document 9) does not go here, because it represents a loan being made to the company and not sales (see Liabilities).

Returns Compartment

In this compartment you sort items that have been sold and returned. You subtract their value from the sales total. There are no items of this type in the exercise, so that compartment is empty.

Cost of Sales Compartment

Checks 1002, 1004, 1005, 1012, 1015, 1021, and 1031 represent the purchase of items intended for resale and are, therefore, cost of sales items (totalling $2750). Because No-Entry Accounting emphasizes cash management, cost of sales items are expensed as soon as the canceled check arrives from the bank.

The IRS does not permit cost of sales items to be written off immediately (so you cannot, for example, avoid tax liabilities by stocking up on inventory at the end of the year).

Liabilities Compartment

If there are any loans, the loan papers, deposit receipt showing loan proceeds being deposited into the company checking account, canceled checks showing loan payments, and an amortization schedule, if available, belong in the Liabilities compartment. A loan packet is established for each loan. For Joe's Cafe this month, checks 1033 and 1043 represent loan payments. Reduction of loan principal and interest payments are separate transactions from an accounting perspective, although both are paid by a single check. The No-Entry Accounting practice is to note on the check the amount of principal reduction and file the check in the Liabilities compartment. A memo showing the interest portion of the payment made by each check (and including check number, loan number, date, and amount) should be sorted into the Business Interest compartment (memos labeled 1033M and 1043M). Document 5, a promissory note showing the interest rate, loan amount, and maturity date and Document 9 (a deposit receipt showing that loan proceeds were deposited in a company account) are also part of the loan packet.

Check 176 represents a loan from Joe to the business and should be placed here. A memo showing telephone expenses and referring to this check in the Liabilities box should be prepared and sorted into the Utilities/Telephone compartment.

The net change in liabilities this month was $1650—$2100 was borrowed, and $450 was paid off.

Draw Compartment

The Draw compartment is for any document that represents removal of cash from the business for personal use. For this example, it totals $2820 and should contain:

- Document 2, a charge card receipt for a dress purchased by Joe's wife. Because there is no notation indicating that the dress was a uniform to be used for company business, the transaction is a draw.

- Checks 1042 (college tuition), 1026 (home mortgage payment), 1041 (payment of Joe's son's Little League fees), 1017 (transfer of funds to Joe's wife's checking account) are all clearly personal expenses, as is 1016 for cash, because there was no notation indicating its use for business expenses. As personal expenses, you treat these amounts as draw.

A quick total of the Draw compartment tells how much cash was taken from the business that month. This can be a shocking experience, when 30 checks come from the bank and 25 of them end up in Draw. Many people prefer to maintain separate business and personal accounts, but this is not strictly necessary so long as accurate records are kept of draws. Sometimes bank charges and bookkeeping can be substantially reduced by keeping all funds in one account. Corporations must used separate accounts.

Capital Compartment
This compartment is used only by corporations, and this case study assumes that Joe's Cafe is a proprietorship (draws are not permissible in corporations!). If your business is a C corp, initial and subsequent deposit receipts from the sale of stock would be sorted here.

Outsort Compartment
Check 1018 is the most common type of outsort. It represents a payment of a charge card bill, but it is a duplicate record of the receipts. The charge receipts should be sorted into the appropriate compartments, because they define the specific business nature of the expense. The canceled check is kept here only as record that the company paid the charge card bill.

Ads & Promotions Compartment
Check 1019, for a newspaper advertisement, is sorted here.

Bank Charges Compartment
Bank charges are generally listed on the bank statement, and handwritten memos of these charges (service charges, overdraft charges, purchase of checks, bank drafts and so on) should be sorted into this compartment with the usual annotations of date, account number, nature and amount of charge.

Car and Truck Compartment
Documents 6, 10 and 17 are cash receipts ($30 in total) for gas that was used on company business.

Depreciation of vehicles that are company owned would be computed with the depreciation spreadsheet (see Chapter 6) and entered monthly directly to Schedule C. Line 13, Depreciation. If a vehicle is personally owned its business use can conveniently be recovered at the per-mile rate established by the IRS. A log must be kept showing the business purpose and mileage and each month the log or a memo supported by the log can be sorted to this compartment.

Wages Compartment

Check 1014 is a payroll check and distinguishable as such by the gross, FICA, state, and withholding notations. These notations meet all the audit requirements for payroll records and eliminates the cumbersome spreadsheets used in pegboard systems. If payroll is more than an employee or two, a different type of check with the payroll notations preprinted would be advantageous.

Check 1014 is a net check: FICA, and state and federal withholding taxes have already been subtracted.

Check 1035 is for contract labor. Check IRS Publication #334 for withholding information considerations. Check 1029 is another ordinary paycheck and is treated just as Check 1014. The total for the Wages compartment is $800.

The gross pay total is needed every quarter to report taxes withheld and deposited on the 941 form. Generate and write the total in the margin of the company copy of the 941 form. Two methods for so doing are discussed on page 222. The margin method is somewhat easier than the memo method.

Unemployment insurance and workmen's compensation insurance are both parts of the business owner's cost of labor, but they are sorted into the Insurance compartment. See Chapter 17's discussion of payroll for more information.

Insurance Compartment

Checks 1001 and 1009 (totaling $125) were for insurance. Check 1009 is to the Secretary of State for unemployment insurance with the premium tied directly to the amount of wages paid. Workmen's compensation insurance is handled by an insurance company ("Major Insurance Company"). These two types of insurance can add more than 12 percent to the hourly wages.

Business Interest Compartment

Memos numbered 1033M and 1043M should be prepared by hand and sorted into the Business Interest compartment. The companion checks 1033 and 1043 will, of course, be found in the Liabilities compartment and represent repayment of loan principal. Repayment of principal is not, of course, a business expense (you are in effect buying back someone else's temporary and partial ownership of business assets) while payment of interest is a cost of doing business and as an expense reduces profits (and tax liabilities).

Office Supplies/Postage Compartment

Document 7 is a cash receipt for copies made. Check 1023 is for supplies, and Document 11 is a postage cash receipt. The total is $61.54.

Rent Compartment

Check 1003 for $1000 is for rent.

Repairs Compartment

Check 1039 covers repairs to the cooler. Document 14 is a cash receipt for jump starting the company car (or this could apply to a personal car if it was being used for business). Some people sort Checks 1037, 1024, and 1045 to the Repairs sections, which is permissible, but I recommend sorting them as miscellaneous expenses. There will, of course, be no differences in profit figures whichever way they are sorted.

Supplies Not For Resale

Items in the Supplies Not For Resale compartment are purchased for the business's use, but are not intended for resale. Checks 1020 (dishwasher supplies) and 1027 (pans) belong in this category, because neither supplies nor pans are sold to customers. Of course, even stationery stores use pencils and typewriter ribbons— what matters is whether the item is for internal use or for resale, not whether it possibly could be sold. Remember that if an item costs over $500 and can be used for several years, its cost may have to be recovered through depreciation rather than as a direct expense.

Taxes Compartment

Check 1008 ($300) is for a sales tax deposit and represents money collected by Joe for the state. See the instructions on your state and possibly local forms for recording and reporting.

Check 1013 is a federal deposit check. Check 1032 is payment for a permit. The tax checks are stored in the appropriate tax packet. The permit check goes behind the tax tab in permanent storage.

Travel/Entertainment Compartment

Document 1 is a charge receipt for a business lunch. Document 3 is a charge receipt for attendance at a business convention. Document 12 is a charge receipt for air fare to the convention, and Document 15 records the charge parking Joe's car while he was at the conference. The total for this compartment is $365.

Utilities/Telephone Compartment

Check 1011 is a payment of an electricity bill for $150. Document 176M should be found here as well. The source document, Check 176, is from Joe's personal account, but because the notation indicates that it is for the restaurant's gas bill, it represents a business expense. It would be best to take this check as a loan to the company and sort it into Liabilities. A memo should be generated indicating that a utility bill was paid by personal check and the memo sorted into Utilities/Telephone. If the small business owner is regularly subsidizing the business by paying its bills, it is important that such transactions be faithfully recorded so that the owner will know how much is being invested in the business in this indirect manner. Some people may prefer to write a check to the business that is clearly marked as a loan and then pay business expenses with checks drawn on the business account. Whatever method you use, for both income tax and personal planning reasons it is imperative that you know how much you have invested in a business.

Licenses/Permits Compartment

Licenses, permits, and various miscellaneous fees fall under Line 27a of Schedule C. Depending on your type of business, there can be a wide variety of such fees. For Joe's Cafe, the total for this month is $50.

Miscellaneous Compartment

Checks 1037, 1024, and 1045 are all small amounts that are clearly expenses but that are not judged worthy of a separate account. Don't waste your time by establishing a large number of tiny accounts, but if some expense occurs with frequency or if you think it needs to be monitored, there is always room for another sort compartment.

Completing the Answer Sheets

There are many important reasons for getting through the four answer sheets. The purposes are

- To establish the amount of clerical work you or your bookkeeper perform preparing financial statements once you extract data from daily transaction documents and enter that data into ledgers and journals.

- To establish that this significant amount of work is eliminated by No-Entry Accounting.

- To prove that your final profit and loss paperwork is available using No-Entry Accounting long before you would have the information from "posting" the numbers using other systems.

- To illustrate that once you tally the collected data, much of your tax work becomes a mere copy job.

- To reveal how most cash management data gets buried when you use accrual accounting.

- To establish that a significant portion of tax data is buried when you use pure cash accounting.

- To show that typically cash analysis is an afterthought—if it ever happens— and that businesses are misfocused on preparing tax reports.

- To prove that although the complete cash picture is not available until after taxes and profit calculations are final, your priorities throughout the year must be cash management first, profit second, and taxes third.

- To make the point that no other accounting system requires less effort or provides easier access to a set of records that is perpetually audit ready.

Schedule C for Joe's Cafe

Completing this part of the exercise will show you that filling out a year-end tax form is mostly a copy job and not something to fear. You will also see some of the differences between the monthly income sheet and Schedule C, which must be filed with the IRS.

Figure 10.6 is the completed Schedule C for Joe's Cafe. Notice that there is no Assets line on Schedule C. Assets and liabilities are balance sheet items and do not directly enter into the calculation of profit and loss or of tax liabilities. In fact, the absence of a line number indicates that a compartment does not deal with profit and loss. References to line numbers that help you keep track of income versus balance sheet transactions. There is no place to enter Liabilities on Schedule C, but the cost of carrying a Liability (interest and any nonrecurring loan costs) is an expense and is reflected in Line 16 of Schedule C.

Depreciation, however, does play a role in calculated profits and must be accounted for to the IRS's satisfaction. The IRS demands an accrual method of accounting to avoid obvious abuses such as allowing a business owner to escape tax liabilities by building an empire through writing off long-term investments as a current-year expense.

Depreciation is a noncash transaction (no check is written for depreciation) and requires no sort compartment, but an appropriate value must be entered on Schedule C Line 13, and Form 4562 must be filed to describe in detail how the owner has treated the various depreciable assets. IRS Publication 334 is a valuable aid to completing Form 4562. As you noted in the earlier discussion of assets, the depreciation for this month could be any of $8, $17, or $500.

Draw does not appear on Schedule C, because it is not a business expense. For a sole proprietorship, the owner is free to put money in or take money out, but neither type of transaction makes its way onto Schedule C. Likewise, capital is not involved with Schedule C, nor are those items that went into the Outsort compartment.

The biggest difference between sort sheet answers and Schedule C is Part I Line 4, Cost of goods sold and/or operations (from Part III, line 8). The arithmetic used for Part III is based on the accrual method of accounting (see the discussion in Chapter 6 of Schedule C, Part III), which allows goods purchased for resale to be expensed only when they have been sold. Consequently, computing cost of sales requires a physical inventory. Physical inventory must be done at least once a year per tax law, but for some businesses it should be done much more often, perhaps even monthly for a concern such as Joe's Cafe. With frequent inventories the owner will not only be able to more effectively manage cash (by, for example better controlling the time and quantity of purchases) but will also have a realistic estimate of current tax liabilities. Good cash management coupled with effective inventory control should prevent any unpleasant surprises at tax time and help you to avoid paying too much tax too early in the year.

In calculating Line 16 of Schedule C, you must separate mortgage interest and all other interest payments. These separate types of interest are of little meaning to the business owner but help the IRS detect likely abuses when a business owner tries to write off what should be a personal expense as a business expense.

The IRS has also been concerned with excessive writeoffs of entertainment as a business expense. Consequently, on Line 24, Travel, meals, and entertainment, only 80 percent of entertainment expenses can be written off as a business expense.

Joe's Cafe does not require the use of a home office, so he cannot list any deductions for that. The actual amount deductible is usually not known until year

SCHEDULE C (Form 1040) Department of the Treasury Internal Revenue Service (0)	**Profit or Loss From Business** (Sole Proprietorship) Partnerships, Joint Ventures, Etc., Must File Form 1065. ▶ **Attach to Form 1040 or Form 1041.** ▶ **See Instructions for Schedule C (Form 1040).**	OMB No. 1545-0074 1990 Attachment Sequence No. 09

Name of proprietor JOE	Social security number (SSN)

A Principal business or profession, including product or service (see Instructions)	B Enter principal business code (from page 2) ▶ 30 79

C Business name and address ▶ JOE's CAFE (include suite or room no.)	D Employer ID number (Not SSN)

E Accounting method: (1) ☒ Cash   (2) ☐ Accrual   (3) ☐ Other (specify) ▶ ....

F Method(s) used to
value closing inventory: (1) ☐ Cost   (2) ☐ Lower of cost or market   (3) ☒ Other (attach explanation)   (4) ☐ Does not apply (if checked, go to line H)

		Yes	No
G	Was there any change in determining quantities, costs, or valuations between opening and closing inventory? (If "Yes," attach explanation.)		✓
H	Are you deducting expenses for business use of your home? (If "Yes," see Instructions for limitations.)		✓
I	Did you "materially participate" in the operation of this business during 1990? (If "No," see Instructions for limitations on losses.)	✓	
J	If this is the first Schedule C filed for this business, check here . . . . ▶ ☐		

Part I   Income

1	Gross receipts or sales. *Caution: If this income was reported to you on Form W-2 and the "Statutory employee" box on that form was checked, see the Instructions and check here* . . . . . . ▶ ☐	1	8,500
2	Returns and allowances	2	0
3	Subtract line 2 from line 1. Enter the result here	3	8,500
4	Cost of goods sold (from line 38 on page 2)	4	2,750
5	Subtract line 4 from line 3 and enter the **gross profit** here	5	
6	Other income, including Federal and state gasoline or fuel tax credit or refund (see Instructions)	6	
7	Add lines 5 and 6. This is your **gross income** . . . . ▶	7	5,750

Part II   Expenses

8	Advertising	8	100		21	Repairs and maintenance . . .	21	330
9	Bad debts from sales or services (see Instructions)	9			22	Supplies (not included in Part III) .	22	125
					23	Taxes and licenses	23	543
10	Car and truck expenses (attach Form 4562) .	10	30		24	Travel, meals, and entertainment:		
11	Commissions and fees . . .	11			a	Travel	24a	310
12	Depletion	12			b	Meals and entertainment .	55	
13	Depreciation and section 179 expense deduction (not included in Part III) (see Instructions). . .	13	17		c	Enter 20% of line 24b subject to limitations (see Instructions) . .	11	
14	Employee benefit programs (other than on line 19)	14			d	Subtract line 24c from line 24b	24d	44
15	Insurance (other than health) .	15	125		25	Utilities	25	250
16	Interest:				26	Wages (less jobs credit)	26	800
a	Mortgage (paid to banks, etc.).	16a			27a	Other expenses (list type and amount):		
b	Other	16b	600			MISC. 50		
17	Legal and professional services	17						
18	Office expense	18	62					
19	Pension and profit-sharing plans .	19						
20	Rent or lease (see Instructions):							
a	Vehicles, machinery, and equip. .	20a						
b	Other business property. . .	20b	1000		27b	Total other expenses	27b	50

28	Add amounts in columns for lines 8 through 27b. These are your **total expenses** . . . . ▶	28	4,386
29	**Net profit or (loss).** Subtract line 28 from line 7. If a profit, enter here and on Form 1040, line 12. Also enter the net profit on Schedule SE, line 2 (statutory employees, see Instructions). If a loss, you MUST go on to line 30 (fiduciaries, see Instructions).	29	1,364
30	If you have a loss, you MUST check the box that describes your investment in this activity (see Instructions). . .	30a ☐ All investment is at risk. 30b ☐ Some investment is not at risk.
	If you checked 30a, enter the loss on Form 1040, line 12, and Schedule SE, line 2 (statutory employees, see Instructions). If you checked 30b, you MUST attach Form 6198.	

For Paperwork Reduction Act Notice, see Form 1040 Instructions.   Schedule C (Form 1040) 1990

Figure 10.6. Completed Schedule C for Joe's Cafe

end, so the amount may not have been deducted from the regular monthly income statement. An estimate could be used throughout the year, with final figures computed just before Schedule C is filed. Chapter 8 provides a form that helps you to calculate these expenses—be sure to keep records of all pertinent personal expenses for the home in the permanent storage box behind the Home Office tab.

Other items that may be significance to a business are shown on Lines 27a, b, c, and so on. If these items are of sufficient concern, name some blank sort box and storage tabs to fit the needs of your business.

No Entry-Accounting Income Statement for Joe's Cafe

The No-Entry Accounting income statement provides essential *cash management* data as compared to Schedule C *tax* data. When maintained over a span of years, these monthly statements can show you how your business is changing or how the environment you operate in is changing by comparing current monthly and year-to-date data. One of the key attributes of successful business owners is the ability to adapt quickly to changes in business conditions, and these statements give you a detailed view of what is happening with your business. Figure 10.7 gives the completed This Month column of the income statement for Joe's Cafe.

As you would expect, the major difference between monthly income statements and Schedule C accounting is in the calculation of cost of sales. If no inventory is required for your business (for example, if yours is a general contracting firm that does all work through subcontractors, or a firm that purchases items specifically for each job), then No-Entry Accounting provides everything needed for Schedule C. Be advised that the treatment of No-Entry Accounting for cost of sales may cause a variance in taxes due each quarter and at year end. By using the No-Entry income statement as is, the net profit result is "cash profit" and can therefore be carried directly to the cash analysis (described in Chapter 13) as a net cash in for the operating period. The profit computer using Part III of Schedule C cannot be.

There is probably also no need to separate mortgage and other types of interest on a monthly basis. If your business requires extensive entertainment and entertainment will be different because the Schedule C deducts 20 percent from entertainment at year end.

Cash In and Cash Out Sheet for Joe's Cafe

Figure 10.7 shows the completed income statement for Joe's Cafe. The starting place for this or any cash analysis is to ask whether the firm made a profit. Joe's Cafe did: $1364. All of this profit will appear in Joe's checkbook, because the profit was calculated using a cash method rather than accrual.

Is this profit reasonable by business standards? Figure 1.5 suggested that 3 percent net profit is on the high side for retail establishments. Because Joe's net profit of $1364 was based on sales of $8500, the percent profit is $1364 ÷ $8500 = 16 percent, which certainly seems healthy. However, Figure 3.1 noted that the accounting rules for sole proprietorships do not include a wage for the owner/operator. Because $1364 is a low monthly wage for managing a restaurant (assuming this was a full-time or nearly full-time job), once Joe "pays" himself a salary there is nothing left over as the owner's profit. This is reflected in Figure 10.8, which shows the numbers for cash received and spent.

Income Statement

	This Month	%	Year To Date	%
			Date _____	
Sales				
Category A	8,500	___	_____	___
Category B	_____	___	_____	___
Returns	(_____)	___	(_____)	___
Total Sales	_____	___	_____	___
Cost of Sales				
Category A	2,750	___	_____	___
Category B	_____	___	_____	___
Total Cost of Sales	(2,750)	___	(_____)	___
Gross Profit	5,750	___	_____	___
Operating Expenses				
Advertising	100	___	_____	___
Car and Truck	30	___	_____	___
Commissions	_____	___	_____	___
Depreciation & Section 179	17	___	_____	___
Wages	800	___	_____	___
Insurance	125	___	_____	___
Interest on Business Debt	600	___	_____	___
Legal, Professional	_____	___	_____	___
Office Supplies, Postage	62	___	_____	___
Rent & Leases	1,000	___	_____	___
Repairs & Maintenance	330	___	_____	___
Supplies Not For Resale	125	___	_____	___
Taxes & Licenses	543	___	_____	___
Travel, Meals, Entertainment	365	___	_____	___
Utilities, Telephone	250	___	_____	___
Bank Charges	_____	___	_____	___
Donations	_____	___	_____	___
Office Expense	_____	___	_____	___
Laundry, Cleaning	_____	___	_____	___
_____	_____	___	_____	___
_____	_____	___	_____	___
_____	_____	___	_____	___
Miscellaneous	50	___	_____	___
Total Operating Expenses	(4397)	___	(_____)	___
Net Profit or (Loss)	1353	___	_____	___

© 1984 by Robert E. Fleury

Figure 10.7. Completed Month's Figures of the Income Statement for Joe's Cafe

Cash In from	Amount	Cash Out to	Amount
Cash Profit	$1,353	Draw	$2,820
Loan Proceeds	2,000	Debt Retired	450
Personal Loan	100	Cash Register	500
Depreciation	17		
Total:	$3,470	Total	$3,770
Cash surplus	$		
Cash shortfall.	($300)		

Figure 10.8. Completed Cash In and Cash Out Sheet for Joe's Cafe

Of course, the record does not show all. Joe's Cafe is rented, and rent is included in the net profit. What if Joe is living in an apartment over the restaurant? How much is Joe spending on his monthly grocery bill? What if Joe's Cafe is situated in a building owned by Joe, and Joe is renting from his own property trust? What if Joe's Cafe is just part of Joe's Truck Stop or is situated right next to Joe's Motel?

However, in the absence of some benefit not apparent in the profit and loss statement alone, and assuming that this enterprise is Joe's main business activity, Joe may have a problem. His $1353 profit may represent nothing other than an entrepreneur who has purchased a job. To more accurately assess Joe's situation, it will be useful to look more closely at what is happening to Joe's cash. It would be useful to review the Schedule C (Figure 10.6) and the sort sheet (Figure 10.5) to see where Joe's cash came from for the month and where it went. You should come up with numbers like those in Figure 10.8.

Cash came in from $1353 in profits form the business, a $2000 loan that was deposited in the company checking account, another $100 loan that was made when Joe paid a utility bill with personal funds, and $17 in noncash depreciation expenses from the cash register purchased. The total cash received was $3,470.

The uses of cash began with $2820, which Joe drew for personal needs. Principal reduction of a loan balance used $450 in cash (interest was expensed through the $1,353 net profit). The cash register purchase did not pass through the profit and loss statement except as a depreciation expense of $17. The cash register was purchased for $500, and $17 came back as depreciation expense.

The $300 shortfall in cash represents what is only the beginning of a more serious problem. By drawing $2,820 from a business that made only $1353 in profits, Joe had a cash shortfall, even though he borrowed an additional $2000. That loan has locked $2000 in future profits into the debt-to-equity transfer. No outside accounting service could pick this problem up, because it stems more from personal considerations than business ones. It could not be discovered without using cash analysis.

Another problem lies waiting in the wings. None of the $1,353 profit has yet been contributed for the earnings-to-equity transfer. That is, the community has delivered equity in the form of a market (customers), a community infrastructure (roads, schools, and so on), and a free enterprise atmosphere (police and fire

164

protection, civil defense, and a retirement plan) for which some payment is due. In Joe's case the payments due are as follows:

- Self-employment tax (social security for self-employed people), which under current law is 13%, for a total of $1,353 x 0.13 = $176.

- Sales tax, which Joe has presumably been collecting but has not yet paid. Assuming the tax in Joe's area is 2 percent, his liability is $8500 x 0.02 = $170.

- Assuming Joe averages $1,400 a month in profits, his annual profit would be $16,800. If Joe has no other source of income, he would likely not owe any federal tax. He might, however, owe state income tax. If the state tax is 2 percent, for this month he would owe $1,353 x 0.02 = $27.00.

- Because Joe is in a rented space, no additional property tax would be due. He might, of course, owe for local taxes, but you can assume not.

Joe's total tax obligation from $1,353 in profit is $373, which means that 27 percent of monthly profits must be paid in the form of taxes so that the entrepreneur can continue to receive this community equity.

If Joe has just started this business and if he is a typical beginning entrepreneur, he will wait until year end before he attempts to figure his taxes. By that time the total obligation will be $4,476 ($373 x 12 months). If Joe did not put aside $373 each month (leaving only $980 to live on), this large tax bill will trigger the Cycle of Demise. Joe will be shocked and amazed at the sudden onset of such a large tax bill. Of course, the obligation is not sudden—only Joe's knowledge of the amount has come about suddenly.

The unpaid taxes are only a part of the float that comes due soon. What about the phone bill that was generated during the month that will come due next month? What about the meat, vegetables, and supplies for which a bill has not yet been received? The accumulation of these various obligations—personal and business—gives rise to the need to complete the monthly cash analysis form. It covers the half of the cash cycle that the profit and loss process ignores. The cash-basis profit and loss statement is the history of cash flow. The cash analysis statement is the future of cash flow. Only with both of these documents can Joe, or anyone else, make informed decisions and guide the business to success.

Summary

Take a look back to review what you have been exposed to with the case problem. These are a real and complete set of transactions from a living, breathing business. The "posting" of expenses is real clerical work that should be done monthly. In the absence of the No-Entry Accounting filing system, it must either be done by some other manual method or be duplicated with a computer. To summarize the whole picture, consider this. Any accounting system mused must provide for these three considerations.

1. The process must be complete through providing detailed cash analysis information.

2. The process used must provide for accuracy with debits and credit or double adding machine tapes of computed amounts and account numbers, if they are used.

3. The process must provide an efficient audit trail so efficiencies gained with one part of the system, such as check writing, are not given back through handling exceptions, and awkward time-consuming handling of audits and queries.

The problem with existing systems is that they are very good at pieces of the puzzle, but the handling of exceptions invariably overwhelms the effectiveness of the efficient parts. No-Entry Accounting eliminates the posting and creating of an efficient audit trial without ever duplicating effort. To the small business owner this translates directly to time available for other projects without sacrificing the completely informed state that is required for success.

Preparing the case problem should have left you with the recognition that the preparation of tax forms is probably only 5 percent of the tax job, much of which is simple copying. The other 95 percent must usually be done in-house before forms can be completed. The act of performing this work is itself the source of the knowledge base so necessary for success. If you leave it to others, your knowledge base erodes.

You should now be aware that the information of most value to the entrepreneur (cash management information) is masked to some extent by either cash or accrual accounting. No-Entry Accounting puts the focus on cash accounting to facilitate the most efficient collection of cash data, but provides for the accrual contribution to the equation that stems from tax time. At the same time it provides most efficiently for handling exceptions and is unparalleled in terms of simplicity, daily usability, and a complete audit trail.

You will find very few failing businesses run by those who are at home with the Joe's Cafe case problem. So, the secret to success is no longer a secret. When you learn and use the contents of this case problem, you will have acquired the entrepreneurial navigation skills required to succeed.

Chapter 11

Valuing a Business:
Ace Trucking Company
Case Study

This chapter presents a second
case study: Ace Trucking Company.
The case study is intended to help you
learn how to value your small business, especially as a prelude to selling it. The approach I show
here can also help you value a business you may buy. So
to set the stage for valuing Ace Trucking Company—and
vicariously, your own business—take some time to learn the ins
and outs of the sale of a small business.

Buying and Selling a Small Business

Small businesses are constantly up for sale. Even most of those that are not
advertised can be purchased. Experience has shown that many owners are disillu-
sioned with the long hours and what seems to be the small returns their businesses
provide. Owners of these businesses are often looking for a way out. Most entrepreneurs begin with a grand perception of the easy money available from a small
business. This perception lingers—even with some owners who have failed miserably.
Sellers of such operations try to recover their losses by passing along their illusion
to possible buyers. Enough buyers believe the dream that there is an unending string
of business failures.

Preventing the First Pitfall: Inflated Purchase Price

Perhaps as many as a third of the small business owners I have had the opportunity
to question had no chance to succeed from the day they bought their businesses—
the only question was how long the ventures would take to fail. The most common
difficulty is that the business does not generate sufficient cash both for normal
operations (including salaries for the owners and others) and to meet the buyout
costs. The Cycle of Demise is triggered before the ink on the contract is dry.

The problem is that some owners are able to sell their businesses on contract to
unsuspecting, ignorant buyers. The very hint of a contract sale is the first warning

that you, as a prospective buyer, need to watch for. Almost no one will sell a business on contract if a bank will finance the sale. The reason banks do not finance most business purchases is because the loans are not bankable. This means that a prospective borrower has insufficient cash flow or collateral (or both) to meet the requirements of regulated lending institutions. A nonbankable loan is one in which full and timely repayment is not certain. If foreclosure becomes necessary, the collateral provided is insufficient to satisfy the outstanding debt. The certainty of repayment regarding a prospective loan does not get any better by setting up the loan outside banking channels through buying on contract.

From the buyer's point of view, insufficient collateral or insufficient cash flow means for practical purposes that the business has too high a price. The most common technique used to convince a buyer that a business is worth more than the records indicate is to convince the buyer that skimming is taking place and that it is lucrative. "The reasons for not showing all this extra cash in the accounting record are obvious," the seller exclaims! It is left for the buyer to imagine what really goes on behind the scenes. Buyer beware! If a claim is not verifiable in a business's tax record, it's not true!

From the seller's perspective, selling for an inflated price on contract has its perils, as well. If a business has some asset value, it can be lost as a result of financing a purchase that is priced too high.

The buyer's first hint of trouble is coming to grips with a lack of cash. All the income seems to be going to the seller for the monthly contract payments. Once the buyer is tapped out, he or she becomes disenchanted with the entrepreneurial condition. The new owner lets the business run down, partly from hopelessness and partly as a reprisal for the injustice he or she feels. In the back of the new owner's mind hides the thought that the contract purchase will never be paid for. Long-time customers become disgruntled and go elsewhere. They may even be run off. Facilities deteriorate or are intentionally damaged. Of course, the contract payments stop, and the buyer walks out on the deal.

The seller is left with a facility in shambles. Lost customers may not be retrievable. Finally, the seller is left with a need for more cash than the cash that was received from monthly payments and the initial downpayment. Perhaps months of future mortgage payments will add to the cash problem, with no tenant income to cover them. The buyer loses whatever money and time were invested. The buyer's credit rating will also likely suffer.

Both the buyer and the seller, therefore, are hurt by their lack of knowledge regarding what a business is really worth and what it takes to make a business run. Both buyers and sellers have a genuine interest in setting a fair price. The typical small business deal is not meant to swindle one side or the other; business deals can become a competition between different levels of ignorance. The level of ignorance on one side actually contributes to the ignorance on the other side to make the wrong joint decision. When a buyer and a seller's joint decision is placed into practice, the wisdom of their collective decision falls out. If their collective wisdom permits the profitable operation of the business, monthly payments can be made on time and in full to beat some long odds.

In my experience, a successful business that could be purchased with a bankable loan is seldom for sale. Such business owners are among the "millionaires" who have successfully trained others to manage their businesses in their absence. They have achieved high annual incomes without having to work any longer. The entrepreneurial dream, therefore, is obtained by diligent, knowledgeable, long-term commitment. Buying a business from a troubled operator at 10 cents on the dollar often doesn't work. Selling out to an unsuspecting buyer at 150 percent of real value doesn't work either. So here's how to improve your odds of doing the right thing.

Setting a Realistic Value

A small business owner or buyer can compute some approximate value of a business using the following formula.

Assets

Market value of assets _____

Outstanding loan balance − _____

Net value of assets _____

Profits

Current year (annualized) _____

Last year _____

Year before last _____

Total profit _____

Average profit (Total ÷ 3) _____

A range of prices

Net value of assets _____

3 x annual profits _____

10 x annual profits _____

The value of the business, then, is equal to the paid-up (same as net) value of its assets or from 3 to 10 times its average net profit. The choice between 3 times the net profit and 10 times the net profit depends on the business's potential. Have profits increased each year? The more likely the business is to continue or increase profits under a new owner, the more likely the price will be at the high end, or 10 times the yearly net profit. If profits are most likely to decline, the low-end price is more likely.

Another favorable factor promoting a high-end price is the likelihood that business assets may appreciate considerably in the future. For example, a hot dog stand sits at the edge of town. The local high school district is considering building a new high school on the adjoining property. If the new high school is built there, the value of the property on which the hot dog stand sits will rise and so will the value of the business.

Determining the Affordability of a Business You Want to Purchase

If a selling price is reasonable, is it affordable? Here is an easy way to check it out. If a cash shortfall is computed, there needs to be some very compelling reason to proceed with a purchase. Regardless of the profitability of a business, the value of its assets, the diligence of its owner, and so on, one thing is certain: If a business runs out of cash, it will fail.

Enter the following numbers to determine affordability of the business you are considering:

1. Monthly cash required for personal requirements (that is, for you and your family to live on)   _____
2. Monthly payment for purchase contract, including interest   _____
3. Other monthly cash requirements   _____
4. Total monthly cash requirement   _____
5. Subtract proven monthly cash profit computed using cash accounting method   – _____
6. Monthly cash surplus (shortfall)   _____

It is difficult to conceive of all the ways cash can run out of a business. This is especially true if a business is being operated by an owner who is ignorant of the concepts in this book. Paying too high a purchase price is just one way.

The Ace Trucking Company case study that follows applies the buying and selling concepts just outlined. If you are considering either buying or selling a small business this case study may be of use to you.

Ace Trucking Company: Purchasing an Existing Business

This case examines the purchase of a business as an example of the cash-handling principles that have been covered throughout Part II of this book. The Ace Trucking Company is for sale. It has two trucks valued at approximately $20,000. The trucks are more than 10 years old, but both are very serviceable and are being used daily. The dump truck hauls decorative stone for landscapers and occasionally some sand or gravel. The boom truck hauls pallets of material such as mortar, cement blocks, and palletized stone. The boom is the more expensive of the two and is in the best condition. A new truck of similar size and capability would cost $65,000 to $70,000.

Ace's business is based on a contract with a local quarry. The first contract's term was six years. The contract has just been renewed for two additional years. Ace's owner, Brett states that the contract is very secure, because it requires an interstate commerce permit, which Ace Trucking owns. More importantly, the boom truck is the only one commercially available within 30 miles. All the other boom trucks in the area are owned by competitive businesses. The quarry has found it very difficult to obtain one of these trucks, even on an emergency basis. Brett explains that as long as the service is reasonable and timely, the contract will be renewed indefinitely.

The revenue for the first six years is plotted in Figure 11.1. The only problem encountered in the last six years occurred when the prime rate reached 20 percent and caused the building of homes and offices to slow considerably. The forecast is for steady growth, particularly for the boom truck.

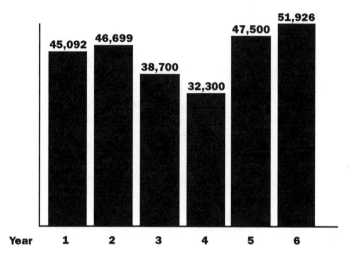

Annual Sales Volume

Figure 11.1. Ace Trucking Sales History

Another advantage of the business is that it is busy only eight months out of the year. Only May, June, July, and August have so much business that a part-time driver is necessary. The rest of the months, Brett does all the driving and completes the work in fewer than 40 hours per week. Brett's daughter was able to earn enough to pay most of her college tuition by helping out during the summer. Figure 11.2 shows that the owner has nearly four months a year with little or no work.

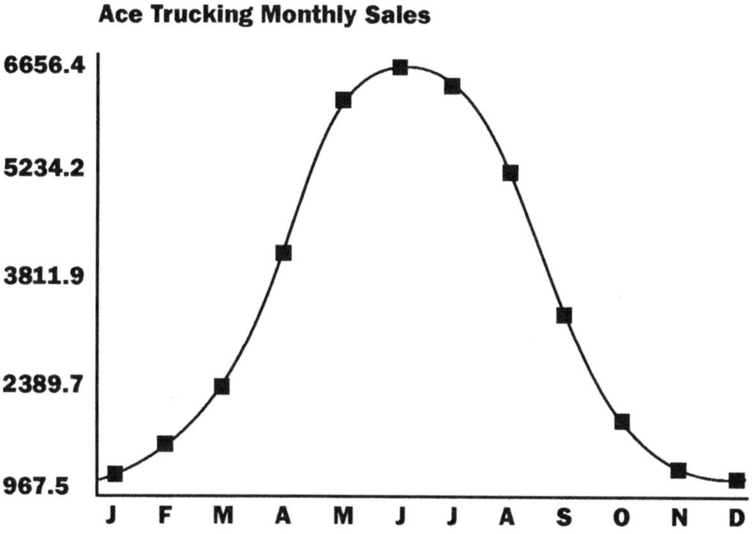

Ace Trucking Monthly Sales

Figure 11.2. Plot of Ace Trucking's Monthly Revenue

171

The net profit margin has grown to 65 percent since the revenue reached almost $50,000. The three-year average profit was closer to 50 percent, however. There is ample truck time available so there is no anticipated need for additional equipment.

The contract includes an escalator clause that permits the hourly rate to be adjusted annually on the anniversary, and quarterly, if fuel prices increase sharply. The hourly rate has been increased five out of the six years with no animosity.

Brett wants $50,000 in cash to sell Ace Trucking. He has found a prospective buyer, but of course the buyer does not have $50,000 in cash. He does have $15,000 in cash, however, and he and his wife own their home. The net collateral available in the home is $40,000. The buyer has had a good job in the city for a few years that has paid him gross wages of $30,000. The job has netted about $2,000 a month, which his family finds sufficient to meet their needs.

How would you advise the prospective buyer? How would you advise the prospective seller? Would you buy a business, any business, under similar conditions?

Valuing the Business

The first consideration for the prospective buyer is how much *cash* the business generates. The revenue chart for Ace Trucking shows a range from $32,000 to $52,000, with a definite upward trend. For the purpose of this question, assume $48,000 as the revenue generated annually, which seems reasonable to expect over the next couple of years. The net profit margin for the last year of operation was 65 percent. The business is a sole proprietorship, so conventional accounting does not provide a salary for the proprietor himself. Therefore, the 65 percent margin must account for *both* the real profit margin and the fair wage the proprietor should earn doing the job he is doing. Therefore:

Gross Revenue	$48,000
Net Profit (%)	x .65
Net cash available from operations	$31,200

Considering How to Finance the Purchase

A second consideration is arranging sufficient financing to make the purchase. The buyer has $15,000 of his own, which he is willing to use for a down payment. The estimated value of the trucks is $20,000. The ICC permit and the two-year contract also have some value and are, in fact, essential to the business operation. However, a lender will probably not give collateral credit for these items, so we will not either. From the bank's point of view, we see:

Purchase price	$50,000
Downpayment	- 15,000
To be financed	$35,000

A $35,000 loan could be collateralized by the bank holding title to the $20,000 worth of trucks and by taking a second mortgage on the $40,000 equity the buyer has in his home. The bank could show $60,000 in collateral for a $35,000 loan. In addition, loan officers could take comfort in the fact that the buyer has also placed $15,000 of his own cash into the business and obviously thinks enough of his chances to put his home on the line, as well. It is likely that the buyer would be able to get financing, probably in the form of a five-year $35,000 loan, secured by the trucks and the home. Suppose the terms were five years at a rate of somewhere around 13 percent interest.

Therefore:

Net cash proceeds from operations	$31,200
First-year interest and principal	- 9,557
($7,000 principal plus 13% of	
$35,000 interes	$21,643
Annual personal requirement	-24,000
Self-employment tax on $31,200	- 4,212
First-year cash shortfall	($6,569)

This scenario assumes there is no income tax due in the first year due to business interest, depreciation, and investment tax credit, plus deductions for personal items such as a wife and three children, mortgage interest, property taxes, sales tax, and other itemized deductions. During the second year, there will likely be some income tax, because the investment tax credit would be gone. The second year shortfall could well be greater than the first.

At this point, the buyer and his accountant, if the buyer has one, have concluded that Brett is asking too much for his business. They calculate that $30,000 is a more appropriate selling price, thus requiring only a $15,000 loan. The numbers now look as follows:

Net cash proceeds	$31,200
Less self-employment tax	- 4,212
Less annual personal requirement	-24,000
First-year debt retirement	
($15,000 x 13% = $1950 interest)	- 1,950
First-year principal	- 3,000
First-year cash flow shortfall	($ 1,962)

The buyer believes that he will be able to make up this shortfall by doing side jobs in the off months, so he makes a counteroffer to buy the business at $30,000.

Brett is, of course, very disappointed at the prospect that his business is only worth $30,000. Before he accepts this view, he does some math of his own.

Net cash proceeds *at least*	$33,200
(Considering the last year was	
$52,000, instead of $48,000, which	
the buyer used)	
Less self-employment tax	- 4,482
Less annual personal requirement	-24,000
Less first-year interest & principal	- 9,557
First year cash shortfall	($ 4,839)

Brett takes the time to point out several factors that the buyer and his accountant had overlooked. First, the $33,200 income was from just eight months of work. Therefore,

1. Brett knows that he has never earned less than $4,000 in the off season, and his earnings have been as high as $10,000. Assume a cash contribution annually of $5,000.

2. The buyer would save the cost of transportation to and from the city. Gas, tolls, parking, repairs, and perhaps lower insurance premiums could provide $800 per year in cash not available before.

3. Depreciation of up to $10,000 (using Section 179) would combine with an office in the home deduction on the order of $1,000 to yield a first-year tax avoidance of approximately $3,000 ($1,000 from self-employment and $1,700 from withholding).

So, the real numbers are as follows:

Off-season wages	$5,000
Transportation savings	800
Tax avoidance	3,000
Cash surplus	$8,800

Brett maintains that this surplus is more than enough to carry a $35,000 loan instead of a $15,000 loan.

As you can see, a purchase price somewhere between $35,000 and $50,000 is workable for the buyer. The closer the price is to $35,000, the more likely the buyer is to obtain financing. The closer to $50,000, the greater the likelihood the seller will need to sell on contract and take the risk of financing the sale himself.

Summary

Learning how to value a business is an important part of building a business. In essence, the value that someone else would place on your business is like a report card for your hard work. The primary barometer that buyers and bankers use to determine value is profitability. Current and past profitability are primary determinants in setting the value of a business. It's important to note, however, that there is rarely a single precise value for a business. A business (like most anything else) is worth as much as someone else is willing to pay for it. If you are buying a business, that means you should concern yourself not just with value but also with affordability.

There are two ways to fail before you start: paying too high a price to purchase a business and buying a business you can't afford. Often, these two problems coincide, with calamitous results.

Chapter 12

Changing Over to
No-Entry Accounting

As I've discussed previously, for the majority of small businesses, the accrual accounting picture is the opposite of what the owner needs to see in trying to optimize the chance for success. To recap the reasons why:

- The practice of accrual accounting dictates the need for at least three times as much work when compared to the work in cash basis accounting.

- The results of accrual accounting are designed to fit nicely into a tidy, in-balance package, neatly trimmed of its peaks and valleys. This trimming and balancing essentially masks any cash control data.

- To obtain data about your actual cash situation in an accrual system, you must completely regenerate the income statement using the cash method. The cash analysis statement (Figure 13.1) shows that cash profit is necessary information for a complete cash picture. Cash profit or loss during a period is typically a large part of this picture; cash analysis is worthless without it. Using cash basis accounting, though, you only need to duplicate the financial statement process to report year-end taxes if accrual accounting was selected as the method for reporting your company's finances on Schedule C.

Reinstating Cash Accounting for Day-to-Day Transactions

Accrual accounting has little to recommend its use for millions of typical small business enterprises. Okay, what can you do about it? First, if you have not yet begun, start with the cash method. If you have already begun and are on the accrual method you *can* change back—at least for your basic transaction accounting. You can use cash basis accounting throughout the year and revert to accrual accounting only for developing the final statement: Schedule C. The other possibility is to write the IRS for permission to change your method.

The math required is written into the Schedule C, Part III. The cash basis figure is the one you use throughout the year for cash management data; the accrual figure is used each time you take a physical inventory. Using both accounting systems in this way enables you to accurately forecast your taxes due and achieve greater overall accuracy of your cash position.

The No-Entry Accounting method recommends immediately expensing all purchases of inventory intended for resale, regardless of whether these items have been sold. Doing so results in a taxes-due variance between cash and accrual numbers, because some inventory may not have been sold. Income is shown lower—there are higher expenses, because all purchases were expensed immediately when some items remain in inventory. Lower income means lower income tax. A year-end tax surprise could result. The No-Entry Accounting system recommends a monthly physical inventory. If you do complete the count, compute the cost of sales using *both* methods so that the cash position will properly reflect cash flow from cost of sale purchases *and* taxes due.

If you want to use cash basis through the year and continue to report on the accrual basis, here are the differences:

- Accounts receivable—those sales that have taken effect (for which the product or service has been delivered)—will have to be counted even if the cash has not yet been received.

- Cost of sales will have to be generated under accrual accounting if your business has inventory for resale. This work is no different under either system, though, because year-end tax reporting requires a physical inventory and mandatory use of the accrual method for computing cost of sales even if you selected the cash method of accounting for the return. The cash method used for taxes is, therefore, really a modified cash basis.
  Note: This text has in several chapters pointed out that businesses that keep inventory in stock for resale must use accrual accounting for cost of sales, even if they use cash accounting on Schedule C.

- Any expenses—such as insurance—that have been paid for and not completely used must be adjusted on the Schedule C. An annual insurance policy costing $1,200 is completely expensed in cash basis accounting once it is paid. If the check is returned in July with the June bank statement, only six months of the prepaid insurance will have been used up. The $1,200 expensed under cash accounting will have to be reduced to $600 on the Schedule C, because six months of the coverage remains unused. This kind of adjustment is necessary for accrual reporting of any prepaid expense.

- Any expense that has been incurred but for which no cash has as yet changed hands would also have to be adjusted onto the Schedule C. For example, as of December 31 employees have worked two weeks on a job that have not yet been reflected in the form of a paycheck. The paychecks are due on January 2, for example. The labor expense not yet paid would have to be added to the cash basis labor computed through the year when the numbers are transferred to the Schedule C. The same is true for materials and other expenses that have been incurred but for which cash has not yet changed hands.

- All outstanding checks and deposits (those in float) that represent business expenses and income will have to be subtracted and added, respectively, to the cash basis totals before they are transferred to the Schedule C.

It looks like a lot of work to switch between the two systems, and it is! However, it is surely more simple to switch to accrual accounting once a year than to do it each month. And it is worth the time for you to be aware of where your money is going all year long.

The Importance of a Cutoff Date

No-Entry Accounting, as a standard practice but not as a mandatory practice, uses the documents that have been generated during the monthly bank statement period. The date of the bank statement becomes the cutoff date each month. If your bank returns the canceled checks, no extra work or separation of documents is necessary. Simply generate the monthly statements using the returned documents and any miscellaneous receipts collected since the last statement was prepared. If your bank does not return the canceled checks and provides carbon sets for checks in your checkbook, take care in your statement preparation to use only the check copies that have cleared the bank.

If your former accounting system used the end of the month as the cutoff date, the resulting financial statements will vary from those that use the bank statement date. Often the bank cutoff date and end of the month are days apart. When you are a new No-Entry Accounting user, change over to bank statement dates from month-end statement dates during a period when the resulting statements will vary only slightly. A month when the calendar month and the bank statement date may coincide or where few additional transactions have occurred would be best.

Changing from a Computerized General Ledger to No-Entry Accounting

The changeover from a computerized ledger system to No-Entry Accounting is very simple indeed. Simply prepare the No-Entry Accounting financial statements using the instructions given in Part II and add the resulting totals to the year-to-date account figures from the existing system. If you have used a spreadsheet type program, simply change the spreadsheet titles to those used with the No-Entry Accounting system. You can use your computer to print neat copies of monthly statements instead of using the fill-in-the-blanks system. If account numbers were used on your spreadsheets, change them to coincide with the Schedule C line numbers.

New users sometimes choose to generate entirely new year-to-date statements under No-Entry Accounting. This procedure serves as a good practice run and results in the records for the entire year being in audit-ready condition. First-time users will be amazed at the speed at which an entire year can be prepared under No-Entry Accounting. If you regenerate year-to-date totals, prepare an income statement through month three, then four and five, then six through eight, and then the balance of the year. These statement dates coincide with the report dates for IRS

Form 2210, which permits both corporate and personal related taxes to be deposited as earned rather than on an even quarterly basis. Using the Form 2210 can be very helpful in managing your cash, and the form is easy to use if financial statements have been prepared showing net income through these dates.

Starting No-Entry Accounting from Scratch

Here is a checklist to use if you have never set up a business accounting system.

1. Call the IRS 800 number and order a free copy of IRS Publication 334, *Tax Guide for Small Businesses.*

2. Create your own sort box and permanent storage box or order your No-Entry Accounting materials using the order form in the back of this book.

3. If your business owns any equipment or property to be used in the business, read the depreciation information in Chapter 6 and in Publication 334, and list all your depreciable assets on the depreciation spreadsheet. Compute your monthly depreciation expense as indicated and directly enter that amount monthly on the No-Entry Accounting income statement, line 13. When a change takes place—which is seldom with small businesses—recompute the depreciation amount and enter it each month. Depreciation is an item you report in detail in your annual tax filing. The Form 4562 is used to make this report. The accounting and tax cycle flow chart (Figure 18.1) reminds you to complete this form as a supplement to deductions taken on Line 13 of the Schedule C at year end. See Publication 334 for more details if necessary.

4. If you intend to operate an office in your home, read Chapters 8 and 13, study the form included there for your calculations. The documents you need for reporting home office expenses can be accumulated through the year as they are handled the first time and stored in the Office in the Home section in the permanent storage box. Computing the deduction at year end, then, will take only minutes rather than the hours it may take just to find these documents if they are not collected throughout the year.

5. Use blank copies of the cash analysis statement (Figure 13.1), balance sheet (Figure 8.5), and the income statement (Figure 8.4) to develop a forecast of your anticipated venture. Simply fill in lines that will have meaning to your business. The process of completely thinking through your venture can be enlightening.

6. If you do not already know, learn how to balance your checkbook. The monthly process begins with balancing the checkbook. Instructions are included on your bank statement.

7. Begin collecting every business document as transactions happen. If they involve anything but checks, sort these documents immediately into the sort box for storage until the bank statement arrives. Include cash receipts, charge card tickets, bills of sale, amortization schedules, loan papers, purchase agreements, and all other reports of transactions. Once the first bank statement arrives and the checkbook is balanced, sort the checks together with the documents already in the sort box and tally them to create the financial statements. The accounting and tax cycle flow chart will guide you through the

monthly, quarterly, and annual accounting, filing, and tax processing for business and personal state and federal taxes. Bear in mind that state reporting requirements vary, and so you may need to verify and alter the state and local reporting requirements on the flow chart.

8. Keep copies of all bills that do not represent paid cash receipts in a single file folder. No particular order is necessary. The only purpose for keeping these documents is as proof of business expense supporting canceled checks should an auditor demand it. Most always, however, the canceled checks or paid cash receipt is sufficient.

Summary

Now you can see that getting started with No-Entry Accounting will take much less time than it takes to read this book. Simply collecting every business document and learning to use receipts and checks properly to generate your own warning system is 90 percent of the solution to *the* entrepreneurial problem of getting your business through the periods when more cash is needed than is available. Learning to deal with your banker—the subject of Chapter 16—will help with the other 10 percent.

Part III

Cash Analysis

The purpose of this section is to familiarize you with the basics of cash management. Cash analysis includes both forecasting and looking back at your cash position. To understand the concept, I begin this part with a delineation of the sources of a cash fund, as described in Chapter 13. Chapter 14 develops the uses of the cash fund. Chapter 15 puts the two together to provide for forecasting cash requirements and looking back to understand how you have used or misused cash. This part also gives insights into where to look to find the cash you can use to deal with a cash short situation.

Cash analysis is often relegated to the "nice to know" category by small business owners who are thoroughly overworked. But understanding where you *now* are in terms of cash, planning for where you will be, and analyzing your company's own records can make a tremendous difference to the overall financial success of your firm.

Chapter 13

Sources of Cash

This chapter is intended to familiarize you with the basics of cash management. It begins by delineating the sources of a cash fund. (Chapter 14 will show you the uses of the cash fund.)

Cash, as used here, refers to two things. One is actual currency—that is, cold, hard, green cash. However, for the purpose of this discussion, goods or services that can be obtained and used without the immediate payment of cash are also considered to be the same as cash. Using the telephone for a month without having to pay until 30 days later is one example.

Cash Analysis

Cash analysis is a key tool for managing your business. It is not meant to be esoteric or unwieldy. It is simply a statement of the cash funds available minus the cash required, which enables you to assess your cash surplus or shortfall—in a nutshell, your cash position.

The cash analysis form shown in Figure 13.1 has several uses. When you assign it a period such as a month or a quarter, it serves as an outline for your short-term cash requirements plan. When used at year end, it becomes the form for reconciling the year's use of cash. It helps you analyze where cash came from and where it was used. A look at the viability of a new business can be had by filling in a cash analysis form and a No-Entry Accounting income statement, with forecasts or estimated data. The specific purpose of the cash analysis form through these various uses, then, is to help you understand enough about your cash position to steer clear of the Cycle of Demise.

Small businesses are frequently cash short. Even successful small business owners may be rich on paper (that is, they have high net worth) but may be cash

Cash Analysis

Cash Requirements Through _____

1.	Outstanding Checks, Bank Reconciliation	_____
2.	Self-Employment Tax[a]	_____
3.	Federal Payroll Tax Deposit	_____
4.	State Payroll Tax Deposit	_____
5.	State Unemployment Deposit	_____
6.	Federal Unemployment Deposit	_____
7.	State Sales Tax	_____
8.	Est. Qtr. Income Tax Deposit	_____
9.	Notes Due (Debt Retirement)	_____
10.	Insurance Prepayment	_____
11.	Property Taxes	_____
12.	Bills Due in Forecast Period	_____
13.	Forecast Cash Loss[b]	_____
14.	Inventory Growth	_____
15.	Accounts Receivable Growth	_____
16.	Post-Dated Checks Already Issued	_____
17.	Operating Reserve	_____
18.	Minimum Personal Requirements (Draw)	_____
19.	Overdrafts Already Written	_____
20.	Other _____	

Total cash required for the period: _____

Cash Available Through _____

1.	Outstanding Deposits, Bank Reconciliation	_____
2.	Checking Accounts	_____
3.	Savings Accounts	_____
4.	Accounts Receivable Collection	_____
5.	Forecast Cash Profit[c]	_____
6.	Borrowed Money	_____
7.	Notes Receivable	_____
8.	Capital Deposits	_____
9.	Inventory Reduction	_____
10.	Post-Dated Checks To Be Issued	_____
11.	Depreciation, Home Office Expense (Anticipated)	_____
12.	Overdrafts	_____
13.	Other Income	_____

Total cash available for the period: _____

Cash Shortfall _____

Cash Surplus _____

[a]For sole proprietorships only: 15.3% of profit deposited quarterly.
[b]Write in estimates on a blank profit and loss form. Record loss here.
[c]Record a forecasted profit here.

Figure 13.1. Cash Analysis Form for No-Entry Accounting

poor. Cash analysis enables you to better manage this most precious resource: your cash. Note that beyond what's available to you in the bank, the form details a number of other sources of cash. The rest of this chapter discusses these sources of cash.

Cash Profit

Cash profit is the source of cash entrepreneurs most hope to obtain: not accrual profit, but *cash* profit. To arrive at a *cash* profit figure, the monthly accounting must be done on a cash basis. If accrual accounting is used, cash profit must later be backed out in an additional accounting operation.

Other sources of cash essentially go from zero to some positive value. Cash profit, however, can swing into the minus range as a loss and become a consumer of cash instead. The double-edged nature of profit as a source of cash is the reason it must be the focus of entrepreneurial attention. The moment between profit and loss can be compared to a lighted room. Visualize the light switch being suddenly turned off. It is either light or dark with very little in between.

This on-or-off nature of cash profit dictates the need for a monthly profit and loss statement. If the statement is done monthly, it can help you create more accurate forecasts for the same months in future years. Even the smallest businesses can benefit from this monthly regimentation and the information it provides. The month-to-month lack of accurate knowledge regarding the true cash profit position of a business is probably the most common trigger mechanism for the Cycle of Demise.

Checking and Savings Accounts

Bank accounts are, of course, the most immediate source of cash available to a business operator. Both business and personal accounts are commonly involved in small businesses. It is important to keep the various accounts separate and in balance so that nonproductive overdraft charges and other account expenses are minimized.

Corporations must be certain that business and personal accounts do not become intermingled; proprietorships are permitted to intermingle personal and company accounts as their needs are best served. The No-Entry Accounting system provides for appropriate separation for proprietors at statement preparation and tax time.

Deferred Payment of Accounts Payable

Putting off paying the bills due is a widely used means of providing operating cash. It provides no cash directly and is included as part of the "bills due in the forecast period" notation on the cash analysis form. The deferred payment for goods or services results in free cash when the goods or services are sold but have not yet been paid for. An account flush with cash from this process can cause the unknowing entrepreneur to become lulled into a false sense of success. The entrepreneur who runs a business by the balance in the checkbook is particularly vulnerable to overusing this source of cash.

Deferred payment of accounts payable is essentially an interest-free loan. The term of this loan varies based on the industry involved and the creditworthiness of each business. Some businesses are allowed 60 or 90 days to pay for their purchases. Most businesses get at least 30 days. Still others with poor credit must pay cash and, therefore, do not have access to this interest-free loan.

Interest-Free Loan Example

A look at a single vendor will show the effect of deferred payment, but this same effect will be felt across the sum of all vendors' credit within a particular business. Assume that an entrepreneur just opened a restaurant and ordered a one-week supply of meat. The meat vendor discovers that the company's credit is good and has given 30 days' credit. The first week's purchase is $300. The meat vendor prepares a delivery invoice in the amount of $300 that the restaurateur signs, indicating that the meat had been received.

The first week draws to an end, with the restaurant having served and been paid for all the meat on hand. The meat vendor delivers again at the beginning of the second week. The restaurateur signs another delivery invoice. This process continues through the fourth delivery, as summarized in Figure 13.2 (see X). The fourth delivery coincides with the meat company's 30-day billing cycle (at A1), so a statement is prepared listing all four deliveries. Such a statement is typically mailed to each of the customers. The meat vendor expects that once the statement is received, the restaurateur will promptly write a check and send it to the meat vendor. In practice, this process typically takes two weeks. Therefore, the restaurant check does not reduce the restaurateur's bank balance for *six weeks* from the first purchase (A in the figure).

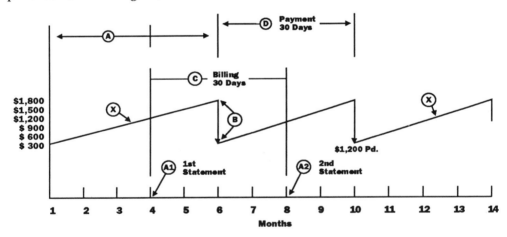

Figure 13.2. Deferred Payment of Accounts Payable

The restaurant's bank account would have swollen from the cash generated by having been paid for six weeks' worth of meals using the meat. This cash would have come in at the fully marked-up price, and not just the cost price.

From C, the 30-day billing cycle develops. The next statement will be received in just two weeks, because two weeks have passed since the first statement or bill was received from the meat vendor (A1 and A2). It will include the four deliveries from the second month in business. If the vendor is prompt with the statement and

the restaurant is prompt with the check, the check will be drawn on the restaurant account approximately 30 days after the previous check. Hence, the 30-day payment cycle (D).

The average cash fund contribution generated from the 30-day cycle from this single vendor based on the price paid is $300 times 4 weeks, or $1,200 (B). Presumably, all the meat was sold at a markup of at least four times. Therefore, meat sales from the first four weeks generated cash of $4,800 ($300 at cost times 400% markup = $1,200 times 4 weeks sales = $4,800).

The sum of money owed ($300 weekly meat purchase times four weeks = $1,200) and cash in hand of $4,800 combine ($1,200 plus $4,800) to present a $6,000 cash management situation. If the same principle is extended over all payables such as utilities, other suppliers, and rent, a large operating cash fund can be generated even for small businesses. In general, however, the larger the business, the larger the deferred payment of accounts payable cash fund.

It is common to find businesses with no monthly accounting statements being run on the premise that, "If there is cash in the bank account, everything is okay." The entrepreneur tends to treat this cash as just reward for operating a business. The cash is often spent before the final accounting results show that at 10 percent profit from $4,800, only $480 was just reward ($4,800 times 10 percent, or 0.1 = $480). What if profit for the restaurant was only 2.5 percent or even 0 percent? If more than the real cash profit dollars—whatever that amount might be—was spent on other than business expenses, the Cycle of Demise may be triggered.

The actual size of the deferred payment fund will vary monthly and therefore should be monitored monthly. Even businesses with a relatively consistent monthly income will fluctuate as annual insurance premiums come due or as a note payment comes due. It may also fluctuate as the owner's personal need for cash varies, such as during the Christmas holidays or at vacation time.

Cyclical Businesses

For the cyclical business, cash management is a big problem. Sufficient cash must be generated in a few months to carry the business obligations for an entire year. The deferred payment cash fund cycle begins and ends with each season. The major problem is that the cash borrowed against future business is easy to get and feel comfortable with as a new season begins. As the season ends with sharply declining revenues, however, there is often insufficient cash to cover the bills from the boom half of the cycle. This is particularly true for new businesses or for businesses with owners who do not use monthly accounting and therefore interpret large amounts of cash as large amounts of profit.

Abusing Interest-Free Loans

During the first few years, most proprietorships and small corporations do not earn sufficient profit/income to be required to pay income tax. How then do they survive? How do they feed their families and seem to do well enough to win the respect of their peers?

Cash Analysis

The answer lies in the deferred payment of accounts payable. The owner of a business whose annual gross revenue is only $50,000 could develop a 30-day fund of several thousand dollars. Extended to 60 or 90 days, it could be much larger. This fund bears no interest and requires no principal reduction. It may be borrowed against forever, as long as the uses of cash in total do not exceed the sources of cash.

The overuse of deferred accounts payable has a subtle dark side. It harbors a triggering mechanism for the Cycle of Demise. Deferred payment of Accounts Payable can be compared to a garden hose or a rope (as in Figure 13.3) that has been whipped, sending a loop rolling along its length. The earlier restaurant example depicts week 6's incoming cash as being available for week 1's bills. The size of the rope's loop represents the total cash available from this source. The business owner can in effect, if not in fact, put the entire cash proceeds of the first five weeks directly into his or her pocket. This is possible as long as the cash from week 6 pays all the bills generated in week 1, the cash from week 7 pays all the bills from week 2, and so on.

Figure 13.3. The Rolling Cash Fund

The roll can continue indefinitely, as long as total uses of cash do not exceed cash sources and bills due are paid on time. The real size of the loop—and therefore the size of the cash fund—is in a constant state of flux, however. If the size of the loop declines, as when a loss occurs, the cash from week 6 may be insufficient to cover week 1's expenses. The business owner will have to borrow on week 7's cash to cover the shortfall. The potential for failure develops the moment the size of the loop decreases and some other source is not available to cover the shortfall.

Accounts Receivable

The money owed to your business is a source of cash in two ways. If you prepare a short-term—perhaps 30-day—forecast, any cash from accounts that are about to be collected would certainly be counted as a source. In the overall perspective, however, accounts receivable is really only a source of cash if total receivables are in a state of decline. The decline would yield cash if one paid up receivable is not replaced by a new receivable (as is the case when a business closes). If a business uses accounts receivable, it must be able to fund the cash operating costs associated with continuing in business while the company waits for the cash payment. This funding is a *use* of cash rather than a *source* of cash until the process stops growing.

188

Inventory

Inventory can certainly be used as a source of cash. This is no simple task, however, because keeping exactly the right items on hand in the right quantity is in itself a science. A small error in overstocking or purchasing the wrong items can tie up large amounts of cash. It is not uncommon to see an entire year's profits (and therefore, a significant amount of cash) tied up in the "paid-for value of inventory" that did not sell.

The sidewalk sales seen during the summer are examples of how the business owner attempts to unlock cash. The items on sale are typically ones that did not sell at full price during the high-demand season. The astute business owner knows that it is better to sell something at cost, or sometimes even at a loss, than to have cash unavailable to fund purchases for the next season.

When it becomes necessary to use inventory as a source of cash solely for the purpose of generating cash, consider several points:

- How much cash is needed?
- For what period of time is it needed?
- Which items can most effectively be used to generate cash?
- Can inventory be reduced on a permanent basis or must it be replaced promptly?

The simple process of thinking through these questions may make the decision obvious. Perhaps there is no way to generate the cash necessary through inventory. If there are items in inventory that can be eliminated permanently, there is no reason why they should not be, and so on.

The difficulty in using inventory as a source of cash is knowing for certain that it was the source of a cash increase. A detailed knowledge of inventory beforehand is necessary to determine whether a change actually took place. If extra cash appears at month's end in the form of higher profit, the business owner must know from where it came. What was the source of this extra cash? In order to know that inventory was the source of cash, one must know what the total value of the inventory was at the end of the previous month. Last month's figure is then compared with the total value of the inventory at the end of the current month. If the total value went down, it means that a declining inventory has become a source of cash.

No-Entry Accounting provides a hint that inventory has been reduced by the lack of canceled checks in the cost of goods sold category at month end. If inventory had been replaced when sold, the replacement purchase may have resulted in canceled checks in the Cost of Goods Sold category.

Example A:

Sales	$1,000
Cost of Sales	- 500
Gross Profit	$500
Operating Expense	- 300
Net Profit	$ 200

In example A, sales were generated from inventory, and the inventory was replaced. This fact is indicated by $500 worth of cancelled checks that found their way into the Cost of Sales category.

Example B:

Sales	$1,000
Cost of Sales	-0
Gross Profit	$1,000
Operating	
Expense	- 300
Net Profit	$700

Example B shows the same level of sales, but no canceled checks in Cost of Sales. This indicates that inventory was not replaced. The result was an increase in profit compared with Example A, which will be realized as cash in the bank account.

This observation is masked, however, by the time it takes to replace inventory. In this example, the $500 cost of sales in Example A may have been the payment of items purchased one or two months earlier. The zero cost of sales in Example B may have developed because the check written in payment for inventory had not yet cleared the bank.

The only reliable way to know that inventory has been reduced and is therefore a source of cash is to take a monthly physical inventory. It may have been reduced even more than cost of sales indicates through theft, damage, or spoilage. Perhaps what remains is useless because of lack of complementary parts, or for some other reason.

The symptom of a problem that this example exposes (extra cash in the bank account) represents a danger to the small business owner. You must have a genuine understanding of how the cash appeared and when it might be needed in the near future. In the absence of that understanding, you may be tempted to spend cash you do not really "have."

Employee Withholding

Withholding tax is often a contributor to the cash fund. It is not included on the "available" side of the cash analysis form because it does not provide cash directly. It falls under the umbrella of the deferred payment cash fund, but this category demands special attention. This cash source results when employee wages are earned and taxes are withheld from paychecks, but the sum of all employee withholding is too small to require deposit. No deposit is required until the sum of withholding equals $500 in any calendar quarter. (Withholding includes income tax and social security contributions.) If, for example, at the end of the second month of a quarter, $490 has been withheld, no deposit is required until the 15th of the fourth month. At that time the entire amount is due. The amount of these withheld taxes is available to use for other expenses until the taxes come due. This situation can be compared to an additional employee who need not be paid for three and a half months. In theory, the amount could reach $1,999, but in reality it is usually less than $1,000. Figure 13.4 shows how the cash builds up.

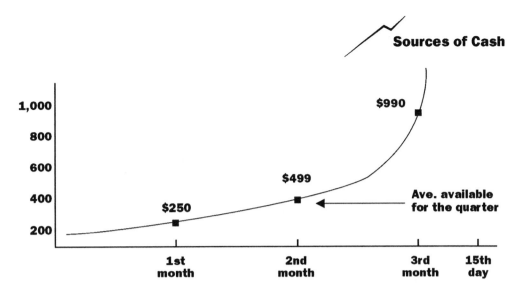

Figure 13.4. Deferred Payment of Withholding

The permissible time delay decreases as the amount withheld increases. Once withholding reaches $3,000 in any month, a business has just three working days to make the deposit.

Employer taxes due to be deposited with the government can easily reach 42 percent of gross payroll when the employer's contribution to social security and unemployment insurance is included. Figure 13.5 gives the math for determining the percentage. An employer can choose pay dates and structure work loads in a manner that permits optimum use of this source of cash. But borrower beware!

The federal government applies almost no front-end pressure on the owner who withholds money from employee pay checks. Months of deposits withheld from employee checks and not deposited may be due before the government initiates an inquiry. The government simply relies on the honesty of the owner until a violation of such trust becomes apparent.

Pressure is absent from the employee side as well, because employees expect to have taxes withheld as a condition of employment. This lack of checks and balances makes the use of cash created from employee withholding a rather dangerous trap. There are two major areas of ignorance that apparently lead the unsuspecting business owner into this trap. The first is that no one seems to be checking, and it is therefore easy to use this source to cover an unplanned shortfall in cash. Second, few business people realize that the *net* paychecks they write represent only some 56.5 percent of their payroll expense (Figure 13.5).

It is routine to find business owners who have ignored the deposit for several months before the government begins an inquiry. By this time, a business could have built an obligation of 43.4 percent times the gross payroll, times several months' wages. When interest and penalties are added to the amount due, it can—and does—come as a whopping surprise.

Probably because of the lack of front-end controls, the back-end controls often prove overwhelming when this scenario develops. The government has the power to attach wages, open safety deposit boxes, and seize property. All of this can be

Cash Analysis

Non Union Construction

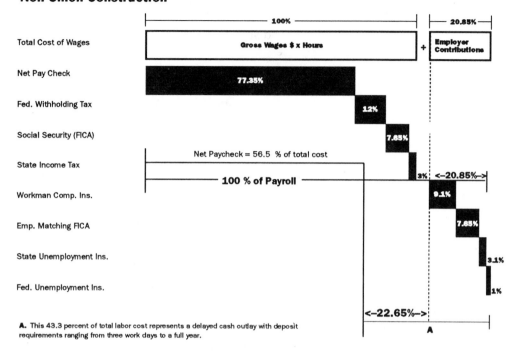

Figure 13.5. Actual Payroll Expenses

accomplished with almost no legal entanglement relative to what a business supplier might have to go through to collect a delinquent account. So what appears to be easy cash for a business in trouble is really the *last* well into which the business owner should dip. The owner knows no heat like that of the government looking for payment of back taxes!

And so it should be. It is the *employees'* social security deposits and the *employees'* taxes that were withheld. If the employer does not pass the money along, it is the employee who loses. Virtually every business owner that I have talked with who has fallen behind on tax deposits has said he or she would never do it again. It is very costly, and the practice invites continued government attention.

Loans

Loans are another source of cash for businesses. Short-term loans are typically used for such purposes as financing seasonal inventory purchases, making payroll tax deposits, meeting short-term operating expenses, and so on. Long-term financing is used to purchase such assets as property, heavy equipment, and businesses themselves.

Banks and savings and loans are a primary source of loans, but business owners borrow money from just about any source that will loan them money. They borrow from themselves, their families, relatives, friends, prospective investors, life insurance policies, and IRAs.

This source of cash could be better used in most businesses. A common problem encountered is that business owners wait until they are in trouble before they go see the banker. Instead, the need should be forecast and the banker visited *before* the need actually arises. Owners in crisis situations give little thought to retiring the debt and providing for the added cost of operation incurred by the interest expense. These problems stem from the lack of regular and timely financial statements. Without knowing the actual condition of both the profit and the cash position of a business each month, the business owner can only put out fires as they start, rather than prevent the fires from starting in the first place. The forward-looking use of the local bank can be of considerable help.

The cost of borrowing money can itself be a trigger mechanism for the Cycle of Demise. If the debt repayment and added interest expense are too difficult to meet for the business owner, the resulting cash drain can cause the triggering shortfall. Bankers do not structure loans with this objective in mind, but it can happen. It occurs primarily because the business person did not look far enough ahead or think a problem through sufficiently to know how much to ask for in the first place and for what period of time.

Notes Receivable

Amounts owed to the business might be an occasional source of cash. This refers to any amount that has been loaned out and that is due to be repaid. Perhaps only the interest on such a loan is due, but it may be a significant source of cash.

Depreciation Expense

Depreciation expense is a source of cash, in that depreciation is a monthly expense that is subtracted from sales, thereby reducing the profit, but no check is ever written for depreciation expense (discussed in Chapter 6). Therefore, the actual outcome is that cash in the bank from monthly operations will be higher than the contribution arrived at by computing the monthly cash profit. This amount is equal to the depreciation expense. (Any noncash expense such as an office in the home will cause the same fall out. Depreciation, however, is typically the largest of these considerations.)

For example,

Sales	$10,000
Cost of Sales	- 5,000
Gross Profit	5,000
Operations Expense	- $3,000
Depreciation Expense	- 1,000
Net Profit	$ 1,000

Because no check was written for depreciation, the actual cash generated will be $2,000 rather than the $1,000 shown as profit. For this reason, depreciation is known as a noncash expense. The noncash basis of depreciation contributes to the problem of cash management. The tendency is to treat cash in the bank as profit. The feeling that a profit is being made leads to unwise spending and excessive draw on the part of the owner.

Cash Analysis

The Sale of Assets

Selling off assets can sometimes be used as a source of cash. Occasionally, a business finds itself with too much land, too large a building, too many trucks, or too much equipment. The sale of such items can not only provide cash but sometimes help streamline a business and make it more likely to succeed by freeing up cash that is locked in equity.

In actuality, this source of cash is seldom used, however, because most businesses have insufficient assets with which to operate. That is, they need a half truck more, or a larger building, and so on. The possibility needs to be planned for, however, just as with any other source of cash. If salable assets do exist, the owner should know their market value. This value is used to keep the balance sheet current. Being on top of the market value of one's assets also helps in receiving top and timely dollar for them, should they be needed to generate cash.

Office in the Home

A home-based office is another noncash expense. When you perform a cash analysis, the office in the home is a cost avoidance opportunity. An office at home is also a tax reduction opportunity, which also increases cash flow. The business owner must have a location in which to perform the necessary paperwork of the business or the actual business. This work can be done at home, where the overhead has already been paid. Therefore, you avoid the cost of office space. The tax laws recognize the necessity of paperwork, and that the costs associated with it are, in fact, a business expense. This is true regardless of the office location.

This tax position permits you to expense the cost of running an office at home, thereby reducing the business profit. By reducing business profit, you also reduce self-employment tax and income tax. In both cases, this is true despite the fact that you would have had these expenses anyway. This is just one small example of how the tax laws are written to favor the entrepreneurial risk takers. An office in the home computation form is included in Figure 13.6 for your use. Note that an office in the home usually cannot be deducted if you have a physical place of business outside the home.

Capital

Capital is the initial deposit of cash used to start a corporation. Later contributions from unremoved corporate profits and investor stock purchases may increase capital. This source of cash differs from the ones previously discussed in that the only hope of return is to successfully operate the business involved. The objective is to multiply the cash invested by increasing the value of the business. Once increased, the stock is meant to be sold for a profit.

Capital as a source of cash differs from other sources for another reason. It typically involves large, unsecured amounts of cash that cannot be obtained from banks or other financial institutions. There is no repayment schedule, as with a loan or a lease. The capital investment is usually not backed by a certain such as with a home mortgage. A business may sometimes provide for dividends on invested

To meet the requirements of an office in the home, the office must be:

1. Exclusively used as your business office. It can be a whole room or part of a room, but it must be used exclusively for business.

2. Furnished with a business telephone, desk, chair, filing space, etc.

3. Used as such regularly. Note: The use of the home for other business purposes applies as well. The same form may be used with a note explaining the business use.

Calculation of Office in The Home Expense

Residence mortgage interest expense _____

Residence property taxes _____

Business telephone (if not already
deducted on P & L) _____

Residence gas usage or other heating fuel _____

Residence electricity usage _____

Garbage collection, water & sewage charges _____

Residence repairs (only those which affect the
residence as a whole, such as roofing or exterior
painting job, plumbing, etc.) _____

Casualty losses such as storm damage _____

Residence insurance _____

Total cost of residence operations _____

Repairs or other expenses solely for business use.* _____

Use this method to calculate your office expense.

Calculate the percent of square footage your office occupies, as compared to the whole residence. Multiply this percentage times the total cost of residence operations to arrive at your office expense.

You may choose the method which generates the greatest benefit. The portion of interest and taxes not taken here may be taken on the 1040 form Schedule A, so that the entire interest and tax deduction may be taken.

* These repairs may be expensed in their entirety and should be excluded from the above calculation. Add in total to the calculated office expense (line 18, schedule C).

Figure 13.6. Office in the Home Expense Computation Sheet

capital, but these dividends are seldom sufficient return. Generally speaking, once capital goes in, it does not come out until the business is sold for a profit.

Most businesses begin with a capital deposit from a single source: the owner. As the business grows and prospers, it requires more and more cash for equipment, inventory, building, and so on. If a business has cash to invest in itself, it is generally wise for it to do so. This eliminates additional expense in the form of interest and the pledging of assets on loans. The need to dilute the ownership by selling shares can be avoided as well.

When cash needs can only be met from outside the business, businesses enter into partnerships or become corporations and sell shares. The owner of such a business must decide whether the expected return from capital cash is worth the dilution of ownership. It must be decided whether 100 percent of a small business is worth more or less than some smaller percentage of a larger business. The greatest fear most small business owners have with outside capital is the possibility of losing control.

Post-Dated Checks

The post-dated check is a source of cash used all too frequently, even though its use is illegal. A post-dated check is one whose date of payment is off in the future. It is used on the theory that the check is not valid until the payment date arrives, and therefore, the writer's bank will not cash it until then. If the bank will not cash the check until some future date, the check writer believes, it is not necessary to have enough money in the account to cover the check until just before the payment date arrives. The practice of writing a check on an account that does not have sufficient funds to cover it is illegal in every state. Why, then, is it done?

Most post-dated checks are provided with the recipient's knowledge. The recipient typically has extended the payor credit of one type or another, and the debt has not been settled. The post-dated check is accepted when the recipient believes that the only way full payment will be received is to wait. The payee feels that a signed check that will—one hopes—become "good" at some future date is a better alternative than proceeding with collection through the courts.

The problem with the post-dated check is that it is only used by businesses that are experiencing a severe cash crunch. The vendor who accepts the post-dated check has little way of knowing whether the cash crunch is temporary and manageable or permanent and terminal. How many other post-dated checks might the payor have out already? Is there any hope of the payor generating sufficient cash to meet the obligation when it comes due? If the post-dated check is for a substantial amount and it is accepted by the payee, the payee subjects the success or failure of the payee's own business to the unknown ability of another party to perform. The payee may be indirectly placing his or her business into the hands of one who has already demonstrated an inability to manage cash. The business owner who uses post-dated checks has probably already triggered the Cycle of Demise and is unaware of it. The failure by such a business to meet the post-dated obligation could well trigger the Cycle of Demise in a second business: the one that accepts the post-dated check.

Summary

Sound cash management requires a thorough understanding of both the sources and the uses of cash. That is, in order to make money, you've got to know where your money comes from and where it goes. This chapter detailed the many ways in which you can "get" cash. Some of these sources of cash are nonobvious. Some are more than a little risky.

The cash analysis form enables you to assess the impact each of these sources has on your business. Religious use of this process is the single most important thing you can do to ensure your business's success. The assumption is that if you know and understand your cash position, you will avoid acts of ignorance that could trigger the Cycle of Demise.

Chapter 14

Uses of Cash

The *uses of cash* are the ways in which cash flows out from a business. As you saw in the case study of Chapter 10, outward cash flow is obscured in ordinary statement preparation. An up-to-date knowledge of where your cash is going and how much is going there is the single most important factor for success in business. It is assumed that your knowledge of a tight cash position and how tight cash positions cause businesses to fail will prevail on you to make financially sound business decisions.

Net Cash Loss

A *net cash loss* is the use of cash from which there may be no return! The loss results from spending more money for the operation of a business than the business returns as revenue. All the other uses of cash—an increase in inventory, draw for personal use, debt retirement, and so on—have some redeeming value about them. They provide more paid-up inventory, less debt, money in your pocket, or some other benefit. A cash loss, though, is money down the tubes.

It is difficult to imagine what a cash loss is like. The experience, however, is something the entrepreneur will likely never forget. The real effect can be compared to one of taking a job for which the hourly rate is some minus amount, say -$10 per hour. At the end of a 40-hour work week, the worker would be left with having spent time and energy for a week only to owe the employer $400!

The most effective way to avoid a loss is to be diligent with accounting and cash management. Regardless of the size of a business, preparation of a *monthly* profit and loss statement and a regular cash requirements forecast is a must. Should a loss become unavoidable, you can then at least manage its severity.

Net Increase in Inventory

A *net increase in inventory* is a common use of cash that takes two forms. The first is a *planned growth,* including expanded and additional product lines or perhaps additional outlets. The second is *unplanned growth* that results from overstocking, damage and waste, theft, and the gradual accumulation of items that have not sold. This second use of cash is most undesirable.

The gradual creep of undesirable inventory locks up cash in a form that deteriorates with time. One dollar's worth of this season's undesirable inventory may be worth only 30 cents next season. The same dollar's worth of inventory goes to zero if it is stolen or spoiled. If any significant portion of a given inventory is locked up in such a way, the business is choked off from its cash supply, and the Cycle of Demise may be triggered.

The basic intent of inventory management from the cash flow perspective is to keep inventory constant so that, once established, it is neither a use nor a source of cash. The only way you can hope to accomplish this balance is to know exactly what the value of a particular inventory really is. The only way to know exactly is to conduct a regular—that is, monthly—physical inventory. The point here is that to build an inventory to a size where it becomes unmanageable from an accounting point is not good business.

Remember that the calculation of a final net profit figure is at *best* only as good as the most erroneous contributing figure. The accurate calculation of cost of goods sold (commonly 50 percent of the total picture) depends on the accurate calculation of the value of inventory. If the value is only a guess, an inaccurate assessment introduces error into the cost of goods sold figure. Net profit, then, is only a guess based on a possibly significant error from a large contributing factor. Any cash forecast or net profit figure developed from such a situation would more often be wrong than right.

The value of inventory is not a factor used to calculate profit with No-Entry Accounting. This is because only canceled checks for cost of goods purchases are used to calculate profit. Doing so provides you with a direct look at the cash position that is the focus of No-Entry Accounting. The need for a quick and simple look at cash position that this treatment of cost of sales provides does not diminish the importance of a monthly physical inventory. A knowledge of the amount of cash that is tied up in inventory is of equal importance. You cannot know whether inventory was a use of cash without knowing whether the inventory level has increased or decreased. The chance for a successful business to emerge from an estimated inventory environment decreases with time. Estimated inventory simply is not good enough. It does not provide sufficiently accurate evidence regarding the degree to which inventory may have become a use of cash.

Draw

Draw is the opposite of capital. It is money taken out of the business for nonbusiness-related expenses. The purpose for which it is taken is immaterial. Sometimes you

simply take money from the cash drawer for personal use. Sometimes you write a check from the business checking account and treat it as salary. Other times you pay personal bills from the company's checking account or withdraw company's inventory for personal use. All these transactions represent draw.

Only one of the transactions just described is likely to appear in the company's financial statements. The check that you write for salary will become evident in the company's books. Sometimes the oversight is accidental; other times it is by design. The problem in either case is that the financial statements are then in error, often significantly in error, which causes a variety of problems.

When you remove cash from the sales register, you create several problems. First, unless you write a receipt that shows the exact amount you take, the day's sales will be understated by the amount of the withdrawal. This causes the sales figure for which sales taxes are computed to be understated. Say you take $200 a week and your sales tax is 6 percent; the understated tax will be $200 times 6 percent, or $12. If this amount remains unreported, you essentially defraud the state government of $12 x 52 weeks, or $624 per year.

Second, withdrawing the cash means the total sales go underreported. This action results in understated profit, which results in understated income and self-employment taxes. If these taxes go unreported (perhaps $2,000 on $10,400 in revenue using the previous example), you become a tax evader over a small amount in the eyes of the federal government, as well. Another problem you create when draw is not fully reported is that the historic financial record will be understated month after month, and perhaps year after year. This procedure means that you will not be able to prove claims about the real value of your business when it comes time to sell the company. The sale price of a business will range from 3 times to 10 times the net profit of the business or the value of its assets, whichever is the greatest. If unreported draw causes your business to show no—or very little—profit, you have inadvertently devalued the business. Therefore, each dollar removed and unreported can cost you $10 at the time of sale.

Probably the most compelling reason to record all draws is that in the absence of such recording, you'll eventually mislead yourself. Whether your draw is real cash or goods or services that later need to be paid for with cash, makes no difference. The lack of an accurate record on draw has caused untold numbers of businesses to inadvertently trigger the Cycle of Demise.

The case of paying personal bills from the company checkbook is different. In a sole proprietorship, it is permissible. The problem is that business and personal expenses have different tax treatments and they must at some point be separated. The No-Entry Accounting system adequately provides for this separation by identifying these checks as draw. Nonbusiness disbursements are sorted into the Draw compartment. Simply totaling the items in the Draw compartment will yield the draw figure that you must have to analyze your uses of cash. Writing personal checks from the company checkbook is quite a different matter for a corporation. A court has held that to do so implies that a business is not being operated as a corporation, and as such, the firm loses the ability to operate under corporate law.

Debt Retirement

Debt retirement is a major use of cash. Virtually every business has some sort of debt that it is working to retire. Some debt is retired monthly. Other debt is retired in lump sum payments at the end of some period of time such as a quarter, semiannually, or annually.

The monthly payment is the easiest to manage, because it is regular, like rent, and does not slip from your mind. But one reason businesses borrow money is to cover monthly shortfalls in cash. The lump sum type payment is best in this situation. It permits you to hold out for a seasonal sales peak or for the collection of a large account receivable.

These lump sum payment loans tend to get lost in the day-to-day operations and can cause a cash crunch when they come due. The larger the lump sum and the longer the period between principal reductions, the more difficult a cash management problem it becomes. You need to plan ahead so that large cash outlays do not come together at the same time.

Probably the single most difficult aspect of debt retirement is its "sinkhole" nature with regard to cash. When you use monthly statements, you may recognize the symptoms but may not understand the problem. A typical comment might be, "I have a good business, my statements show a good annual profit, I'm worth more than I used to be worth, but I never seem to have anything left over. I can't even take a vacation."

The core of this dilemma lies in the transfer from debt to equity. Almost every business must finance some part of its cash requirement. The financing may be a mortgage on the building from which the company operates. It may be a loan to finance major pieces of equipment, franchise fees, or inventory. The resulting interest expense is deducted to arrive at net profit, but debt retirement never *appears*. Only cash provides for debt retirement. Therefore, a business that earned a $35,000 cash profit during a year and retired $15,000 in debt has cash of just $20,000 remaining to cover personal taxes and owner draw for the year.

The negative swing in cash from $35,000 to $20,000 might be reflected in two different places. The first is the checkbook, where $15,000 in checks for the repayment of loans would have reduced the balance. Even this effect may not be noticeable, because the principal reduction may have been $1,200 monthly. The cash balance might have been relatively constant the whole while. The second indication that debt was retired might be an increase in the net worth on the balance sheet. This change, too, may not be evident; the decrease in liabilities may have been offset by a corresponding decrease in the asset cash. If so, the net worth would not change.

When the negative change is reflected in the checkbook, the cash is gone and cannot be used for business or personal expenses. When debt is retired as shown on the balance sheet, cash has been traded for equity and is also gone. Cash used for debt retirement is essentially locked into the value of the business and is not available until the business is sold.

Nowhere does the profit and loss statement or the balance sheet show that the business owner who retires debt might have a problem. The accountant sees only the data in the statements, and the problem is not visible from that perspective. All the owner can do is recognize the symptoms. The $20,000 left to finance personal requirements for the year is likely insufficient. Most owners would be living as though $35,000 were available rather than the actual amount—$20,000. If they do so unknowingly, they risk draining off business cash and triggering the Cycle of Demise.

Consider this:

$35,000	cash profit
- 15,000	debt retirement
- 5,355	15.3% self-employment tax
- 5,250	minimum income tax
$9,395	cash in hand for personal use

Only a handful of business owners could handle their personal expenses for an entire year on just $9,395. You can begin to see why accounts payable float is so important to a business owner. You can also see how unrecorded draw can become a major factor as the owner attempts to meet cash shortfalls by living out of the cash drawer or off company inventory.

Can a business that earns a $35,000 annual cash profit go bankrupt? It certainly can! Taking on too rapid a debt retirement program is just one way this can happen.

Accounts Receivable

Accounts receivable is a use of cash in businesses that make charge sales. The use of accounts receivable dictates the need for a major managerial effort to keep the sum of receivables from triggering the Cycle of Demise. Consider that a receivable does not exist until a business is in operation and provides labor, facilities, and a product, and then makes a sale. The business has had to use cash for rent, payroll, the purchase of salable inventory, and so on, to arrive at the point where some amount is receivable. To have come that far and not receive fair exchange in the form of cash dictates the need for still more cash. The additional cash is required to run the business while the owner waits to receive the cash from the account receivable. The longer that the receivable is extended—30 days, 60 days, 90 days—the greater the drain on a business cash fund.

The greatest problem develops when a receivable becomes uncollectible. The business owner loses not only the cash for the receivable and the expenses of producing the receivable but any costs incurred in the collection process as well. The business may have also incurred an interest cost from borrowing cash to use while waiting for the receivable to be paid.

It has repeatedly been shown that it takes great effort to manage accounts receivable. Only a small percentage of the business owners I have had occasion to deal with have had the ability and energy to effectively manage accounts receivable. If a business can avoid maintaining any accounts receivable, it should certainly do so.

If your business must maintain accounts receivable, consider the following:

- Shrinking the time you carry receivables (even small changes such as reducing the length of receivables from 30 to 20 days may have positive impact on your cash position).

- Developing solid methods for monitoring receivables (this is an area where many small business owners fail).

- Sending monthly statements and dunning notices for overdue accounts.

- Using a collection agency if all else fails.

Effective management of your receivables is essential to the success of your business.

Cash Purchase of Assets

The cash purchase of assets can be a significant use of cash. Certain businesses are asset intensive, such as the trucking and excavating businesses. Others require the purchase of land or facilities. Most of these purchases require substantial cash downpayments. The business owner needs to weigh each purchase against the need for operating cash to prevent committing too much cash to assets.

Consider that once cash goes into an asset, it generally stays there until the business is sold. Cash spent on an asset essentially becomes locked into the value of the business. The same argument is true for the portion of a purchase that is financed. A highly leveraged purchase (one with a small downpayment) commits future cash profits to the repayment of this debt.

Summary

The uses of cash require constant vigilance. This vigilance can only come from business owners themselves. In order for you to make money, you need to know how you use cash, and you have to take control of those uses.

Chapter 15

Cash Forecasting

Cash forecasting is probably the single most valuable tool you can use to ensure the success of a business, especially a new business. The cash position of a new business is often in jeopardy before the first profit and loss statement is even prepared. Perhaps 30 percent of all new business ventures are, from inception, chronically cash short and fail within months from this single cause.

How, then, do you avoid the largest of all pitfalls in the hopes of making a new business succeed? The process begins with the income statement, repeated here as Figure 15.1, and the cash analysis form, Figure 15.2. Together, these forms keep you apprised of your cash position and the viability of your business venture. Having a firm grasp of your cash flow and the financial health of your company is the starting point for forecasting cash income and expenses in the future, collectively known as *cash forecasting*. We will begin exploration of cash forecasting with the profit and loss statement.

Forecasting Using Your Income Statement

The income (profit and loss) statement is essentially an outline or list of your major business expenses. Each line must be reviewed so you can reach a realistic estimate for each expenditure—first for one month, and then for the rest of the year. This type of forecasting is fairly straightforward. You are familiar with the expenses of your business. Look at each category of expense. What do you expect to spend on that category (for example, advertising) next month? You can use your business's history as a value. For a new business, use a *realistic* (I stress the word) estimate. It will probably not hurt you to be somewhat conservative in your estimates . . . expenses always seem to be somewhat higher than any owner expects.

Each month's forecast will vary because of some known changes, be they air-conditioning in the summer, year-end bonuses in the winter, or the slow season in

Cash Analysis

Income Statement

Date _____

	This Month	%	Year To Date	%
Sales				
Category A	_____	___	_____	___
Category B	_____	___	_____	___
Returns	(_____)	___	(_____)	___
Total Sales	_____	___	_____	___
Cost of Sales				
Category A	_____	___	_____	___
Category B	_____	___	_____	___
Total Cost of Sales	(_____)	___	(_____)	___
Gross Profit	_____	___	_____	___
Operating Expenses				
Advertising	_____	___	_____	___
Car and Truck	_____	___	_____	___
Commissions	_____	___	_____	___
Depreciation & Section 179	_____	___	_____	___
Wages	_____	___	_____	___
Insurance	_____	___	_____	___
Interest on Business Debt	_____	___	_____	___
Legal, Professional	_____	___	_____	___
Office Supplies, Postage	_____	___	_____	___
Rent & Leases	_____	___	_____	___
Repairs & Maintenance	_____	___	_____	___
Supplies Not For Resale	_____	___	_____	___
Taxes & Licenses	_____	___	_____	___
Travel, Meals, Entertainment	_____	___	_____	___
Utilities, Telephone	_____	___	_____	___
Bank Charges	_____	___	_____	___
Donations	_____	___	_____	___
Office Expense	_____	___	_____	___
Laundry, Cleaning	_____	___	_____	___
_____	_____	___	_____	___
_____	_____	___	_____	___
_____	_____	___	_____	___
Miscellaneous	_____	___	_____	___
Total Operating Expenses	(_____)	___	(_____)	___
Net Profit or (Loss)	_____	___	_____	___

Figure 15.1. No-Entry Accounting Income Statement

Cash Forecasting

Cash Analysis

Cash Requirements Through _____

1.	Outstanding Checks, Bank Reconciliation	_____
2.	Self-Employment Tax[a]	_____
3.	Federal Payroll Tax Deposit	_____
4.	State Payroll Tax Deposit	_____
5.	State Unemployment Deposit	_____
6.	Federal Unemployment Deposit	_____
7.	State Sales Tax	_____
8.	Est. Qtr. Income Tax Deposit	_____
9.	Notes Due (Debt Retirement)	_____
10.	Insurance Prepayment	_____
11.	Property Taxes	_____
12.	Bills Due in Forecast Period	_____
13.	Forecast Cash Loss[b]	_____
14.	Inventory Growth	_____
15.	Accounts Receivable Growth	_____
16.	Post-Dated Checks	_____
17.	Operating Reserve	_____
18.	Minimum Personal Requirements (Draw)	_____
19.	Overdrafts	_____
20.	Other _____	_____

Total cash required for the period: _____

Cash Available Through _____

1.	Outstanding Deposits, Bank Reconciliation	_____
2.	Checking Accounts	_____
3.	Savings Accounts	_____
4.	Accounts Receivable Collection	_____
5.	Forecast Cash Profit[c]	_____
6.	Borrowed Money	_____
7.	Notes Receivable	_____
8.	Capital Deposits	_____
9.	Inventory Reduction	_____
10.	Post-Dated Checks	_____
11.	Depreciation, Home Office Expense	_____
12.	Overdrafts	_____
13.	Other Income	_____

Total cash available for the period: _____

Cash Shortfall _____

Cash Surplus _____

[a]For sole proprietorships only: 15.3% of profit deposited quarterly.
[b]Write in estimates on a blank profit and loss form. Record loss here.
[c]Record a forecasted profit here.

Figure 15.2 No-Entry Accounting Cash Analysis Form

August. Take care not to overlook any major fluctuations you can predict. Once you arrive at your expected expenses, consider your expected sales to calculate the revenue forecast. The expense forecast is then subtracted from the revenue forecast. The positive (or negative) result is the forecast of cash available from business operations. Essentially, you are predicting what a year-end statement would look like given the current state of affairs of your business.

What Your Profit and Loss Statement Never Told You

The profit and loss statement, however, is only one source of information for a cash position statement; it is not comprehensive. Take a look at all the business expense pitfalls your P&L never warned you about.

Debt Retirement

A profit and loss statement does not provide for debt retirement. That amount of cash to be used to reduce a loan balance (the principal) must be provided for. If the principal retirement is not on a monthly basis, as with an installment loan, take care to forecast the required cash in the month or months that it falls due.

Draw

Another cash consideration is owner draw. How much cash must you draw from the business to meet personal expenses each month? Accounting, per generally accepted accounting practices, does not provide for owner wages in a sole proprietorship. The owner receives no paycheck. It is assumed that the owner will draw out the profit from the business as his or her needs require. If the sole proprietorship has insufficient profit to meet the draw, the owner risks draining enough cash from the business to trigger the Cycle of Demise.

If the business is one of the many that obtain an accounting only quarterly or annually for income tax purposes, you can draw your business right into bankruptcy before it becomes obvious that a problem exists. Use of the cash forecasting procedure discussed here will help you to know a cash crunch is coming, so that you can steer your business around it.

The "owners" of small corporations are often its employees as well. Draw becomes a periodic paycheck that must immediately provide for taxes and social security payments. There is less opportunity to float withholding taxes and social security in a corporation than in a proprietorship, especially in the early years when profit is small.

Inventory and Accounts Receivable

A third major area that needs consideration is a forecast of what the business owner intends to do with inventory and accounts receivable. Both of these items are sinkholes for cash. Buildups of both inventory and accounts receivable invariably require more cash than monthly net profit provides. To keep these items from sinking a profitable business, you must have a detailed definition for the limits of each. The sources of cash that will fund any increase in these must be identified before the buildups happen.

For example, Barbara decides to extend $10,000 in accounts receivable to the customers of her new business. Her plan is to generate $100,000 in sales during the first quarter of operation. If she optimistically hoped to generate a 10 percent net profit, she is already in trouble:

Sales	$100,000
Net Profit	x 10%
Cash	$ 10,000
Less accounts not yet received	(10,000)
Cash from first quarter operations 1	0

The entire first quarter of operation must be funded from Barbara's personal finances. If the receivables do not come in or if the hoped-for profit proves to be only 5 percent, the Cycle of Demise will surely be triggered.

Employee Expenses

A fourth consideration is payroll add-ons, the employer's matching social security deposit, unemployment compensation insurance, workmen's compensation, self-employment tax, and the owner's quarterly estimated withholding tax deposit. It is common practice in small business to let these items simply "fall out" at year end when the owner takes a basketful of papers to an accountant to get the tax returns done. If there has been a loss, neither the owner's social security payments nor income taxes are due. If the company earned a profit, self-employment tax is due. The current rate of this tax is 13.02 percent. This amount is due *regardless* of personal deductions. If the profit is sufficient, income tax may be due as well. The proprietor is permitted to subtract personal deductions from profit in figuring the amount of tax due. So, although the business may have made a profit, it may not be sufficient to require the payment of income tax.

The major tax problem with most small businesses is that the owners do not know in December whether they owe any tax and if so, how much. This knowledge void occurs because the owner has not done the proper accounting throughout the year. If tax is due, the payment is generally put off until April 15, which is the filing deadline. A cash crunch develops in April, when all the ordinary expenses come due, in addition to the entire tax bill for the previous year, plus interest and penalties. If the tax burden is not planned for, it can and often does trigger the Cycle of Demise.

Summary

Nothing you can learn to do will benefit your business as greatly, with as little effort, as will a monthly cash forecast. The more often it is done, the easier it gets to produce. The closer you are to your real cash position, the more informed your decisions will be. More informed decisions lead to a greater opportunity to succeed.

Part IV

Surviving Small Business

The entrepreneurial problem is, "How can I get my business through the periods where more cash is needed than is available?" As with most business problems, the process of completely defining the problem is 90 percent of the solution. That is, simply knowing precisely what your business's problem is makes the solution simpler. If your fax machine doesn't print a document, there could be thousands of causes, from a blown fuse to noise on the telephone line. But say you have the presence of mind to check the machine's error message about the paper supply and find that the machine has run out. This specific definition of the problem instantly eliminates all but one of the possible causes. You now can proceed with the remaining 10 percent of the solution: getting another roll of paper and loading it in the fax machine.

But how do you go about completely defining a business problem in the absence of something so simple to understand as an "Out of Paper" message? The answer lies in the proper use of accounting. The cash analysis statement, the income statement, and the balance sheet are the error warning system for the going concern.

Those who already operate a business and have little or no knowledge of these three statements are doing the equivalent of relying on a fax machine without ever checking whether it still sends and receives documents.

The most prevalent and destructive belief I have encountered in talking with thousands of small business owners is, "My accountant is taking care of all that financial stuff. Why do you think I pay for the service?" To take the position that the accountant is taking care of all the financial considerations for you is like saying the fax machine is taking care of itself.

The problem with this gross misconception is that the machine doesn't report the error until *after* you have missed getting that important document. Only pure luck will keep the machine working while your critical documents get through. As with the accountant, the machine doesn't *prevent* problems, it just reports them once it's too late.

With this analogy in mind, what then is the fastest, most effective way to define *the* problem within a specific individual business? How do small business owners assemble and learn how to use the error warning system that enables their businesses not only to survive but also to thrive and grow?

Chapter 16

Getting Along with the Banker

Contrary to popular belief, banks do like to make loans—loans are their bread and butter. The majority of bank income is derived from interest earned on loans, many of which are made to small businesses. But if this is the case, why don't all business owners get the loans they think they need?

A brief look at how a bank operates may help you to understand the basics of obtaining a loan. The more you know about banks and bankers, the easier it is to deal with banks successfully.

Banks are not in business to gamble. Banks use their deposits—other people's money—to generate income through loans. The depositors and bank regulators expect these funds to be kept safely. This means that loans must conform to standards that are known to result in the successful loaning of money. The loan application process is a measure of an applicant's ability to repay a loan against these known standards. The small business owner needs to consider his or her own loan application in light of these standards, before he or she submits it to a banker. Well, then, what standards does a banker consider?

Five C's of Credit

When a loan application is made, the information is analyzed by comparing it to what are generically known as the "Five C's of Credit." What follows is a brief summary of these criteria.

Character

Following are some issues bankers consider:

- What about the applicant's character? Is the applicant an honest and trustworthy individual? The applicant's reputation among vendors who have already extended the individual credit is one measure of trustworthiness.

- How well have previous obligations been handled?

- How does an applicant's former employer or other applicant reference feel about the applicant's character?

- Is the applicant secure with his or her existing source of income?

- Does the applicant exhibit good work habits?

- Is there stability in the applicant's life?

- Are projects always finished once they are started? Is the applicant's direction consistent or erratic?

Family and personal problems can enter into the perception of one's character. In smaller towns, for example, the business and banking communities have access to personal information through business contacts at golf clubs or service organizations. Applicants' "public image" may precede them as rumors pass regarding a possible divorce or a drinking problem.

Capacity

Following are some issues bankers consider:

- What is the applicant's capacity for repayment? The bank wants to know how a loan will be repaid.

- Where will the money come from? Is projected cash flow great enough to support the repayment and the borrower's other commitments?

The capacity question is an assessment of whether repaying a loan will create an undue hardship upon the borrower. The banks assume that if a hardship might develop, their interests would take a second seat. The assumption is that a borrower in trouble would pay for rent, groceries, or other such personal choices before a loan payment would be made. Marginal capacity to repay a loan makes providing the loan too risky for a bank. Marginal capacity is any developing situation that might cause change. This includes a situation that at present might look good but that in the future may change significantly. For example, "If this big deal comes through next year, everything will work out fine." The banker immediately sees a red flag. "What happens to my money next year if the big deal falls through?"

In the absence of a detailed plan demonstrating what would be done if the big deal falls through, no loan will be granted.

Capital

Following are some issues bankers consider:

- How much capital is supplied by the borrower?

- Is the borrower well capitalized? That is, how much risk does the borrower take in the business for which the loan is sought?

A bank may provide 100 percent financing on a business venture but only if the borrower puts up significant personal collateral so that the bank is not at risk. If the borrower is not willing to risk personal funds, why should the bank take any risk?

Collateral

Following are some issues bankers consider:

- What is the borrower's alternate source of repayment should the intended method of repayment somehow falter?

- What home equity or liquid assets could the owner—or the bank—tap?

Many small business loans are collateralized by the equity the borrower may have in a personal residence. This means that a borrower is willing to turn over his or her residence to the bank for sale if all other sources of capital for repayment dry up. The bank uses proceeds of the sale first to pay off the loan and any other cost incurred in the process.

Note: If this type of sale becomes necessary for any type of collateral, plan on no leftover cash. A lending institution will sell collateral for only the amount the bank has coming to the first buyer who comes along with the required amount. It makes no difference to the banking institution whether a residence should bring another $20,000 or $30,000 if sold at the top of the market. The lender is not looking to solve the borrower's problems at this point. It is only looking to clean up its loan portfolio as quickly as possible.

Putting up a personal residence as collateral satisfies the requirements of the banking regulators and also goes a long way in addressing the capital commitment mentioned earlier. If a borrower is willing to put up his or her own home as collateral, the banker will get a strong indication that the borrower certainly intends to repay, and is confident of repaying, a loan.

Sometimes this strong indication is still not sufficient. The lengthy and expensive legal problems involved in actually obtaining a home in lieu of a failed repayment plan are more of a bite than the banks are willing to take. Banks also fear the negative community impression associated with taking a homeowner's property.

There are, of course, many other types of collateral. The equipment or property an entrepreneur is purchasing with the borrowed money can become part of the collateral. It is seldom 100 percent, however, because the value of such purchases often declines the moment the purchase is complete. If the bank has to repossess such collateral, it cannot afford to hold out for top dollar from just the right buyer. The bank may have had to wait months or years just to reach the point where the law would permit repossession.

Fire sale prices result from the need to dispose of the matter quickly. It is, therefore, not surprising to see a return of only 10 or 20 cents on the dollar of an original purchase price when all the recovery costs are considered. Business inventories or accounts receivable are sometimes used for collateral. A stock or other investment portfolio may be used. The collateral of a second party may be used if a second party, such as a parent or other relative, cosigns for a loan. In general, the amount of collateral a borrower must provide—whether a fraction of, double, triple, or quadruple the amount of the loan—is in direct proportion to the banker's perception of the applicant's ability to repay.

I once received a $10,000 loan on my signature alone. When the maturity date arrived and I could only repay a portion of the principal, I was required to put up nearly 300 percent of the balance in collateral.

Conditions

Following are some issues bankers consider:

- What are the conditions of both the national and local economies?
- Is there anything happening locally, nationally, or internationally that could adversely affect the business?

The bank itself may have reason not to grant a loan. Perhaps the institution's loan portfolio is too heavily geared to one industry or another, and the bank cannot afford to take on another loan of the same type.

Banks make loans to creditworthy businesses and individuals every day. Few applications are perfect, but the Five C's of Credit are used to evaluate every one. In order to make these evaluations, the bankers need information. The larger and riskier the application, the greater the need for detail and confirmation of the information provided. The borrower is responsible for supplying this information. It is helpful if everything necessary is provided *before* the banker has to request it.

Giving the Bank the Right Information

To keep the entire bank staff informed, a loan officer builds a file of an applicant's loan and business information. The file is subject to periodic review by bank officers and regulatory examiners.

It is very important for a loan applicant to be well prepared, both in knowing what to expect and in having the proper information at hand. If an applicant is making an initial visit, he or she will want to prepare what amounts to a sales presentation. After all, the borrower is trying to sell his or her creditworthiness to the bank. Regardless of how many previous visits the applicant has made, thorough preparation is absolutely essential.

Follow these steps in preparing for your loan request:

1. Always call ahead for an appointment. You need to work within the framework of the banker's work schedule. Emergencies do happen, but the last-minute need to see a banker whose appointment book is full for the day is perceived as a lack of prior planning. Exercise professional courtesy as well as an ability to plan ahead by making an appointment.

2. Allow sufficient lead time to process the loan before you require the funds. It generally takes a few days to complete the loan's paperwork. Some loans take weeks. The loan officer checks your references and verifies other information. The logistics within the bank of getting everyone involved in a decision together can take time. Bankers are often legitimately skeptical of businesses needing immediate cash. Never wait until the last minute!

3. A written request makes a more professional appearance. Presenting a proposal personally, rather than having an accountant or attorney present it, conveys the impression of a knowledgeable borrower. A loan application

should always be for enough money to accomplish what needs to be done without going back later to ask for more. Show the banker on paper how much money is needed and why. Show what may be required should things not go exactly as planned.

4. Never ask how much can be borrowed. Asking how much can be borrowed immediately conveys the impression that you need every dollar you can get your hands on. From the banker's point of view, few "good" loans are ever made to people who are scraping for every dollar they can get.

5. Take all the proper information and supporting documentation to the application interview. Having it all together proves that you really know what you're doing. It can also save time in the approval and processing of a loan request.

Here is a basic list of items necessary to prepare your paperwork:

- Personal information—essentially a resume and a personal credit information form.
- Professional information regarding key employees.
- A list of key advisers—attorney, accountant, insurance agent, and so on.
- General information about products, markets, major customers, suppliers, competitors, physical facilities, employees, and anything that is pertinent to the loan application.
- Financial information about the company, including the Form 1040 for the last three years, if available, and the current No-Entry Accounting balance sheet.
- A No-Entry Accounting cash analysis showing how the prior year's cash was used and a forecast of how the cash in the coming year will be used with the loan proceeds. Make sure to explain in detail how much money you want, what it will be used for, and how you plan to repay the loan.
- A list of credit and trade references.

Naturally, not every item of this list applies to every loan application. If some information has been previously supplied, there is no need to duplicate that effort. But in general, it is better to have too much documentation than too little. The degree of preparation and the degree of openness about sharing the information are very important to the impression you create.

Following are some do's and don'ts for loan protocol:

- Do not haggle over the interest rate, especially before the loan is approved. Check the rates at several banks before you select those at which to apply.
- Do not spend the money before the loan is approved. A loan may not be granted for some unforeseen reason, or the amount loaned may be reduced.
- Do not spend the money for something other than the purpose for which it was granted. Borrowing money under false pretenses is fraud.

The more complete the request, the more convincing the presentation, the more professional the impression, the more likely is the chance that a request will be granted as put forward.

Following are several points to be concerned with once the initial loan has been made:

- Do not surprise the banker. Bankers hate surprises. If there is some change the bank should know about, you as the borrower are the one to make the loan officer aware of it.

- Always share the bad (or potentially bad) along with the good. Once you receive a loan, be sure to keep the banker updated relative to the plan presented with the application.

- It is not wise to change banks just for a better interest rate. This has always been true but is even more so today with the predominance of variable-rate loans. Unless a bank is way out of line over a substantial time period, you gain little from changing banks. This is especially true if a business is doing very well. Some financial institutions try to attract successful businesses with special interest rates but overprice other services. Also, these rates are very short-lived. Exercise loyalty to bankers and institutions you've had good relations with.

A banking relationship encompasses (or certainly should encompass) more than a simple "purchase" relationship that is determined by a one-time price. The importance of a good banking relationship to a business cannot be overemphasized. Develop the type of relationship that permits a free flow of information in both directions. Both the borrower and the banker benefit.

Summary

Try to do as much business with one banker as possible. It's best not to scatter business all over town unless none of the banks is large enough to handle all the transactions alone. If at all possible, deposit accounts should be with the same banks as the loans. The more business a firm can give a bank, the more important the business becomes to the bank. Talk to the banker frequently, not just when money is needed. Build a personal relationship. Then, when times get tight, there is a friend in your corner instead of an adversary.

Chapter 17

Some Simple Systems
to Start With

Businesses require accounting modules that feed data to the general ledger module. The common modules are payroll, accounts receivable, and accounts payable. This chapter describes a simple way to provide for these modules until your business grows past their usefulness.

General Ledger

The *general ledger* is the portion of an accounting system that deals with the financial statements, namely the income statement (profit and loss statement) and the balance sheet. No-Entry Accounting is essentially a general ledger package designed for simple, rapid preparation of these documents. It goes beyond this level, however, by providing you with directions for navigating the tax system and by serving as a perpetually audit-ready record filing system. It is this portion of accounting that the typical accountant would prepare for clients. Some entrepreneurs feel that the general ledger and taxes are too complicated and time consuming to deal with on their own. This approach harbors the seeds of failure, because it prevents the entrepreneur from getting close to the information about his or her business that is most required for success.

Many entrepreneurs hate working with figures and paperwork—so be it. But entrepreneur beware! Seeking an outside service before an entrepreneur becomes minimally competent at maintaining a general ledger may double or triple the odds against success. Remember, cash management—the essence of small business survival—is based heavily on the general ledger portion of an accounting system.

Payroll

Payroll is a business financial application that small business owners seem to find difficult. This probably stems from the fact that a large part of the tax work a business is required to perform arises from payroll. I once had to teach accounting practitioners a sales pitch designed to land new monthly fee clients. The pitch rambled through the number and name of each form that needed to be filed monthly, quarterly, and annually. This review made the whole process sound terribly complicated and technical. When one hears the entire list of payroll forms recited in a single paragraph, it seems endless. In fact, payroll accounting is not complicated and is not very technical. In practice, the small business owner will spend just minutes each month getting this work done rather than hours. Understanding payroll paperwork is easy if you take the short amount of time required to learn something new. Most of what you need to know can be learned by simply reading the tax forms.

Payroll tax requirements consist of the following:

Federal
- IRS Form 941: Withholding and FICA, filed quarterly.
- IRS Form 940: FUTA, Federal Unemployment Tax, 0.008 percent of gross wages filed annually.
- IRS Form W2: Wages and taxes withheld for each employee. Includes all taxes withheld—federal, state, and local—done annually.
- IRS Form W3: a total report of the sum of the W2's done annually.

State
- State 941: A simplified version of the federal form in states that have income tax. May be only annual for many small businesses.
- State 940 SUTA: State Unemployment Tax; usually quarterly. Works in conjunction with the FUTA program. Most of the contribution goes to the states.

The payroll process begins when the business owner obtains from the Internal Revenue Service (IRS) a Federal Employer Identification Number (FEIN). The application form can be obtained by calling the local toll-free IRS number. The FEIN is used to report the wages and taxes withheld for each employee of the company registered. Once the number is applied for, the IRS automatically supplies the forms required to report the various taxes. Contact the state government in the same manner so your business will also receive the state forms. The accounting and tax cycle guide (Chapter 18) includes information and direction for the timely, orderly filing of each of the federal, state, and personal forms.

Each employee must complete a W4 form. Its purpose is to determine the number of exemptions an employee is expected to have at year end so that an appropriate amount of tax can be withheld. A penalty will be charged to the employee if the deposited tax is less than 95 percent of the amount due, when it was due. This form must be kept on file as part of the payroll record.

The payroll system described in this chapter does not require any special documents, forms, books, or journals. A typical business check is all that is necessary. The check in Figure 17.1 is an ordinary Joe's Cafe check that is not designed specifically for payroll. It works nonetheless. Notice that the memo line in the lower left corner is used to enter all the pertinent data regarding the pay period for which this check has been written.

| JOE'S CAFE | No. 1047 |
| HOMETOWN, U.S.A. | |

19_____ 70-2406/719

PAY
TO THE
ORDER OF _____ Jane Brown _____ $ 206.25

Two hundred six dollars & 25/100 _____ DOLLARS

AMERICAN NATIONAL BANK
HOMETOWN, U.S.A.

FOR Gr. 250.00, W/H 20.00, FICA 18.75, State 5.00   Joe Smith

---

Figure 17.1. Ordinary Check Use for Payroll

The process begins when the owner or bookkeeper calculates the gross wage (often the hourly rate times the number of hours worked) and enters that gross amount on the check as shown on the memo line in the figure. The first amount is designated *Gr.* for gross pay. This is the amount the employee has earned during the period before any deductions. The $250 amount may have been earned as a salary of $250 per week or it may have been earned as $6.25 an hour for 40 hours, for example.

The next step is to determine the amount of tax to be withheld from the employee's check. The appropriate tax chart is provided by the IRS when the FEIN number is requested. The charts are in a booklet called the "Circular E Tax Guide." To determine the amount of tax, the number of exemptions is obtained from the employee's completed W4 form. The tax chart is divided into sections based on the frequency of the payroll. The sections are weekly, biweekly, semimonthly, and monthly. Given the number of exemptions an employee claims and the pay period, the tax amount can be looked up based on the gross wage for the period. This amount is written on the check as shown in the figure. It is designated by *W/H*, which stands for withholding.

Next, the employee's social security and FICA contribution must be deducted. It can be looked up in the "Circular E Tax Guide" as well. If the chart does not go high enough, multiply the gross wage by 7.65 percent, the current rate. At the end of the quarter when the tax is reported on the Form 941, the employer must match the employee's 7.65 percent for a total contribution of 15.3 percent. This deduction is currently limited to the first $53,400 in earnings for each employee. The 7.65 percent should be entered on the check as shown in the figure with the notation *FICA*.

The timing required for withholding deposits to be made is different from that required for reporting the deposits with the Form 941. The withholding and FICA guide that is part of the accounting and tax cycle guide in Chapter 18 can be found on page 231.

If state or local taxes must be withheld, they should be entered as on the sample check in Figure 17.1. For example, Illinois currently has a 3 percent income tax. The Form Il700 contains a chart on which the tax can be looked up. If no chart is available from your state, simply multiply the percent of the state tax by the gross pay amount.

Once the checks are written for all the employees, the data must be transferred to the federal Form 941. There are two considerations at this point. First, the current federal tax obligation (the total amount due to be deposited for withholding tax and FICA as a result of this payroll) must be recorded at the bottom of the company's copy of the Form 941. The obligation is equal to the taxes withheld (a total of the W/H entries from each check) plus 15.3 percent of the total gross wages. The total gross wage is obtained by adding the gross amount from each paycheck. Do not include an individual's wage over $53,400. Enter the total of the withholding tax plus the 15.3 percent of gross for FICA obligation, in the appropriate date and month column at the bottom of the Form 941.

The second consideration involves gross wages. The total gross wages for the period will be needed when the Form 941 is filed with the IRS at the end of the quarter. To reduce the workload at that time, enter the pay date and the total gross wages for the period somewhere in the margin of the 941, company copy. At the end of the quarter, then, the total of gross wages for the various paydays in the quarter can be totaled from the margin notes without having to review prior payday figures. The total tax obligation at the bottom of the Form 941 is summarized at the end of the quarter and checked against the math on the top half of the form. Once balanced, the data is transferred to the IRS copy.

The taxes due are deposited at any bank; the bank forwards the money to the IRS. The bank deposit receipt is stapled to the company copy of the Form 941 and is stored in the No-Entry Accounting Federal Tax packet for permanent storage. Once the canceled check for the deposit amount is returned, use the following procedure:

1. Prepare a memo ticket for the amount of the deposit that represents the employees' portion of the deposit. (That is the total deposit minus the company's 7.65 percent FICA matching amount.) This memo is sorted into the Wages compartment so that the total wage figure can be computed by adding the net pay checks and the employees' portion of the tax deposit.

2. Prepare a second memo for the company's portion of the deposit, which is sorted to the tax compartment. The canceled check is stapled to the company copy of the 941 to complete the audit trail of the deposit.

3. At the end of the quarter mail the 941 IRS copy directly to the IRS in the envelope provided.

It is wise to write the same figures on the check stub that are written on the memo line of the pay check. An occasional question arises that is easier to answer by flipping through check stubs in the checkbook than by finding a check in the file. If the employee wants to keep a running total of earnings, he or she can copy the data to a personal record before cashing the check. A complete "payroll journal" results from sorting the net pay check into the wages compartment. Total wages can be computed by adding the gross amount recorded on each of the returned and canceled checks. The same is true for each of the other taxes and miscellaneous deductions.

At year end the checks can be separated by employee to help prepare the employee W2's and the W3. The W3 is simply a total form for all the W2's. The IRS automatically mails the required forms at year end.

The canceled payroll checks will be stored in the permanent storage box behind the wages tab. The result is a record that is in sequence for the year alphabetically by employee just as though the record were generated by a computerized payroll system. This system has the added advantages of being faster than reentering all the data for computer compilation and having the sorted checks represent an immediate-access audit trail.

The federal withholding guide is part of the tax and accounting guide under payroll p. 231. Review it each payday to determine whether a deposit is necessary. Some small businesses do not reach the $500 minimum limit through the quarter, so they deposit only once per quarter. Some larger businesses reach the $2,000 level once or twice a month. This level of withholding requires depositing the withheld tax within three working days of the payday in which the level is reached.

Each state and local tax also has limits below which an immediate deposit is not required. Copies of forms, correspondence, deposit receipts, and canceled checks will be stored for these taxes in the State Tax packet. The packet is filed behind the Taxes tab along with the Federal and Personal packets. Supporting forms and instructions are always provided so that the small business owner need not hire outside help.

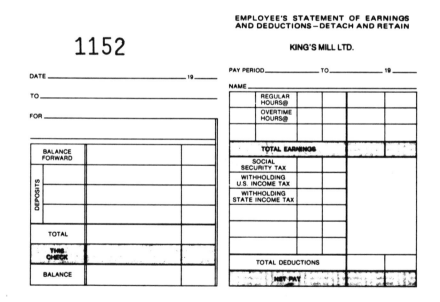

Figure 17.2. Check Design with Stub

Once an employee count reaches five or six, a small business owner may want to move to a different check design to reduce rewriting time. The check in Figure 17.2 is a type that will be helpful as a next step. Notice that the check stub includes space for computing the gross wage and a procedure for computing the net check. The document in the figure is actually a carbon copy of the check that was written over it in the checkbook. The carbon copy eliminates having to write the figures twice as with the plain check, once on the check and once on the stub. With this system, however, the employee keeps the stub that is attached to the check so the canceled check returns without the payroll data on it. The carbon copy must now become part of the payroll record along with the canceled check, because it is the only place where the gross payroll and the deductions have been recorded.

These represent the bulk of the steps involved in doing your own payroll. The forms and filings are routine and straightforward, so that although it sounds complicated and intimidating, payroll is actually doable for most small business owners.

Accounts Receivable

Accounts receivable is a cash trap that the small business should avoid if at all possible. If your business must use accounts receivable, however, keep the record keeping as simple as possible. The simplest system uses a multipart invoice of at least four plies. One copy—not the original—becomes the customer's copy, which serves as a sales receipt. The original, third, and fourth copies are filed in a box or folder marked Open Accounts Receivable. If the business needs a copy for internal purposes such as a shop order, use a five-ply set; if your collections do not require follow-up, a two-part form may be sufficient. If the number of customers is more than a handful, an alphabetical file is helpful. See the sample form in Figure 17.3.

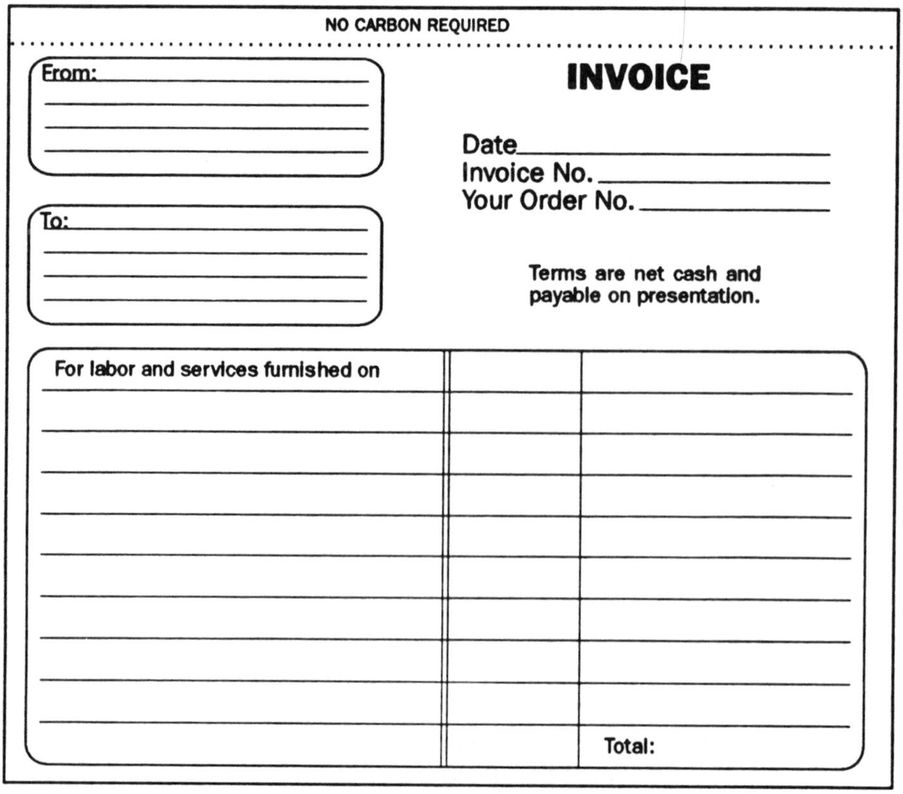

NO CARBON REQUIRED

From:

INVOICE

Date
Invoice No.
Your Order No.

To:

Terms are net cash and payable on presentation.

For labor and services furnished on

Total:

Figure 17.3. Typical Four-Ply Invoice Set

As payment is received in full, the unused copies remaining in the Open Accounts Receivable file should be moved to a "Paid Invoices" file with provision for alphabetical storage. If an invoice is partially paid the payment is noted on the invoice copies remaining. The copies with the notation on them remain in the Open Accounts Receivable file until the invoice is fully paid.

The Open Accounts Receivable file is reviewed every 30 days. Customers with invoices still in the file at the time of this monthly review are mailed the next copy in the set. By the end of 60 days the third copy will have been mailed. The original copy should not be mailed. It serves as a permanent record to remind the business person that the collection matter must be taken up personally.

The receivables total needed for the quarterly balance sheet and the monthly cash analysis report is obtained by taking an adding machine tape of the Open Accounts Receivable balance. It is a good idea to take two tapes or as many as required to get two with the same total. To check the effectiveness with which the receivables are being managed, the file needs to age monthly.

Aging accounts receivable means to categorize the amount due from each invoice by its age:

- An invoice with a date up to 29 days old would be placed in a 0-to-30-day stack. These items are considered current.

- An invoice with a date 31 days old but less than 60 days would be placed in a 30-to-60-day stack.

- An invoice that remains uncollected after 60 days but that is not yet 90 days old would be placed in the 60-to-90-day stack.

- Invoices older than 90 days go in a fourth stack.

An adding machine tape is taken of each stack. The sum of the stack totals should equal the total of all the receivables.

As a rule of thumb, the total of the current items should be equal to the other stacks combined. In other words, current accounts receivable should be at least 50 percent of the total. Any situation where delinquent items—those over 30 days old—are greater than 50 percent represents a cash management problem that warrants constant vigilance. Keep in mind that the older a receivable gets, the more difficult it is to collect. Items that are not paid promptly must be pursued immediately.

The next step for a growing business is to implement a manual receivables system where invoices are posted to customer receivable cards. A running balance is kept by customer, and statements are sent monthly. This type system becomes advantageous when a business has something like 50 repetitive monthly customers. Pegboard systems are available from office supply stores that provide write-it-once accounts receivable systems. This type of system helps to reduce the writing and posting work with carbon statements that prepare the customer ledger and sales or cash receipts journal simultaneously. The user needs to become familiar with conventional accounting to some extent to master this type of system.

Two considerations prompt an owner to move beyond these simple, manual systems. The first is growth in invoices per customer monthly. As a particular customer's account becomes increasingly active with invoices per month, the bookkeeping workload may increase. If the customer transaction volume reaches several hundred transactions per month, using a personal computer is helpful. The second consideration is the number of customers who have open balances at the end of each month. As this number grows larger, the preparation of statements can become a significant month-end chore. The computer may be of some economic advantage in this situation as well. If growth is experienced from both transaction counts and number of customers, a computer can be advantageous for the receivables system.

Computer systems provide users with two basic options: the balance forward option and the open item option. The *balance forward option* requires sufficient computer storage space to store the customer master file and as many customer invoice transactions as are generated in the heaviest month of activity. Growth should also be provided for. When monthly statements are printed the balance unpaid from the last statement preparation is carried forward in total but not in detail. No effort is made to keep track of separate items that remain unpaid from prior months.

The current month items are printed on the new statement item for item and added to the balance forward. A look at all the prior statements, therefore, provides a complete detail of all transactions to date. This method saves a considerable amount of time in applying cash as it is received. This is especially true when partial payments are received or when only a portion of a single invoice remains contested and not paid. The cash received under this system applies cash to the oldest open invoice from the paying customer and moves forward until the cash received is exhausted. Partial payments become lumped into the next balance forward.

The *open item system* provides for reprinting a statement line for each invoice that remains unpaid each time the statements are printed. This system requires considerably more effort, because individual invoices must be credited as the cash is received. This extra work is necessary when a customer has a high monthly volume of individual invoices, many of which may be in the pipeline at the end of each month. Accounts receivable must be treated more like a checking account in this situation. Each item must be reconciled individually. The computer storage space required for such a system is considerably greater, because there must be disk space for every conceivable open item at month's end for each of the various customers.

If you are a computer software shopper, note that some accounts receivable programs are written for the open item user but permit cash to be applied as with a balance forward system. Such a program can be used on an open item basis for those accounts that require open item and more like balance forward for those customers who do not require the detail.

Note: Do *not* move to a computerized system until a solid manual system is in place and working effectively for some months. The project of cleaning up an accounting system at the same time a business is coming to grips with computerization can be ruinous. Many businesses have taken the position that the installation of a computer will invoke the regimentation required to clean up company accounting. I have not seen such a project work. Failure results from not being able to make a clean-cut changeover using accurate balances and a working system in place. The paper flow and people that feed a manual system are the same paper flow and people that must be in place to feed a computerized system. The computer may only provide these people who have the existing paper flow the opportunity to mess up the results more quickly and to a greater extent!

Accounts Payable

Accounts payable is the application that deals with the payment of bills a business owes its suppliers. Except in very large businesses that have hundreds of suppliers, this application can remain manual forever.

The easiest method to use is the *in-box method*. Each day as mail is received, the that which require payment are simply placed into an in-box or an Accounts Payable file. Once a month the invoices are removed and checks are written in payment. The resulting checks end up as the original transaction documents in the No-Entry Accounting system. The invoices paid must be kept in a file of all documents paid for the year. The box or file folder containing the invoices should be labeled with the tax year.

An additional step could be to provide the absolute audit trail. Each invoice could be stapled to the canceled check that paid the invoice, and both could be stored in the permanent storage box. The canceled check is usually sufficient proof of a transaction for audit purposes, so this step may not be warranted. In the event an audit requires the owner to find the invoice that was paid with a particular check, it must be locatable in the tax year file. Certain business owners may prefer to keep these invoices in an alphabetical vendors file, if there is frequent need for review.

The total of your payables is used to complete the quarterly balance sheet. This total is also a significant factor in the preparation of the monthly cash analysis report. As with all such totals, two adding machine tapes with the same total should be prepared before the figure is used.

Summary

The important thing to keep in mind is that recordkeeping is nonproductive, except for the accounting practitioners. It behooves the entrepreneur to keep an accounting system as simple and as fast to handle as sound business practices permit. The objective is to have precisely what you need and not a moment's worth of work more.

Chapter 18

What You Need When—A Guide to Monthly, Quarterly and Annual Accounting and Tax Cycles

This chapter summarizes the essential steps that will enable you to be self-sufficient with respect to your own accounting. Even if you don't elect to use No-Entry Accounting, you still must file all of the forms, and following these procedures will ensure perpetually audit-ready records and will eliminate duplication of work. While this chapter does not assume the use of any of the popular microcomputer-based accounting or "checkbook" systems, these procedures work just as well with those as with totally manual systems. If you have not yet begun to use an accounting system, following these steps will help you learn self-sufficiency before you commit the common early errors. If you already use a system, this summary is a memory jogger to help you recall reports that occur infrequently.

The description starts with regularly monthly activity (Monthly Accounting), which begins by reconciling the bank statement. From here you'll see each accounting and tax function in sequence, right up to storing all documents useful for an audit. Although there may appear to be a lot to do, a typical small business (with 35 or so checks a month) will require no more than an hour a month for everything. If you have not yet done so, you should complete the exercise in Chapter 10 before you tackle your own accounting chores.

Once monthly accounting is complete, the chapter considers necessary monthly reports, including those that must be filed every month and collecting information necessary in preparation for those filed quarterly or annually. Quarterly reports include both state and IRS 941 forms and estimated income tax reports. Finally, the chapter presents a summary of the dreaded annual reports and shows how preparation of annual tax filings is really little more than a copying job, if the monthly and quarterly reports are prepared as suggested.

Monthly Accounting

Balance Business and Personal Checkbooks
If there are charges on your bank statement, prepare handwritten memos with the date, amount, and a description. The statements should be stored at the rear of the permanent storage box. Put the checks into numeric order.

Sort Checks, Memos, Receipts, Deposits, & Miscellaneous into the Sort Box
Totals for each compartment should be transferred to the No-Entry Accounting income statement (Figure 15.1). Do not neglect to prepare all necessary memos. For example, a loan payment has both interest and principal-reduction components that must be sorted separately, even though there is only one check. Likewise, if business expenses are paid with personal funds, be sure to prepare a memo indicating that the payment is a loan to the company. If there is any ambiguity about whether an expense is business or personal, it is easier to resolve it now than it would be at the end of the year. If a transaction could be either, prepare a memo giving a more complete description of the expenditure. If you maintain a petty cash fund, it should be reconciled and all receipts appropriately sorted.

Compute Cost of Sales
No-Entry Accounting uses the cash method of computing cost of sales, so as soon as an item purchased for resale is paid for, the canceled check or cash receipt is sorted to cost of sales and immediately subtracted from sales on the income statement. For purposes of computing taxes, accounting is by accrual and items can be expensed only when the sale is made. Consequently, cost of sales as computed on IRS Schedule C requires a physical inventory. If your business has little or no inventory, the cash method will suffice. Whenever you do physical inventory, compute cost of sales as described on Part III of Schedule C.

Enter Depreciation and Home Office Expense on Income Statement
Details on which assets can be depreciated and which of various depreciation schedules is acceptable are given in Chapter 6. IRS Publication 334, *Tax Guide for Small Businesses*, is a valuable aid in computing depreciation. Once you select a depreciation method, monthly values for each depreciable asset will change no more often than annually, so keeping track of depreciation is mostly a copying job. Chapter 8 provides a form to help you calculate home office expenses. The actual amount deductible is usually not known until year end, but an estimate can be used throughout the year, with final figures computed just before Schedule C is filed.

Complete No-Entry Income Statement
Complete the income statement for the month and for the year-to-date. If your company has been in operation for a while, it is good practice to compare this month to earlier months and this year to earlier years. Complete your cash forecasting forms. Be careful to look for any signs that you have triggered or may be about to trigger the Cycle of Demise. Pay particular attention to future cash needs if you are expecting sales to either increase or decrease (for example, entering or leaving a busy season) or if your business has or will soon have unusual cash needs. Remember that if additional funds will be needed, you should act before the need becomes critical.

One advantage of No-Entry Accounting is that it provides essential information about the cash needs of your business, but to gain this advantage you must learn to use this information (see also the case study in Chapter 10).

Monthly Reports

Sales Tax

Prepare the Sales Tax Forms

Sales tax is levied by some states, some counties, and some municipalities. Any local merchant can tell you where to obtain forms. File copies in the State Tax Envelope in permanent storage.

Send Check and Report to State Taxing Body

States that charge sales tax usually require monthly payments and report of sales.

Payroll

See also Chapter 17. Follow these steps:

1. Compute total gross wages, withholding and FICA, state and local tax.
2. Transfer totals to state and IRS Form 941 and to any local forms.

The IRS Form 941 reports wages obligated by taxes and the tax obligations themselves. It includes withholding tax on income earned in the period and social security contributions. The form is filed each quarter, but entries are made each payday in the section at the bottom of the form. The 941 state form is used in states with a state income tax to report wages. It is generally filed quarterly, but deposits may be required more frequently. Read the instructions with your state forms for details.

If your state does not have a monthly deposit requirement, enter the amount due at each payday in the margin of the company copy of the form. At quarter's end, the total can be computed without having to review the payroll records for the quarter.

If necessary, make federal, state, and local deposits. Each payday, when employee checks are drawn:

1. Record federal withholding and FICA obligations (15.3 percent of gross up to $53,400) on Form 941.
2. Compute total FICA and withholding for the quarter-to-date:

If the total is less than $500 and it is not the third month of the quarter, you are done. If it is the end of the quarter, make a deposit by the 15th of next month.

If the total is $500 or more, but less than $3,000, make a deposit by the 15th of next month.

If the total exceeds $3,000, make a deposit within three days.

To Make a Deposit

1. Draw check and take it with 941 deposit coupon to any local bank. (Remember to save the bank deposit receipt and report copy in your Tax packet.)

2. During month 3, 5, 8, or 12, update IRS Form 2220 (Corporation) or IRS Form 2210 (Partnership or Proprietorship).

The IRS Forms 2210 and 2220 are for the purpose of computing the tax deposits due from corporations and proprietors in each quarter. If no profits were earned, the IRS estimated 1040ES deposits (four equal payments totaling the expected annual tax obligation) are not necessary. You could be charged interest and penalties if you do not make even quarterly payments and have not filed Form 2220 or 2210. Remember that Form 2220 or 2210 must be computed on months 3, 5, 8, and 12 rather than 3, 6, 9, and 12, through which other quarterly reports are typically done.

State Unemployment Tax
Prepare 940 SUTA state unemployment tax. SUTA is state unemployment tax, which funds a program, run in conjunction with the federal government, to provide unemployment compensation. SUTA must be paid for all regular employees.

Quarterly Reports

Month 3, 6, 9, or 12
1. Update your No-Entry Accounting balance sheet.

2. Complete IRS form 941 and state 941 if appropriate. Mail in envelope provided.

3. Deposit any funds required for 941 using deposit coupons federal and state governments provide. IRS 941 deposits are made at local banks; state deposits are usually mailed.

4. Deposit any outstanding tax due that has been computed with Form 2210 or 2220, or 1/4 of estimated annual tax if neither of these forms used, using federal and state 1040ES deposit coupons provided. Form 1040ES OCR explains the estimating procedures and provides a record for the quarterly deposits.

5. Recompute your Real Ratio (see Chapter 4 for details).

Annual Reports

Annual reports for most businesses are dominated by forms required by the IRS to substantiate your claims about tax liabilities. If you have a sole proprietorship or partnership, both business and personal tax forms are filed as a package. The package may include forms such as those pertinent to property you own and are renting to others or farm income, which this book has not considered.

Figure 18.1 is a graphical portrayal of both the forms you must file and an indication of which forms contain information needed on other forms.

After you have filed all tax forms, you need to be sure that all of your records are in "audit-ready" condition, and you should prepare a report for yourself on the financial health of your enterprise.

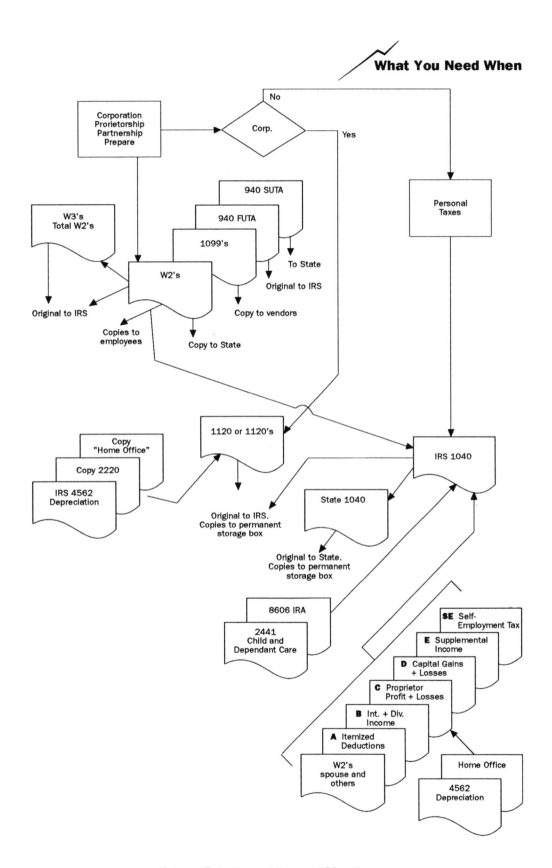

Figure 18.1. Annual Report Filing Process

Storing Your Records

Follow these steps to house your year's transaction records:

1. Place all copies of the tax filings (business and personal) in the permanent storage box.

2. Place all monthly No-Entry Accounting income statements in permanent storage.

3. Place all the quarterly balance sheets in permanent storage.

4. Place the Paid Vendor Invoice folder in permanent storage. Make sure it contains only paid invoices for that year. If some invoices are for paid-in-full assets, move them to the assets tab.

5. Move the Assets and Liabilities compartments (tab and all documents) to the current year's permanent storage box.

6. Move the Warranties tab and associated documents to the current year's permanent storage box.

7. Move any remaining tax reporting forms to the new box.

An Annual Financial Checkup for Your Business

This is a good time to take a long-term look at the financial health of your business. As we have said, having money in the bank is nice, but it doesn't guarantee the basic soundness of your business. You should:

1. Prepare a cash analysis that looks back on the past year and identifies all the sources of cash and all the uses. It should tie out to cash in your bank accounts. Determine

    a. where you are with regard to the debt-to-equity transfer. What percent of income is encumbered by debt retirement?

    b. where you are with regard to the labor-to-equity transfer. What portion of a reasonable wage have you taken home?

    c. where you are with regard to the node of profitability. If you are not generating free cash, what steps can be taken to get you there?

2. Develop a cash forecast for the coming year, factoring in any new cash needs. Establish a line of credit early to meet any forecasted shortfall.

3. If you have achieved several consecutive years with earnings at the $45,000 level, explore ways in which incorporating may be an advantage.

Ordering Information

Send your order for the No-Entry Accounting materials along with check or money order in the amount of $39.95 to:

> No-Entry Accounting
> 36 W 794 Stonebridge Ln.
> St. Charles, IL 60175

Your No-Entry materials consist of:

- The No-Entry sort box.
- Two Permanent Storage boxes capable of storing approximately 1500 documents each.
- Two sets of permanent storage tabs.
- A two year supply of memo tickets.
- Three tax packets describing the documents to be stored therein. There are:
  Personal Tax Packet
  State Tax Packet
  Federal Tax Packet
- Master copies of the No-Entry report forms including, the cash analysis form, the income statement, the balance sheet, the office in the home form, and the depreciation spread sheet.

Rush orders please send an additional $5.00 for priority shipping and handling. Allow three to six weeks for processing. Prices are subject to change without notice.

Mr. Fleury is available for seminars and workshops. For further information and scheduling in your area, please contact:

> Sourcebooks Trade
> P.O. Box 372
> Naperville, IL 60566
> (708) 961-2161
> FAX: (708) 961-2168

About Sourcebooks Trade

In 1990, Sourcebooks Inc., started its trade division, Sourcebooks Trade. Our goal was to provide easy-to-understand, empowering how-to books for today's consumers. We began by developing practical business and finance books. Offering a wide range of expertise, we now also include titles in the areas of marketing, current affairs, self-help and reference designed to make consumers' lives easier. **Our Sourcebooks Trade Titles include:**

The Basics of Finance: Financial Tools for Non-Financial Managers
by Bryan E. Milling

Ideal for every businessperson without a financial background who now aspires to management responsibility. Written in readable language, *The Basics of Finance* offers tools to help non-financial managers master financial information including understanding annual reports, interacting with financial personnel and using financial analysis to better understand the business world. It features 31 fundamental principles of financial management clearly and concisely explained, and includes simplified case histories illustrating each principle.

The Basics of Finance is an essential desk companion for any manager with direct or indirect financial responsibility ... and a key tool for professionals aspiring to the corner office.

> 210 pages ISBN 0-942061-18-7 (paperback) $14.95
> ISBN 0-942061-25-X (hardcover) $24.95

Cash Flow Problem Solver: Common Problems and Practical Solutions
by Bryan E. Milling

Thousands of business owners have discovered that the *Cash Flow Problem Solver: Common Problems and Practical Solutions* is a tool of surpassing value in the day-to-day management of a firm's cash flow. Now in its third edition, *Cash Flow Problem Solver* is a proven bestseller and has helped over 20,000 business owners **improve their cash flow and benefit from effective cash flow management.**

Cited as one of the three books on the "Smart CEO's Reading List" in INC Magazine. Selected as an alternate of both the **Business Week Book Club** and the **Fortune Book Club.** *Cash Flow Problem Solver: Common Problems and Practical Solutions* is a profits-oriented approach to cash flow management. In addition, *Cash Flow Problem Solver* **provides a results-oriented, step-by-step guide with tools and specific tactics to assure positive cash flow and to help boost a firm's profits.**

> 296 pages ISBN 0-942061-27-6 (paperback) $19.95
> 0-942061-28-4 (hardcover) $32.95

Creating Your Own Future: A Woman's Guide to Retirement Planning
by Judith A. Martindale, CFP and Mary J. Moses

Planning your future can be a wonderful and trying experience all at the same time. As authors, Judith Martindale and Mary Moses found, creating a simple, more relaxed and enjoyable retirement takes patience and hard work. "Critical decisions must be made well in advance to turn a dream into a comfortable reality," say Martindale and Moses.

The authors argue that although retirement planning is important to everyone, factors unique to women, such as, shorter work lives due to child rearing, longer life expectancy, differing health needs than men, among others, make appropriate preparations essential.

> 256 pages ISBN 0-942061-09-8 (paperback) $14.95
> 0-942061-08-X (hardcover) $28.95

Finding Time: Breathing Space For Women Who Do Too Much
by Paula Peisner

Finding Time: Breathing Space For Women Who Do Too Much is a terrific book for today's women who always seem to be doing more than they have time to do. Balancing careers, families, homes, and outside interests, women are feeling out of control and stressed.

This book is for all women who want to take control of their own time and make more of it. The book shows women how to identify and eliminate actions by themselves and others that rob them of their most precious asset... time.

"Comprehensive and insightful - easy tips to understand.
Taking even a few of these tips to heart should allow some breathing space."
— Sandra N. Bane, Partner, KPMG Peat Marwick.

"Provides a wonderful insight into a working woman's management of time.
A very practical primer. I found it very useful."
— Anita R. Gershman, President and CEO, World International Network

256 pages   ISBN 0-942061-33-0 (paperback) $7.95

Future Vision: The 189 Most Important Trends of the 1990s
From the Editors of Research Alert

"... the ultimate guide to the new decade."—*American Demographics*

"... a valuable tool and a bargain."—*Media Industry Newsletter*

"... a stunningly complete summary."—*Executive Trend Watch*

"... especially useful."—Robert Tuefel, President, Rodale Press

Future Vision gives substance to the dynamically changing forces that are reshaping the American marketplace. Its unique presentation of both the facts and the fictions presents readers with an evenhanded perspective of what will happen next... with enough detail for them to see the implications of their own work.

Presented in a usable, readable format, this guide examines key trends in areas including: Money, Media, Home, Leisure, Food, Environmentalism and the Workplace. No outdated trends or thinking... just the cutting-edge numbers drawn from hundreds of sources.

256 pages ISBN 0-942061-16-0 (paperback) $12.95
0-942061-17-9 (hardcover) $21.95

The Lifestyle Odyssey: The Facts Behind the Social, Personal and Cultural Changes Touching Each of Our Lives. . . From the Way We Eat Our Cookies to Our Desire for a Better World
by Eric Miller and the Editors of Research Alert

The Lifestyle Odyssey touches all social and cultural changes affecting our American lifestyle it takes us on a journey — a pathway describing a new American lifestyle. Beyond the obvious demographic shifts, American society is changing the way it chooses to live. The cumulative effect of those choices will give way to a "new" American lifestyle. All of us have experienced these changes to some extent. *The Lifestyle Odyssey* crystallizes the loose feelings that these changes have engendered in many Americans and outlines what else we may expect.

"Whatever your profession or personal investment program, somewhere in this remarkable new book lurks a fact or a trend that will change what you do. **If you have but one life to live, read this book,**" says John Mack Carter, editor-in-chief of *Good Housekeeping* Magazine.

304 pages ISBN 0-942061-36-5 (paperback) $15.95
0-942061-31-4 (hardcover) $32.95

Outsmarting the Competition:
Practical Approaches to Finding and Using Competitive Information
by John J. McGonagle Jr. and Carolyn M. Vella

Competitive intelligence can help you understand where your product or your company stands with respect to your competition, and can give you some advance warning of the stirrings in your competitor's offices—without doing anything illegal or unethical. The first book to show both what information you need and how to get it.

". . . competitive intelligence is essential for any business. . . **Now you can develop this important business skill with the help of** *Outsmarting the Competition*."

— *Adweek's Marketing Week*

"Please measure your CI (Competitive Intelligence) index right now. You may be courting disaster." — *The Wall Street Journal*

"(John) McGonagle and (Carolyn) Vella. . . have written another excellent business book; this one will help any businessperson understand the marketplace and the competition."

— *Library Journal*

". . .**provides sound advice on how to obtain inside knowledge.**" — *Entrepreneur*

"The book is so comprehensive that few marketing managers will be able to take advantage of all its suggestions." — *Business Marketing*

A must for any businessperson's library

388 pages ISBN 0-942061-06-3 (hardcover) $29.95
ISBN 0-942061-04-7 (paperback) $17.95

The Small Business Survival Guide: How To Manage Your Cash, Profits and Taxes
by Robert E. Fleury

The Small Business Survival Guide includes discussions on: planning for and filing taxes • cash flow analysis and management • understanding and developing financial statements • methods of taking and valuing inventory • how to value a business for buying and selling • managing your payroll & recordkeeping • PLUS...**NO-ENTRY ACCOUNTING...a means of doing and understanding your own accounting, without double-entry bookkeeping**

With two full case studies, lots of examples and forms, this book takes the mystery out of managing the financial side of a business.

"Innovative, this book can help you gain control of your cash flow."
—Jane Applegate, Syndicated Small Business Columnist, *Los Angeles Times*

256 pages ISBN 0-942061-11-X (hardcover) $29.95
ISBN 0-942061-12-8 (paperback) $17.95

Small Claims Court Without A Lawyer
by W. Kelsea Wilber, Attorney-at-Law

Small Claims Court Without A Lawyer is an invaluable guide to understanding the small claims system. It allows you to file a claim and get a judgement quickly and ecomomically, without an attorney's assistance or fee. Written in clear, uncomplicated language, this useful new book includes details about each state's small claims court system, so that wherever you live you can use it to successfully file a claim and see that claim through to a judgement.

"An excellent primer for individuals or small businesses attempting to collect their own debts." — Arthur G. Sartorius, III, Attorney-at-Law.

"The easy-to-read format is comprehensive but offers the basics necessary for the non-lawyer to proceed and succeed!" —Drew W. Prusiecki, Attorney-at-Law

224 pages   ISBN 0-942061-32-2 (paperback) $18.95

To order these books or any of our numerous other publications, **please contact your local bookseller,** or call Sourcebooks at 1-800-798-2475.

You can also obtain a copy of our catalog by writing or faxing to:

Sourcebooks Trade
A Div. of Sourcebooks, Inc.
P.O. Box 372
Naperville, IL 60566
(708) 961-2161
FAX: 708-961-2168

Thank you for your interest in our publications.